阿尔法·文图斯
海上风电场 Operation offshore

序

风能是一种清洁的可再生资源，风电是最具发展潜力的新兴能源，大力发展风电等可再生能源是推动世界新一轮能源革命、推进世界经济转型发展的必然要求。近年来，不少国家纷纷推出风电等新能源战略，风电产业发展超乎预期，中国风电产业发展更是后来居上，2012年全球新增风电装机4471万千瓦，中国新增风电并网装机容量1500万千瓦。2012年全球新增海上风电装机约129万千瓦，累计装机约541万千瓦。中国2012年新增海上风电装机12.7万千瓦，海上风电累计装机约34万千瓦，位居世界第三位。根据相关预测，2020年前全球风电装机将以每年20%的速度增长，风电发展处于重要战略机遇期，而且海上风电将会成为重点发展领域。

中船重工是我国最大的造修船集团，拥有国内实力最强、最齐全的配套研发与生产体系，具备强大的机、电、液、控综合一体化装备制造能力，形成了从叶片、齿轮箱、发电机、控制系统，到机座、机架、塔筒、轮毂等全系列制造能力，是我国唯一一家具备较完整风电装备研制生产体系的企业。立足风电产业发展规律，借鉴国际风电产业发展经验，中船重工风电开发走出了一条由提供配套，到总装生产，再到进军风场、建设风电产业基地的发展路径，形成了风电全产业链竞争优势，走在了中国风电产业发展的前列。

面对海上风电的巨大潜力和发展趋势，国家已将海上风电纳入加快培育和发展的战略性新兴产业范畴，同时列入"十二五"发展规划。中船重工作为全球知名的海洋装备及配套供应商，汇聚了国家海上风电工程技术研究中心、国家能源海洋工程研发中心等一流的科研力量，研制了世界上第一台海上风车安装船，具有发展海上风点装备制造业的科研、制造、配套优势和丰富的海洋工程项目经验，目前正在自主研发5兆瓦及以上海上风力发电机组、风电储能设备等重大配套设备，将会引领中国海上风电产业持续快速发展。

德国是全球风电产业发展的领先者，在发展风电装备制造业、建设海上风电场、并网发电等方面进行了许多有益的探索。阿尔法•文图斯海上风电场项目是德国花费了20多年时间，耗费了大量人力、财力、物力，最终收获成功的一项重大项目，这座海上风力发电场成功并网发电，标志着德国利用可再生能源进入了一个新纪元。德国在阿尔法•文图斯海上风电场项目中，取得的成绩来之不易，积累的经验弥足珍贵，成为我们学习和借鉴的标杆。我们应树立全局观念，拓展国际视野，运用战略思维，以更大的决心和勇气、更强的欲望和追求，向全球领先者学习，与其同台共舞，在激烈的国际竞争中顽强拼搏，推进实现中国风电产业又好又快发展。

以此为序，期望中国风电产业的明天更精彩！

中国船舶重工集团公司副总经理

董 强

2013年7月，于北京

中文版前言

阿尔法·文图斯来自希腊文"一阵风",这使我想起了汉高祖刘邦的诗句"大风起兮云飞扬……",可谓是豪情万丈。在海上建造风力发电平台是人类利用海洋资源的又一个创举,这不仅仅在欧洲和美洲国家,中国也在积极准备涉水前行。

在陆地上,中国的风能设备催生了一个新兴产业,如果忽略其中许多技术上的问题,当人们看到这个行业如此迅速地发展,确实是令人鼓舞的。

然而,正如本书原版前言中所述,海上风能不只是陆上发电厂的简单延伸,而是一项独立的、高度复杂的技术开发,具有自身特殊的环境条件。与已有收益的陆上风能相比,海上风能要面对完全不同的挑战。

改革开放使我们有了更多的机会接触到发展中的先进技术。2010年5月我在访德期间,德国BVA能源技术出版社的同行热忱向我推荐这部刚刚出版的新书,这对我以及国内关注海上风能发展、从事海上风能研究开发的人来说,正是一个机遇。当时,我就与德国同行讨论该书的中文版版权引进许可。回国后,马上组织专业翻译进行翻译,又邀请了德国劳氏船级社上海公司的技术专家进行了审校。经过了最终的编辑、定稿、付印,终于用几个月的努力换得了一个令人满意的成果。

本书记录了由德国政府资助的海上风能项目的整个实施过程。这个项目采用了目前世界上最大的5兆瓦海上风能机组。在项目实施过程中,经历了漫长的时间和多次接近失败的考验。再一次告诉人们,科学实践的道路是不平坦的。

书中作者已经把未来的中国海上风能市场列入待开发领域。

随着中国风能事业的发展,许多人都在勾画着未来中国海上风电场的蓝图,并且正在筹措资金,引进设备和技术。通过翻译这本书,希望帮助国内的专业读者,深入了解海上风能平台的建造过程,从中汲取经验,推进我国海上风能项目顺利进行。

在本书的翻译出版过程中,得到了中国船舶重工集团公司和中国船舶信息中心等单位的大力支持,在此表示衷心感谢!

中国造船工程学会《船舶工程》编辑部主任

宋新新

2013年7月,于上海

感谢以下单位对《阿尔法·文图斯》中文版编译工作的支持

（排名不分先后）

协办单位
中船重工（重庆）海装风电设备有限公司
东方电气集团东方汽轮机有限公司
邦飞利传动设备（上海）有限公司
中国熔盛重工集团控股有限公司
德国劳氏船级社（中国）有限公司
中国船级社质量认证公司
国家海洋局第三海洋研究所
南通润邦重机有限公司
重庆齿轮箱有限责任公司
南车株洲电力机车研究所有限公司
广东明阳风电产业集团有限公司
上海中集海洋工程研发中心
中国电力工程顾问集团华东电力设计院

支持单位
中国水电顾问集团华东勘测设计研究院
武昌船舶重工有限责任公司
山海关船舶重工有限责任公司
上海泰胜风能装备股份有限公司
江西华伍制动器股份有限公司
北京莱维塞尔科技有限公司
新乡市豫新风电设备工程有限公司
江苏龙源振华海洋工程有限公司
洛阳双瑞风电叶片有限公司
重庆前卫仪表有限责任公司
浙江海洋大学船舶与建筑工程学院
天津大学电气与自动化工程学院

《阿尔法·文图斯》中文版编译出版委员会

(以姓氏笔画为序)

主任委员

董　强

副主任委员

王若文、王建录、刘郑国、叶　华、吴　建、陈　刚、陈　强、李海宁、李彦庆、杨本新、贺小兵、胡安康、赵航宇、郭知彼、常　山、黄世元、童小川、焦　侬、廖康明

委员

孔祥东、历海强、王满昌、王渭龄、史俊虎、孙显辉、胡　昊、李坤胜、张乐平、张兆德、陈启瑢、沈若冰、陈　峰、周铁根、孟　黎、赵书敏、赵敏惠、赵生校、徐大林、高志龙、聂春华、黄人豪、黄京明、曾　沅、程武山、彭祖洋

翻译人员(上海市工程翻译协会推荐)

方思敏、李书甫、杨文英、刘积骅、张　晶、秦鹏鑫、施　璟、徐陈芳、薛　丹、鞠光华

编校人员

孙明芳、殷　利、常卫伟

专业审校人员

德国劳氏集团风能分部(GL Wind, Germanischer Lloyd Group)

项目策划

宋新新

图书在版编目（CIP）数据

阿尔法文图斯海上风电场 /（德）考纳曼
（Koenemann,D.D）著；李彦庆主编. ——上海：上海科学技术文献出版社，
2014.1
书名原文：Alpha ventus
ISBN 978-7-5439-5937-8

Ⅰ.①阿… Ⅱ.①考… ②李… Ⅲ.①海风－风力发
电－发电厂－概况－德国 Ⅳ.①F451.666

中国版本图书馆CIP数据核字(2013)第199485号

阿尔法·文图斯海上风电场
Alpha Ventus Operation Offshore

© BVA Bielefelder Verlag/Germany 2010
Copyright in the Chinese language translation (Simplified character rights only) ©
2013 Shanghai Scientific & Technological Literature Publishing House Co., Ltd.

All Rights Reserved
版权所有，翻印必究

图字：09-2013-580

责任编辑：田立群　应丽春

阿尔法文图斯海上风电场
李彦庆　主编

出版发行：上海科学技术文献出版社
地　　址：上海市长乐路746号
邮政编码：200040
经　　销：全国新华书店
印　　刷：上海普顺印刷包装有限公司
开　　本：225×287　1/特16开
印　　张：12.5
版　　次：2014年1月第1版 2014年1月第1次印刷
书　　号：ISBN 978-7-5439-5937-8
定　　价：298.00元
http://www.sstlp.com

目录 CONTENTS

10	约尔格•库比尔作序：一个合作项目 A joint project Preface by Jörg Kuhbier
13	海上作业 安装5兆瓦风机机组 High above the sea Installation of an M5000
17	牢固的三脚式桩基 Strong tripod
34	访谈：费利克斯•第比尔斯（阿海珐Multibrid） Interview with Félix Debierre (AREVA Multibrid)
41	从梦想到现实 From vision to reality
64	访谈：克努特•雷费尔特博士（德国海上风能基金会） Interview with Dr. Knud Rehfeldt (German Offshore Wind Energy Foundation)
71	能源公司进军海上 Power companies enter the offshore business
76	向深海的危险致敬 Respecting the dangers of the high seas
93	研究和测量技术 Research and metrology
107	岸上工作为海洋工程技术服务 Work on land for technology at sea 海上风能为沿海地区创造新的就业机会 Offshore wind energy creating new jobs in coastal regions 海上能源需要千里迢迢从海洋输送至大陆 Offshore power on a long haul from sea to mainland
116	穿过浅滩和岛屿的电缆 A cable through mudflats and an island
135	在秋季风暴期间迎来激动人心的收尾工作 完成5兆瓦风机机组的安装 Exciting finish between autumn storms Installation of an 5M
145	风机塔架——轻质坚固 Jacket – light yet strong
158	访谈：马蒂亚斯•舒伯特（瑞能系统公司） Interview with Matthias Schubert (REpower Systems AG)
169	未来已经来临 The future has already begun
177	附录 Appendix
178	地理位置示意图 Cartographic overview
180	大事记 Chronology
185	术语 Glossary
189	图片来源 Photo Credits
191	编后记 Postscript

一个合作项目 A joint project
约尔格·库比尔，海上风能基金会执行董事
JÖRG KUHBIER, BOARD OF DIRECTORS STIFTUNG OFFSHORE WINDENERGIE

任何伟大构想的首次尝试似乎常以失败告终，这样的情况同样发生在30年前，当时3台超大功率大型风力发电机"Growian"没能成为风能成功典范的开端。那个项目证明了那些构想无法落实，那时的材料达不到要求，也许它本来就是为了证明这些。

几十年后，旨在推进德国可再生能源开发的第一部法律——1991年的《电网电力馈入法案》获得通过，受此鼓励，风能加速了其在海上的发展。此后进展极为迅猛，令人震惊，尤其震惊了那些视可再生能源为臆想的人，他们认为那是理想世界的梦想家们甚至是可爱的疯子们的臆想。

又过了近20年，我们终于又通过海上风电场阿尔法•文图斯取得了进一步的突破性进展。而且，海上风电不只是陆上风电的简单延伸，而是一项独立的、高度复杂的技术开发，具有自身特殊的环境条件：与已有收益的陆上风电相比，要面对完全不同的挑战。

与此同时，海上风电场在性能和输出可行性方面正在赶超传统的发电厂，从投资需求方面来说也如此。因此，在逐步取代矿物燃料的过程中，海上风能将在未来混合能源中发挥重要作用，而且还能为环保做出关键的重要贡献。然而，这也产生了不可避免的矛盾，事实上，海上风能部分目前不得不和传统能源抗衡一段时间。

阿尔法·文图斯是一个新时代的成功开端，这个试验场拉开了德国海上风能时代的序幕，不久的将来在北海和波罗的海的德国海岸附近将建设更多的风电场。与类似的开发项目一样，此次项目的成功有一大批创始人，在此值得一提的是风机制造商瑞能公司和阿海珐Multibrid公司，早在海上风能的概念阶段就已经投入信心，并且开发了海上专用的5兆瓦风机。德国联邦环境部不遗余力地推进阿尔法•文图斯项目，多次将项目从失败边缘拉了回来。德国联邦海事与水文局（BSH）

It seems that the first attempts at any great idea often end in failure. That's what happened thirty years ago when the three megawatt 'Growian' (an abbreviation of the German: Große Windenergie-anlage – Large Wind Energy Turbine) failed to mark the beginnings of the wind-energy success story. The project proved that it wouldn't work with the concepts and materials of the time – which is quite possibly what it was also meant to prove.

Some ten years later and encouraged by the first law passed to promote renewable energies in Germany – the Electricity Feed-in Act of 1991 – wind energy picked up speed onshore. Its later deve-lopment moved extremely quickly and astonished everyone, especially those who regarded renewable energy as the domain of 'dreamers of a better world' or even endearing madmen.

Almost another 20 years later we have seen a further clear breakthrough on the high seas with alpha ventus. And offshore wind energy is not just the logical continuation of onshore generation but an independent, highly complex technical development with its own special set of circumstances: completely different challenges have to be mastered compared to harvesting wind energy on land.

At the same time, offshore wind farms are catching up with conventional power stations in terms of performance and output availability. This also applies to the investments required. For these reasons, in the gradual replacement of fossil fuels, wind energy at sea will play an important role in the energy mix of the future and will make a key contribution to climate protection. However, this means that conflicts are inevitable; in fact, the offshore wind energy sector has had to cope with these for a while now.

alpha ventus is the successful start of a new era and this test field represents the bright dawn for the offshore wind-energy age in Germany. It will not be long before further wind farms follow in the North and Baltic Seas off the German coast. As always with such developments, the success has numerous founding fathers. Deserving of a special mention here are the turbine manufacturers REpower and AREVA

约尔格·库比尔

也大获赞誉,作为许可证发放管理部门,充分发挥了创新力。最后同样重要的是,Prokon北方能源系统公司投入了巨大的人力财力为阿尔法·文图斯海上风电场取得了许可证,并使其最终能并入国家电网。

本书描述了德国首座海上风电场正式发电之前经历的许多阶段,叙述了参与者们付出的巨大努力,他们相互之间紧密合作,最终获得了他们应得的成功回报。此外,本书也讨论了必须克服的众多困难。作者详细讲述了出色的工程,提到了决策失误,呈现了失望和愉快,像是就发生在眼前,更反映了参与其中的许许多多贡献者们毫不动摇地坚守承诺。

最重要的是,本书记录了阿尔法·文图斯这项在欧洲可再生能源领域里史无前例的广泛合作项目。在这项浩大工程中,多方共同促成了阿尔法·文图斯的成功,其中有德国海上风电场和基础设施股份有限公司(DOTI)及其成员企业EWE公司、意昂公司和大瀑布电力公司;海上风能基金会和电网运营商;各方联合包括政治决策人、行政人员、开发人员、制造商、供应商、物流企业和投资者。每一方的成就都是此次合作取得成功不可磨灭的组成部分。

Multibrid, who placed their belief early on in the offshore concept and developed turbines in the 5-megawatt class especially suitable for operation at sea. Furthermore, the German Federal Environment Ministry, as a never-tiring engine of the alpha ventus project, repeatedly pulled things back from the brink of failure. The German Federal Maritime and Hydrographic Agency (BSH) has also earned itself a great deal of praise, and as the licensing authority has demonstrated a great deal of creativity. Last but by no means least, Prokon Nord Energiesysteme dedicated enormous human resources and financial effort into getting the alpha ventus offshore wind farm licensed and was behind the push for its eventual cable connection to the power grid.

This book describes the many steps that had to be taken before the first offshore wind farm in Germany really did start generating electricity. It tells the story of the titanic efforts made by the individual protagonists who needed to work closely with each other and who were finally rewarded with the success they deserved. Furthermore, this book discusses the multitude of problems that had to be overcome. The authors detail the outstanding engineering work, describe the errors of judgement, bring the disappointments and euphoria alive – and reflect the unwavering commitment of the many dedicated individuals involved.

Above all, this book documents the fact that alpha ventus was a collective exercise of unprecedented proportions in the European renewable energy sector. In this huge undertaking, the Deutsche Offshore-Testfeld und Infrastrukturgesellschaft mbH & Co. KG (DOTI) with its member companies EWE, E.ON and Vattenfall, as well as the Offshore Wind Energy Foundation and grid operator transpower stromübertragungs GmbH, joined forces with political decision-makers, administrators, developers, manufacturers, suppliers, logistics companies and investors to make alpha ventus a success. And the achievements of every individual are what made this collective success possible.

海上作业
High above the sea

装载着海上风力发电机5兆瓦的塔架、发动机舱和叶片的安装作业平台还要经过很长时间才达到高于北海海平面40米的预计高度,队员们一直在JB 114号自升式平台的餐厅里等待着,咖啡供不应求。

平台提升前,大功率拖轮"Banekert"号和"Smit Barracuda"号已将锚抛在数百米之外。马丁•特斯蒂船长根据卫星定位系统操纵着4台锚机,将钢铁平台精确地定位于下一个风机安装点。桩基塔架已伸出海面,上面"AV 7"几个巨幅大字赫然醒目。平台就位后,距指定目标只有一点点误差。船长操作着液压系统,将自升式平台四个角的桩腿降低,进入水下,这里的沙床大约在北海海面以下30米。当四个桩腿到达海底时,平台就可以开始提升了。在海上工作时都说英语,德国人称其为"jacken"。平台提升重量达1000多吨,液压油缸顶着它一点一点地提升时,还发出嘎吱嘎吱的响声,就像一个铁怪物,它的最佳提升速度为0.5米/分。海浪拍打桩腿时发出的沉闷响声告诉船员们,平台正在升出水面。这时,如果海浪过高,极端情况下,平台受浪涌作用力的上下升沉会导致平台受损,甚至会使自升式平台倾翻。然而,现在不会有这样的危险,因为JB 114号自升式平台是由荷兰自升式平台公司在新加坡制造的,其设计能够抵御两米高的海浪。

今天,北海海面非常平静,气候宜人,和煦的阳光照在海面上,丝丝清风掠过,有少许的浪花。这意味今天很可能可以开工,在阿尔法•文图斯风电场开始装配由德国不来梅港的阿海珐Multibrid公司生产的第五台5兆瓦级海上风力发电机。

与此同时,几天前,在东部装配的第四台海上风力发电机现在正在试运转了。当夕阳西下时,大约是7点钟,第五台海上风力发电机的装配工作告了一个段落。Multibrid公司的项目经理迈克尔•克林格将队员们召集到餐厅开个短会。这些队员有机械工和升降机操作员,都是不来梅锐特公司、汉堡全球能源服务中心(GES)和不来梅港的Kronschnabel等专业公司雇佣来的。队员们认真听取了迈克尔•克林格的工作总结和后续工作安排。对这些平均年龄只有30岁的年轻队员来说,无论是留在JB 114号自升式平台上,还是去解塔架的固定绳,或去装配风机,都不需要多说什么,他们知道该怎么做。先提升塔筒S1部分,然后用螺栓固定;随后,也就是将近午夜时分,再将发动机舱紧固件松开,并将其挂在起重机吊钩上提升到预定的高度,这一直要工作到第二天凌晨,才能将发动机舱安装到塔架上并固定。对于这些有多年在陆地上装配风机经验的队员来说,海上安装不是难事,因为这些装配过程都是固定的程序。短会临近结束时,38岁的克林格提到

Waiting. Waiting. And more waiting. The coffee machine in the canteen of the jack-up barge JB 114 just can't keep up with the coffee consumption of the team who are there, waiting. Hours pass before the platform, loaded with the tower segment, nacelle and rotor of the M5000, has reached the planned height of 40 metres above the North Sea. Before the lift could be started, the powerful tugs 'Banckert' and 'Smit Barracuda' took out the four anchors to a distance of several hundred metres. Then Captain Martijn Tersteeg manoeuvred his iron platform and the four anchor winches to their destination using satellite navigation with almost perfect accuracy. The aim is to locate it directly next to the tower segment, already protruding above the surface of the sea, bearing the name of 'AV 7' in huge letters. After getting into position with only a few centimetres 'leeway' he operates the hydraulic system that lowers the support pillars on the four corners of the jack-up barge into the water. The sandy seabed here is about 30 metres below the surface of the North Sea. Once the powerful stilts have reached the bottom the lifting process begins. The working language at sea is English and even the Germans call this "jacken". To the sound of creaking metal the hydraulic pumps heave the steel monster, which together with the freight weighs more than 1,000 tonnes, piece by piece into the air. The best that can be managed is half a metre a minute. The dull sound of waves beating against the underside of the body signals to the crew that the barge is now coming out of the water. This is the most critical moment of the whole jack-up process: if the waves are too high, in extreme cases it may happen that they briefly lift the platform body, which can then become damaged when thumped back down on the support posts. In the worst case the barge may capsize. However, there is no danger of that today, as barge JB 114 has been designed to master a maximum wave height of two metres. It was commissioned to be built in Singapore by the Dutch owner Jack-up-Barges B.V..

The sea is showing its friendly side today. It's warm and sunny, with a light wind gently blowing over the North Sea. There are a few white crests on the waves, a sign for everyone on board that the assembly of the fifth 5-megawatt offshore wind turbine from the manufacturer AREVA Multibrid in Bremerhaven can probably be started today in the test field alpha ventus.

Meanwhile to the east, the fourth turbine, installed a few days previously, is now revolving in a test run. As the evening sun moves slowly towards the horizon, at around seven in the evening things start getting serious. Project Manager Michael Klingele, head of the Multibrid team, calls his staff together in the canteen for a briefing. Calmly and factually he explains what is to happen and how it is to be done in the coming hours. The mechanical fitters and crane operators listen at-

装配工托尔斯滕·扬施克和机电工程师尼尔斯·布兰德、卢茨·格罗赫（从左至右）正在JB 114号自升式平台的咖啡厅里等待下一次作业。
Fitter Thorsten Janschker and start-up engineers Niels Brand and Lutz Grohe (from left to right) are waiting in the JB 114 jack-up barge's canteen for their next assignment.

了一个细节问题，"在陆地上装配风机时，他们忘记将发动机舱轻微旋转了，所以到海上装配时必须首先轻轻转动发动机舱。"

短会结束了，队员们纷纷离去。现在的情况比较乐观。风力在逐渐减弱，风速还不到8米/秒。起重机用吊篮将四名技术人员运送到已经装配好的塔架墩柱上后，又转回来把吊篮送到地面，然后小心地将吊钩放在连接有下一个104吨塔筒段的横梁上。机械工用吊钩钩住缆绳，吊起了32米长、5米宽的部分，并缓慢下降到高出海面的塔基上。一切都正常进行着，过了一小会儿，响起了液力扭矩螺栓扳手作业的哒哒声，依旧挂在吊钩上的横梁和塔筒盖回到了JB 114上。

通常情况下，只有在提升300吨重的发动机舱时，才动用平台上的起重机。就在这时，附近突然出现一艘正在向自升式平台方向驶来的橡胶小艇。这是一艘最适合冰冷天气，且长期以来为俄罗斯服役的探险船，它来将机电工程师卢茨·格罗赫和机电技师尼尔斯·布兰德接送往他们住宿的"Petr Kottsov"号船上。卢茨·格罗赫和尼尔斯·布兰德是Multibrid公司的员工，他们的任务是启动装配好的风力发电机。连接海上风力发电机和电网需要十四天的时间，所以，他们每

tentively to his instructions. They are employed by the specialist companies Reetec from Bremen, Global Energy Services (GES) from Hamburg and Kronschnabel from Bremerhaven. The upcoming work is allocated: the team is told who stays on the barge JB 114, who releases the straps on the tower segment and who goes onto the turbine for the assembly. Only a few words are required before the young team, with an average age of 30, knows exactly what to do. First, lift over tower segment S1, then bolt it tight; later, at about midnight, release the nacelle from its fastenings, hang it on the crane hooks, raise it to the required height and then, working into the early hours of the morning, place it on the tower flange of the segment and fasten it tight. After all, this is 'routine stuff'; each of the technicians has had years of experience in assembling wind turbines – even if only on land. At the end of the short meeting, Klingele mentions a specific matter: "In this case we have to slightly turn (yaw) the nacelle, as they forgot to do this when assembling it on land", explains the 38-year-old.

Then they're off. The conditions are good: the wind has dropped even further, now having a speed of less than eight metres a second. The crane takes four technicians in a lifting basket to the already assembled stump of the tower. Then it swivels back, puts the basket on the ground and subsequently places its hook carefully over a beam to which the

JB 114装载着M5000零件，用两艘船花了12个小时从埃姆斯港运载到阿尔法·文图斯的安装地点。
JB 114 loaded with M5000 components. Towing it from Eemshaven to the alpha ventus installation site takes two tugs about twelve hours.

天一早离开生活船"Petr Kottsov"号，乘小艇去风电场，晚上再返回。他们在JB 114上呆了一整天等候海浪停止，但直到天黑这一时刻才到来。需要留在阿尔法·文图斯风电场的工具包装得满满的，卢茨·格罗赫和尼尔斯·布兰德随意地将它们和其它设备放到吊篮里。随着他们从海面以上40米的缓慢下降，他们对队员们说"一切顺利，待会儿见！"。

当迈克尔·克林格在检查塔架拧紧的螺栓时，负责安装Multibrid风力发电机的海上施工经理弗兰克·梅特巴赫正在为提升发动机舱做准备，发动机舱用绳索固定在50米长、32米宽的JB 114号自升式平台的中间位置。彼得·瓦朗特是由EWE、意昂公司和大瀑布电力公司联合出资组成的德国海上风能实验安装公司的施工总监。此时，这位前德国联邦陆军官员和作战潜水员就像甲板上的主人，他用鹰一样锐利的眼睛监控着工程，所以每个环节都必须按照安全规程操作。

夜已经黑了，天空繁星点点。四台Multibrid风力发电机已装配好，其中两台上的导航灯照亮了夜空；旁边的测风平台FINO 1、护卫船Otto Treplin和生活船"Petr Kottsov"上的灯光也在黑暗中闪烁，它们

next 104-tonne tower-tube segment is fastened. After the mechanical fitters have hung the cables onto the hook, the 32-metre-long and five-metre-wide segment is cautiously lifted by the crane and slowly lowered onto the section already protruding out of the sea. It all goes routinely, and after a short while the hydraulic bolt tensioners are buzzing away. Still hanging on the hook, the beam is returned with the cover of the tower segment back to the JB 114.

Normally the crane standing on the platform would remain still until it needed to lift the approximately 300-tonne nacelle. However, this time a rubber dinghy approaches the jack-up barge unexpectedly; it has come to take two men, electromechanical engineer Lutz Groche and mechatronician Nils Brand, to the supply ship 'Petr Kottsov'. Their job is to commission already-assembled turbines. The long-serving Russian expedition ship, suitable for icy conditions, is now within view of the barge. Time to use the man-basket. The two from Multibrid are to spend a fortnight in the test field and connect the offshore turbines to the grid. They will leave their floating hostel, the 'Petr Kottsov', early each morning in small boats and return in the evening. The team has been waiting on the JB 114 the whole day for this moment; however, they have not been able to transfer until the waves let up and this hasn't been until late in the evening, when it's already getting

阿尔法·文图斯电站的项目经理
迈克尔·克林格
Project manager Michael Klingele
in the alpha ventus test field.

为风电场以及拖船'Banekert'和'Smit Barracuda'提供了照明。自升式平台'Buzzard'上的灯光也非常明亮,上面正在进行六台瑞能风力发电机的基建工作;远处闪烁着油船和货船的灯光。这一切说明,在阿尔法·文图斯风电场周边,有大量往来的船只。施工现场正好穿过位于北纬54度方向风电场的变电站,尽管距离波尔库姆的东弗里斯兰群岛海岸有45公里之远,但仍然有一米半的潮差。

夜空的月亮很美,身置其中,让人感到激动。海风略显大了一点。塔筒固定好了,发动机舱必须及时安装上,因为只有这样,塔筒才能保持平稳。队员娴熟地将绑带移去,发动机舱很快被悬挂到了起重机吊钩上。发动机舱的螺栓非常大,必须用专用100mm扳手才能拧。起重机提升风力发电机的核心部分时,引擎响声不断,起重机的悬臂缓慢向外移动,旋转180度后,把风力发电机提升到开放的塔筒的正上方。起重机操作员无法直接看到风力发电机,只能通过用对讲机联络迈克尔·克林格和装配组,将发动机舱准确地放在塔筒上,对准螺栓的位置。3,2,1,0…巨大的风力发电机安全准确就位了,每个人的脸上都露出了放松的表情。简单整理后,船上队员可以上床休息了,但风塔上的队员们还要奋战一晚,因为他们要对发动机舱的安装

dark. They casually throw their fully-packed bags and other equipment for their stay in the alpha ventus test field into the basket and call back to their colleagues, "All the best, see you later!" as they are slowly lowered from 40 metres over the sea.

While Michael Klingele is overseeing the bolting-on of the tower segment, Frank Mettbach, who has been hired as Offshore Construction Manager to set up the Multibrid turbines, makes the preparations for heaving up the nacelle, which is sitting lashed down in the middle of the 50-metre-long and 32-metre-wide JB 114. The former German Federal Army officer and combat diver is something like a 'lord on deck'. He decides what is done and when it is done. And every move is watched with eagle eyes by Peter Valland, the Construction Supervisor employed by the consortium of investors EWE, E.ON and Vattenfall (DOTI). He has to intervene should safety regulations not be respected.

It is a clear, starry midnight. The navigation lights on two of the four already-assembled Multibrid turbines light up the dark. Next to them there are the artificial lights shining into the night from the research platform FINO 1, the guard vessel 'Otto Treplin', there to keep an eye on the test field during the complete construction work period, the two anchored tugs 'Banckert' and 'Smit Barracuda' as well as from the 'Petr Kottsov'. The powerful on-board lights of the jack-up barge

牢固的三脚式桩基

当一个物体几乎无法用眼睛看见时,就很难看出它的特点。阿尔法·文图斯风电场就是这样。在这里,从远处高于海平面的塔台上可以看见功率强大的风力发电机。然而,安装海上风力发电机最大的一个技术挑战是水下部分:基础施工。

海水很深,一种号称三脚式桩基结构的基座首次用于安装阿海珐Multibrid风力发电机。简单地说,就是把钢制的三脚式桩基的三条腿固定到海床上,为风力发电机提供一个稳固的基座,使风力发电机能够抵御暴风、洋流和海浪的侵袭。三脚式桩基在挪威维达尔的阿克克瓦纳船厂(距特隆赫姆北部50公里)进行生产和焊接组装;然后用自升式平台一次将三个三脚式桩基运送到威廉港。2009年春天,一台起重机把六台风机所用的三脚式桩基一次从威廉港搬运到了施工现场。

每个三脚式桩基都有十层楼那么高,三条腿的长度超过45米。三脚式桩基必须牢固地固定在海床上,所以它们极重,达667吨。三脚式桩基的每个脚都焊接有一个竖直的套管,套管向上伸出。30米长、100吨重的基桩从工作船上的管桩穿过,然后被固定到海床上。如果天气状况良好,安装一个三脚式桩基需要两到三天的时间。但由于天气问题,往往需要更久的时间。因此,从4月23号开始安装,直到6月1号结束,六个三脚式桩基共花费了40天时间才固定好。

人们只能在陆地上,尤其当它在船坞制造时感受到三脚式桩基的庞大尺度。它功能强大,形状笨重。如果近看,你会发现它是由圆锥形套筒做成的,因为这样可以满足稳定性要求。它的三条腿从上到下逐渐变细,焊接在基座的连接件上。

STRONG TRIPOD

When something is mostly hidden from view it's often hard to recognize what makes it special. This is also the case at the alpha ventus test field, where the powerful wind turbines can be seen towering above sea level from a long way off. However, one of the greatest technical challenges in setting up these offshore turbines is under the waterline: the foundation construction.

Because the water is so deep, a so-called tripod construction has been used for the first time for the foundations of the AREVA Multibrid wind turbines. Put simply, a tripod is a standing, three-legged construction made of steel and anchored to the seabed, providing the turbine assembled onto it with a stable foundation against storms, currents and waves. They were built and welded together at the Aker Kværner shipyard in Verdal in Norway, 50 kilometres to the north of Trondheim; subsequently three of them at a time were loaded onto a flat barge and transported right across the North Sea to Wilhelmshaven. From there, a floating crane took the six tripods for the six AREVA Multibrid turbines one at a time to the construction site in spring 2009.

Each of these tripods is as high as a ten-storey building, with the three-legged construc-tion measuring a proud 45 metres. And they really are heavyweights, weighing in at 667 tonnes. So that the tripod has a firm hold on the seabed there is a vertical pipe (pile sleeve) welded onto each foot which protrudes upwards. The 30-metre long, 100-tonne foundation piles are 'thread' through these tubular pipes from a work-ship and then driven into the seabed. Setting up a tripod takes two to three days when the conditions are good. However, as the installation team frequently has to wait for good weather, the period for the complete foundation work can be much longer. It ended up taking 40 days, from April 23rd until June 1st.

The observer can only comprehend what huge dimensions a tripod really has when it is on land, at best in the shipyard where it is being built. It's a powerful and bulky construction. If you take a close look at the shape you'll notice that it's made of conically-shaped tubes, enabling it to fulfil the statics requirements. The three legs taper off towards the foot end, as do the three connecting pieces at the base of the tripod.

进行检查，用螺栓固定好所有部件，准确布好电缆。

现在是早上5点钟，天刚微微亮，一切工作都已经完成了。队员们虽然很累，但心里充满喜悦。起重机把克林格和他的队员们用吊篮送到了JB 114号自升式平台上。"这次安装时间破纪录了，我们的安装技术越来越熟练了。"克林格对后来的安装工作很满意，准备上床休息。

当装配组队员都躺在床铺上休息时，JB 114号的船员又开始工作了。叶轮还在平台上，它的一个叶片伸出平台围栏一大段，为了提升叶轮，自升式平台必须移位。虽然只需10米左右的距离，但起重机吊臂伸开后还是够不着。因此，平台的桩腿必须从北海海床上拔起，然后移到几米外的位置。从拔出到用起锚机重新定位，再将平台提升到海面上，这个过程需花费数小时的时间。当JB 114号自升式平台升到海上25米时，夜班工人才陆续走进餐厅吃中饭。他们有点睡眼惺忪的样子，有人嘀咕道：变天了。天空灰蒙蒙的，风力超过了每秒8米。在这样的天气状况下，不能用起重机提升叶轮。但尽管如此，起重机操作员仍然在下午两点启动了引擎。

平台提升到海面25米后，所有等待的队员又开始忙碌起来。克林格让亚历山大•拉布伦茨定时向他通报风速。亚历山大•拉布伦茨是一位水道测量专家，他在舰桥上负责用仪器收集位置和天气数据。从监视器上仔细地看，可以看到这样一幅美丽的景色：一只长着橙色的嘴、带有斑纹的蛎鹬停在56米长的叶片上，它安详地享受着习习的海风。"这对我们可不是那么好的事，或许今晚的风力会减弱。"拉布伦茨看着监视器说。大约7点钟，克林格来到舰桥，向拉布伦茨询问了天气的预测情况。"现在风速为每秒7.9米"，拉布伦茨回答道。"太快了"，装配组负责人叹了口气说："每隔20分钟测一次风速，如果三次都小于每秒7米的话，我们就可以开始。"这时，提升叶轮的准备工作已经就绪，大量绳索和电缆都已经到位，队员们蓄势待发。

开始工作的指令还没有下达，餐厅已经为夜班人员准备好了热乎乎的饭菜。比利时厨师准备了羊肉、豆和米饭，可选的还有德式糖醋烤牛肉。

大约晚上10点，天色已经漆黑。克林格和梅特巴赫突然发出了工作指令。队员们听到指令，立即就位。一队队员被提升到发动机舱上，其他队员拉动各种绳索和电缆。与此同时，大型起重机吊起叶轮，小型起重机吊起叶轮的一个叶片，把整个叶轮从水平位置移到了垂直位置。起重机操作员倾其所能，尽量避免叶轮和叶片发生碰撞。几分钟后，叶轮被悬挂到了JB 114右舷上3米的地方。一切进展非常顺利。然而，非常戏剧性的一幕突然发生了。吊运过程中，叶轮叶片下面两边的保护条被紧紧地卷到还在海上吊着的叶片外壳中。"把它们顺利弄好真难"，队员们抱怨道。他们试图移开3米长的保护条，但最后还是徒劳。这时，他们突然想出用吊钩和绳索拉拽并摇晃的办法，但当他们使出所有的力量拉拽和摇晃时，保护条仍旧去不掉，时间在一点点过去，气氛十分紧张……一阵强风吹来，能清楚地听到队员们用7种不同语言的抱怨声。直到有人想起拉紧船上的绳索，将其与叶轮叶片的保护条用挂钩连接起来，同时小心地用起重机提升叶轮时，保

'Buzzard', that is conducting the foundation work for the six REpower turbines around the clock, are also shining brightly. There are flickering lights of tankers and freighters passing in the distance. There is no doubt that there's a lot going on in and around the floating construction site alpha ventus – out here on the high seas, directly to the north of the 54° latitude parallel, which at this location runs right through the transformer station of the wind farm. Although 45 kilometres off the coast of the East Frisian island of Borkum there is still a tidal range of about one and a half metres.

The moon is picturesque in the night sky. You can clearly feel the excitement increasing amongst all those involved on site. The wind has risen slightly: the tower segment has now been fastened and the nacelle has to be fitted to it without delay, because only when the tower has the weight of the nacelle holding it down will it have the necessary stability. The team removes the straps with their professional ease. It all goes fairly quickly and very soon the nacelle is hanging on the impressive shackle, which has a bolt so large that a special 100 mm spanner is required. The crane's engine moans and groans while lifting the heart of the wind turbine. The jib slowly moves outwards, turns 180° seemingly in slow motion and lifts the hanging freight directly over the open tower-segment. This is where it gets tricky, where the crane operator – without having a direct view, but in permanent radio contact with Michael Klingele and the assembly team – has to set the nacelle exactly onto the bolts. Three, two, one, zero … the huge object has landed safely. The relief is written on everyone's face. After a bit of clearing up the on-board team can go and lay down in their berths – but the team up there in the tower has the whole night ahead of them, as the technicians have to yaw the nacelle and bolt everything together and cable it all up properly.

It's now five in the morning, slowly getting light, and everything is finished. Tired but contented, the crane takes Klingele and his team in the basket over to the JB 114. "That was done in record time! We're getting better and better at this", comments Klingele happily at the end of this shift and moves off to bed.

While the assembly team are lying in their bunks, the crew of the JB 114 are back in action. In order to lift the rotor, still lying on the platform and whose one blade is protruding a long way over the railing, the jack-up barge has to be moved. It may only require around ten metres – but the crane does not have this reach when it swings out. The supporting pillars of the steel island have, therefore, to be lifted from the North Sea bed only to take up the next position a few metres away. Hours are required to lift the supporting legs, to reposition using the anchor windlasses and then push the platform again out of the water. Just as the JB 114 reaches the 25-metre point over sea level the night shift trundles into the canteen, still somewhat bleary-eyed, for their lunch. There are mumblings: in the meantime the weather has turned, the sky is leaden-grey and there is a wind at the hub height of over eight metres a second. In these conditions the rotor cannot be lifted. Nevertheless, the crane operator starts up the engines at around 2 pm and gets the hook into position.

Then the waiting starts all over again. Klingele has hydrographer Alexander Labrenz, who is up there on the bridge working out all positional and weather data with his equipment, inform him of the wind speed at regular intervals. In the meantime anyone watching carefully will see a beautiful scene: a pied oystercatcher is sitting on the tip of the 56 metre long rotor blade protruding out over board and is holding his orange beak silently into the west wind. "Doesn't look that good at all", says

叶轮升起前的最后准备
Last preparations before the rotor star is hoisted.

Labrenz looking at his monitor. "But maybe the wind will drop this evening. Then we'll have a small window for the rotor."

It is about seven in the evening when Klingele comes up to the bridge. He asks Labrenz what can be expected from the weather. "We're currently at 7.9 metres a second", is the answer. "Too fast", sighs the head of the assembly mission, and adds: "Once the wind figures are less than seven metres in three successive measurements taken at intervals of 20 minutes – then we'll start." Meanwhile, the final preparations for lifting the rotor have been completed. Numerous ropes and cables have been laid out, all the men are in full gear and ready to go… but the go-ahead has still not been given. At least there is a hot meal ready for the night shift waiting for them in the canteen. The Belgian cook has made lamb, beans and rice. And as an alternative there's a hearty Sauerbraten.

At about ten in the evening, it is almost pitch-black when Klingele and Mettbach suddenly give the signal to get going. Everyone gets into position quickly: a team is lifted onto the nacelle, the others pull and move various ropes and cables about, while the large crane lifts up the rotor and the small crane hooks up and lifts one of the blades, thus moving the whole rotor from a horizontal into a vertical position. The crane operators have to demonstrate all their considerable skill so they don't hit anything. After a few minutes the rotor is hanging at a distance of three metres on the starboard side of the JB 114. All well and good. However, all of a sudden a small drama unfolds: the two edge protectors that take the load at the lower part of the rotor blade during transport have sucked themselves tightly onto the outer casing of the blade hanging over the sea. "Devil's own job to get 'em off", curse the men. They attempt to remove a three-metre-long protector – in vain. It's time for improvisation: using hooks, ropes and all their combined strength they pull and shake, but the polyester edge-protectors is stuck fast. Time is running out, but everyone has to keep their nerve. The time-window is tight and getter tighter by the minute … it's frowns all round, and curses in seven different languages can be heard clearly above the gusting wind. It is not until someone has the idea of fastening a chain on board, connecting it to the rotor protector using hooks and at the same time carefully lifting the rotor with the crane that a

护条才被去掉并落入海中。现在要将另一边的保护条也去掉。这一边就容易多了，但叶轮叶片的外表面可能会略微受损。不过只是一点划痕，很容易修补。

工作场面还是很紧张。风速在增加，预计装配风机的最佳时间差点因刚才的突发情况而错过。然而，梅特巴赫不想取消行动，他冲着队员们喊道："继续，继续，继续！"队员们紧张地工作着。起重机吊起叶轮，转动悬臂，当悬臂转到JB 114的船尾时，开始一点一点向上挪动，最终将叶轮固定在左舷侧，也就是正对发动机舱的位置。这时已经是凌晨2点了，风力明显加大了。他们必须选择一个恰当的时机，将叶轮与发动机舱对接上。船上的队员在专注地看着，但只能看到发动机舱正在进行的大致动作。"接上了！"消息通过无线电传了出来，任务成功完成了，队员总算是松了一口气。他们把螺栓全部拧紧，第五台海上风机安装就完成了。接下来几天，这台风机就能正常使用了。作为奖赏，他们要再去喝点咖啡，有些人想再吃点夜宵，听着摇滚乐吃烤菊苣和蒸土豆泥。夜宵过后，队员们捆好布带，卷好电缆，堆放好重重的链条。夜班工人还要继续工作，大约早上7点，叶轮安装完毕，克林格带领装配队回到船上。尽管很累，但他们很高兴。

当安装作业队队员们熟睡时，自升式平台的队员已经为按时返回荷兰港口埃姆斯港口做好了准备。船长在指挥JB 114号自升式平台缓慢下降。这是一个持续数小时的常规作业，但人们仍然争分夺秒，因为时间就是金钱。在一个从四月到八月的安装作业季里，所有时间成本都将累积在一起。在此之上是两艘拖轮的花费，它在整个作业过程中的燃油费高得惊人！但没有它们，自升式平台无法移动。除此之外，必须为船员和安装作业队员提供24小时无间断的后勤保障服务。没有它，整个作业队就将士气低落。

拖船起锚了。一艘拉着JB 114号自升式平台的船艏，另一艘拉着船艉。五台风力发电机渐渐地在水平线上消失。繁忙的航线水道上，到处是集装箱船和货船，好像是灰黄霾下的珍珠项链。再过几个小时，东西弗里西亚海岸的轮廓就依稀可见了。

往西看，西弗里西亚岛Rottumeroog和几个沙滩的轮廓已依稀可见。船队保持着安全距离，缓慢通过波尔库姆滨海区，很多度假的人们在这里享受着阳光浴，有的人胆子大，干脆跳进海里。埃姆斯蒙德风电场已经出现在荷兰海岸，这是欧洲最大的陆上风电场之一。在它的东边，"Banckert"已经把JB 114号自升式平台完全拖进了埃姆斯港。

埃姆斯港是一个工业港口，根据20世纪70年代的计划创建在堤坝内的埃姆斯河西海岸。港口建得没什么特色，但其功能很多。码头区很宽阔，可装卸巨大的风力发电机。港口区为矩形，很宽，为操作和运输连接Mega-Motti提供了足够的空间，Mega-Motti能够把叶轮、发动机舱和塔筒从施塔德和不来梅港运到这里。而选择埃姆斯港的决定因素，是因为它的地理位置靠近阿尔法·文图斯风电场，没有水闸，可以连续使用。

自升式平台停靠在码头时已是晚上。码头边上，阿海珐Multibrid公司的第六台也是最后一台风力发电机正在等候运到阿尔法·文图斯风电场。

possible solution to the problem comes into view. And it works! The protector positively flies off and sinks into the inky depths. Now it's time for the opposite edge. It can be removed easily, dropping away in an uncontrolled manner but slightly damaging the outer skin. Annoying – but thankfully it's only a scratch that can be swiftly repaired.

But the tension remains high. The wind has increased and the predicted time window has almost been exhausted with this operation. However, Mettbach does not want to cancel everything and barks "Go, go, *go*!" at his team. The technicians jump into action and fix cables: the crane

任务完成：叶轮安装完毕的风机。
Mission completed: turbine with rotor.

装运将在第二天早上开始。迈克尔·克林格完成工作，睡了一小觉后，看起来很自信。项目即将完成，先前的工作尽管有很多困难，但还是成功解决了。不过，阿海珐Multibrid公司早就预料到这次工作的艰难，这包括在2008年8月遇到的一次强风暴积累的经验。当时，队员乘坐装有三个三脚式桩基的自升式平台出发前往风电场，在快要到达目的地时，发现浮吊功能不满足承保方的技术要求，所以不得不返回，这是一次痛苦的撤退。这件事遭到了媒体和风能行业同行们的嘲笑。但他们善于总结经验，吸取教训。克林格率领的工程队依然不放弃自己的目

boom swings away, pulls up the rotor, swivels it around the stern of the JB 114 and moves it bit by bit upwards into the dark night. On the port side the delicate huge object is finally positioned face-to-face with the nacelle. By this time it is almost two in the morning and the wind has picked up considerably. Now they have to choose the right moment to dock the rotor onto the nacelle. The men on board are watching spellbound, heads thrown back, seeing only the outline of what is going on up there at the nacelle. The news is radioed down: "It's in!" Mission successfully completed and the relief is palpable. The fifth turbine is

安装作业结束后：清理JB 114甲板。
Finished: tidying up the JB 114 deck.

标。在2008至2009年的冬天，他们提出用起重能力较大的浮吊，并采用新的策略。2009年的工作并没有想象中顺利。比如，桩基安装中需要对三脚式桩基进行调平，但调平工具不起作用，而后续的工作还必须继续，在第二个桩基作业中，现场技术人员立即决定采取其它调平方法，使得接下来的插入、夯实和调整等基建工作顺利进行，这些工作程序是海上风电技术（OWT）公司于2001年制定的。2004年12月，他们在不来梅港北部的河堤后安装了5兆瓦的第一台样机。后来，克林格的队员做了很多次运行试验，虽然试验有失败也有成功，但为海上风机的安装积累了经验。

"我坚信我们的海上安装技术。"迈克尔•克林格在驶回海岸时说。虽已经安装了五台风力发电机，但他并不否认在风电场建设的初期，他也不确定这些风电安装方案是否可行。水下30米有太多的事情无法预测，也没有可以借鉴的经验。除了瑞能公司在Beatrice和Thornton Bank有风电场，世界上还没有人在远离海岸并且如此深的水下安装过风力发电机。对于这位经验丰富的工程师来说，在阿尔法•文图斯风电场安装六台风力发电机，意味着结束了他从2007年进入

up, now all they have to do is bolt it together and it can be commissioned in the coming days. As a reward there is another coffee. Some enjoy another nighttime meal: to the sound of rockabilly music the beaming cook serves up piles of grilled chicory and steaming mashed potatoes. After the meal the night shift continues. Time to tidy up, and the men tie down straps, roll up cables and stow heavy chains. At about seven in the morning the rotor has been completely fitted and the assembly team organised by Michael Klingele return in the basket back on board from the nacelle, tired but happy.

While the team are enjoying their well-earned sleep, the crew of the jack-up barge gets ready to return without delay to the Dutch port of Eemshaven. A procedure that takes, as usual, a few hours. But every minute counts, as time is money. In an assembly period stretching from April to August it all adds up. On top of this are the costs for the two tugs involved, which burn up a considerable amount of fuel while doing the tugging but without which the platform would simply not be manoeuvrable. Moreover, the on-board crew and assembly team have to be catered for around the clock – without the 'full board' arrangement, the atmosphere would quickly go downhill. The captain of the JB 114 presses the knobs and buttons on the command bridge and the jack-up

托马斯·皮亚斯塔、塞巴斯蒂安·德格纳和罗伯特·努克利希（从左至右）在安装完风电场第一台风机后。
Thomas Piasta, Sebastian Degner and Robert Nuglisch (from left to right) after setting up the first turbine in the wind farm.

Multibrid公司就开始的令他兴奋的样机阶段的工作。这里的前老板英格·德布尔激发了他对建造海上风机的兴趣，并鼓动他离开其竞争对手Suzlon Energy公司（他在印度为该公司工作了多年）。"我们经常把赌注押在有包装且较轻的设备上。每样东西都设计得非常紧凑，没有独立的驱动系统，为了节省空间，发电机和增速齿轮箱被紧凑地设置在发动机舱内。而且，我们早已决定选用单级变速箱"。克林格提到Multibrid公司的5兆瓦发电机技术方案时显得非常激动。在接下来的几年，一旦它的生产组装过程不断标准化，发电机就能进行系列投产。克林格对海上风电可观的经济前景和8兆瓦的发电机深信不疑。"还有，我们在这里不会影响到别人，我们正在建设的是大型绿色环保发电厂，其他人还能有什么疑问吗？"他笑着说道。

2009年8月12日，对克林格和他的队员来说是一个非常特别的日子。那天晚上9点15分，第一度海上风电在德国经济特区从Multibrid公司的5兆瓦风力电机中产出并输送到陆上。阿海珐Multibrid的全体员工和所有参加该工作的人员，经过几年的辛苦工作后获得了成功，他们尽情享受着成功的喜悦和巨大的满足。德国能源领域开始走进了一个崭新的时代。

barge is slowly but surely lowered.

Then the tugs weigh anchor and start pulling the flat, square steel monolith back towards the coast. One tug pulls with a thick steel cable from the bow, while to the stern the second tug stabilises it. The five turbines disappear slowly over the horizon. The nautical caravan crosses the busy shipping lane, dotted with container and freight ships like a chain of pearls against a grey-yellow haze. After only a few hours the first outlines of the East and West Frisian coast can be seen. To the west, the silhouette of the West Frisian island Rottumeroog and a few sandbanks are just about visible. Keeping a safe distance, the procession slowly passes the waterfront of Borkum, where the holidaymakers are sunning themselves on the beach and a few hardy souls have even dared to plunge into the North Sea. The wind farm Eemsmond appears on the Dutch coast, one of the largest onshore wind farms in Europe. On its east side the 'Banckert' finally manoeuvres the JB 114 into the port entrance of Eemshaven.

This industrial port was planned in the 1970s and constructed on the west bank of the River Ems within a newly raised dyke. The port is nothing at all for romantics – down-to-earth, but extremely functional: wide quayside areas enable problem-free loading and unloading of the giant wind turbines. Large, rectangular inner harbour basins provide space for manoeuvring and for the transport-combine Mega-Motti, which brings the rotors, nacelles and tower segments from Stade and Bremerhaven to here. However, the decisive benefits of Eemshaven as starting point are its geographical proximity to the alpha ventus field, and the fact that this port has no canal locks and can therefore be used non-stop.

It's already evening when the jack-up barge finally docks and pushes its steel pipes into the bottom of the harbour for mooring stability. On the quayside the sixth and last turbine from AREVA Multibrid is already waiting to be shipped out to alpha ventus.

The loading-up starts the next morning. After catching a bit of sleep and finishing the work, Michael Klingele seems confident. The project is close to completion and the pioneering work has been successfully mastered in spite of all kinds of obstacles. However, AREVA Multibrid has had to learn the hard way. This also includes the experience gathered in the extremely stormy August of 2008, when the team set off with a smaller pontoon loaded with three tripods towards the test field, only having to turn back shortly before reaching the destination because the floating crane did not fulfil the technical requirements that were laid down by the insurer – a bitter setback. Even if they were ridiculed by the media and also by their own colleagues within the wind-energy sector, these pioneers quickly learned from such mistakes. The engineering team around Klingele remained steadfastly goal-focused and created a new strategy in the winter of 2008/09 with larger equipment. But then again, the year 2009 did not always go as hoped. For example, the alignment of the tripods using a certain compensating device, the so-called 'levelling tool' did not work correctly. After completing the second foundation, the on-site technicians had to start work without the levelling tools, which turned out to be just the right decision. The team was then able to carry out the plunging, ramming and shakedown procedures of the foundation, as painstakingly developed by Offshore Wind Technologie (OWT) founded in 2001, with greater and greater ease. However, the team had not only gone through these learning processes on the open sea in the test field: the learning curve had begun years before, as soon as they began setting up the first prototype of the M5000 in December 2004 behind the embankments to the north of Bremerhaven. Since then Klingele's engineering team has practiced in numerous dry test-runs so as to be as well prepared as possible for any eventualities at sea, with all the setbacks and successes that such a courageoguous project involves.

"I firmly believe in the offshore technology", says Michael Klingele during the return to shore. Having installed five turbines he does not even try to hide the fact that, at the start of the construction work in the test field, in spite of all the practice and provisions he did not know for sure whether it would all really work. There were just too many unknowns in waters that were 30 metres deep; there was no past experience that those involved could fall back on. Except for REpower – with the wind farms Beatrice and Thornton Bank – no one in the world had previously set up turbines so far away from the coast in such a depth of water. For the trained industrial engineer, completing the installation of the six turbines in the alpha ventus test field will end an exciting prototype phase that started when he joined Multibrid in 2007. The former boss there, Ingo de Buhr, got him interested in the idea of constructing offshore turbines and enticed him away from the competitor Suzlon Energy, for whom he had been working for some years in India. "We always placed our bets on a capsulated and lightweight system. Everything is designed to be compact. There should be no separate drive train and the generator and rotor bearing were shrunk down into the nacelle so as to save space. Moreover, we made the decision early on for a single-stage gearbox", enthuses Klingele about the technical concept of the Multibrid M5000. Once the manufacturing and assembly processes become increasingly standardized in the coming years, the turbines will go into serial production – Klingele uses buzzwords here such as "horizontal single-blade assembly at hub height." The installation techniques will also be developed further. He has no doubts that offshore wind power has a great economic future and is already looking forward to turbines with an output of eight megawatts. "What's more," he smiles, "we're not disturbing anyone out there and are establishing green power generation on a large scale. What more can anyone ask?!"

That's why the 12th of August 2009 was a very special date for Klingele and his team: late that evening at 9.15 pm, the first kilowatt-hours of offshore wind power flowed from a Multibrid M5000 in the German Exclusive Economic Zone (EEZ) onto land. For the employees of AREVA Multibrid and for DOTI this was, after years of hard work, tremendously satisfying – and the start into a bright new era for the German energy sector.

塔筒分段从自升式平台上升起,进而安装完成。
The tower section is hoisted from the jack-up barge and then mounted.

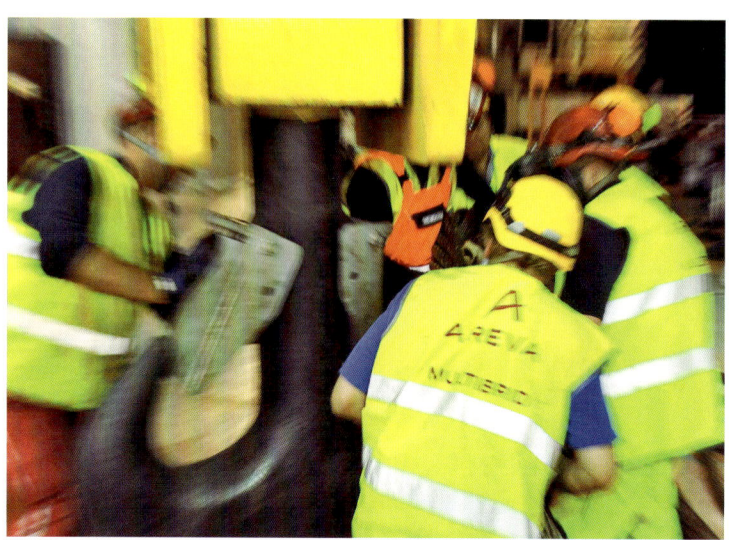

人力作业仍是不可少的。工人们一起起吊将叶轮的钢缆绳套上吊钩。这项工作需要团结一心,每个成员必须依靠团队的力量才能完成。
Manpower is still required. Together, workers tie the rope to which the rotor star will eventually be attached, to the crane hook. Work goes hand in hand, so each member must be able to rely on the team.

直面挑战 Facing challenges
阿海珐MULTIBRID公司行政管理发言人
AREVA MULTIBRID EXECUTIVE MANAGEMENT SPOKESMAN

费利克斯•第比尔斯
Félix Debierre

自从2007年以来，费利克斯•第比尔斯一直担任阿海珐Multibrid公司的首席执行官，负责阿海珐公司的风能工作。他在柏林和巴黎学习过，并以土木工程和国际经济学硕士毕业。他最初就职于法国财政部和金融部门，其间在巴黎、美国和日本工作，随后进入工业界，加入了Nexans电缆集团（a.o.），在中国建立了一家光纤电缆合资企业，后担任全球业务总经理。自2004年以来，他一直在阿海珐公司工作。

阿尔法•文图斯是阿海珐Multibrid公司的第一个大型海上风电项目，这个项目具有挑战性。2009年夏末，当公司的六台海上风力发电机成功安装时，你一定感到非常欣慰。

阿尔法•文图斯项目的结果已经超过了我们的预期。最重要的是验证了5兆瓦能够用于海上发电的事实。在整个项目的实施过程中，我们非常关注安全问题。我想我们可以为我们严格的安全标准感到骄傲。我们对这六台风力发电机实现了快速、专业、无事故安装，外加安装队的初始性能报告，这为我们的未来发展打下了一个良好基础，展示了阿海珐公司海上产品组合的多面性。

阿尔法•文图斯项目对于贵公司未来发展的重要意义是什么？

阿尔法•文图斯项目是一系列海上风电场建设的开端，这些风电场将使用我们5兆瓦的风力发电机。继阿尔法•文图斯风电场之后，即将上马商用的海上风电场，每个风电场将使用多达80台风力发电机，所以我们正在扩大生产能力。阿尔法•文图斯项目已经证明，我们的发展方向是正确的。

5兆瓦风力发电机已经在北海运行几个月了，你能就它的技术性说些什么吗？

六台5兆瓦风力发电机从2009年秋天运行到12月为止，产生了将近3000万千瓦时电能。仅11月下半月，就产生了超过1000万千瓦时电能，可利用率达到了99%。试运行期间取得的这些惊人、显著的成果，已经大大地超过了我们的预期。

从明年为阿尔法•文图斯风电场制定的RAVE计划的研究中，你有什么期望？

我们希望在技术上有所创新，该计划实施后，希望在海上风能的后勤供应和环保方面出台统一的标准。

Félix Debierre has been CEO of AREVA Multibrid since 2007 and in charge of AREVA wind activities. He studied in Berlin and Paris, and graduated as Engineer from the Ecole Poly-technique and the Ecole des Ponts-et-Chaussees (Civil engineer), as well as with a Master of International Economics. He has spent his initial career as a civil servant at the French Treasury and in the banking sector, where he has worked in Paris, the USA and Japan. He joined the industrial world for the Nexans cable group, a.o. to set up an optical fiber cable joint venture in China and later as world-wide business line manager. He has been with AREVA since 2004.

alpha ventus was the first big test of the rough offshore business for AREVA Multibrid. It must have been a huge relief for you when the six turbines from your company were successfully installed in the late summer of 2009.

The outcome of the alpha ventus project has exceeded our expectations. The suitability of the M5000 for offshore operations has now been proven, and that is the most important thing for us. Throughout, our primary focus was on the safety aspects, and I think we can be very proud of our high safety standard. The fast, professional, accident-free installation of the six turbines, plus the initial performance reports of our service team, are a good foundation for future business and demonstrate the versatility of the AREVA offshore portfolio.

What is the significance of the alpha ventus project for the future development of your company?

alpha ventus is the kickoff for a series of offshore wind farms that will use our 5-megawatt M5000 wind turbines. We're expanding our production capacity, because the com-mercial offshore farms that are set to follow the alpha ventus test field will use up to 80 turbines each. alpha ventus has given us the certainty that we are on the right path with our ongoing growth.

Now that the turbines have been opera-ting in the North Sea for a few months, can you say anything as to the technical performance of the Multibrid M5000?

The six M5000 generated almost 30 million kilowatt-hours from their commissioning in the

不来梅港阿海珐Multibrid生产大厅中装配的5兆瓦旋翼叶毂。
The M5000 hub is assembled in the AREVA Multibrid production hall in Bremerhaven.

对于阿尔法·文图斯项目,和瑞能公司不一样,你交付风力发电机就如同"交钥匙"一样,为什么?

在阿尔法·文图斯项目中,阿海珐Multibrid公司提供风机基座并负责安装,然后进行现场风机安装,最后交付给用户。"交钥匙"从字面上讲,就是准备投入运行。我们不能只生产风力发电机,还必须逐步建立必要的供应商体系,并且考虑项目工程物流,诸如如何交付那些常常重达数吨的设备、部件,并使用特种工程船舶在海上安装它们,固定三脚式桩基,然后将六台5兆瓦风

autumn until December 2009. During the second half of November alone, they operated at full capacity and generated over ten million kilowatt hours, with an availability of 99 percent. These surprisingly positive results during test operations have significantly exceeded our expectations.

What benefits do you anticipate from the scientific research in the RAVE programme that is planned for the alpha ventus test field in the coming years?

We're hoping for technical innovations, and we're looking to the programme to result in uniform standards and progress on the logistical as well as environmental questions surrounding offshore wind energy.

Unlike the manufacturer REpower, for the alpha ventus project you delivered your turbines as 'turn-key'. What exactly does that mean?

AREVA Multibrid supplied and installed the foundations and then set up the turbines on-site. We delivered them to the customer 'turn-key', in the

直面挑战 Facing challenges 35

力发电机矗立在海上。总的来说，这是一个巨大的挑战，我很高兴，我们能够控制局面。

贵公司计划坚持交钥匙战略吗？还是在一些情况下，只做一个制造商？

阿海珐Multibrid公司计划给潜在的海上风电场经营者提供多方面的产品组合解决方案。为了扩展市场，加强我们在国际市场上的地位，我们的产品必须具备用户需要的灵活性。我们重点是制造5兆瓦风力电机，并提供维护服务。我们将使5兆瓦风力电机能适应未来海上风电场特殊的需要和技术要求。

不久的将来会对5兆瓦风力发电机做技术改进吗？

5兆瓦的技术改进将与其在我们公司的批量生产同时进行。不同的风电场位置需要不同的改进，我们也将把特定用户的要求纳入我们的高技术产品范围。针对目前的5兆瓦额定输出功率的风力发电机，我们会很快对其改进。

你认为海上风能领域最大的技术挑战是什么？有改进的空间吗？

最大的技术挑战是使海上风机的发电量最大化。虽然5兆瓦风力电机已经具有很高的水平，但是我们依然和用户一起努力，以期进一步改进设备的安装和运行，并且在每一个风电场的全生命周期都这样做。

你也认为海上风能会像过去20年中发展的陆上风能一样成功吗？

是的。各种迹象表明，未来的海上风能和今天陆上的风能一样，同样会获得成功。高功率风力发电机将有更大的能量输出，海上的风力不仅猛烈，而且持续不断，加上成本在不断降低，所以这方面需求将会更大。

如果你的看法是正确的，那么海上风电市场在下一个十年里，哪些国家会发展得最快？

我们正在关注欧洲不同的市场，英国和德国有巨大的潜力。我们也期望在北美和中国有更大的市场。

未来几年，你们计划推出什么类型的风力发电机？除继续生产5兆瓦级产品外，阿海珐Multibrid公司会生产更大的风力发电机吗？

短期内，我们会优先考虑优化5兆瓦的技术，扩大生产能力。在总公司的支持下，一方面继续生产，完成手中的订单，另一方面进行进一

literal sense of the word – that is, absolutely ready to go into operation.

To do this we had to do much more than just manufacture the turbines. We had to build up the necessary infrastructure of suppliers, and also get a handle on the logistical elements of the project. We took care of delivering the components, weighing many tonnes each, and installing them with special construction ships, anchoring the tripod foundation structures and erecting the six M5000 units. All in all it was a big challenge, which I am happy to say we were able to master.

Does your company intend to stick to the turn-key strategy? Or will you also act just as a manufacturer in some instances?

AREVA Multibrid intends to offer potential offshore wind farm operators a multifaceted solution portfolio. In order to reinforce and extend our position on the world market, we need to provide the flexibility our customers demand. Our primary focus is on manufactu-ring and providing maintenance for the M5000. We also adapt the M5000 to the specific sites and technical requirements of future offshore wind farm operators.

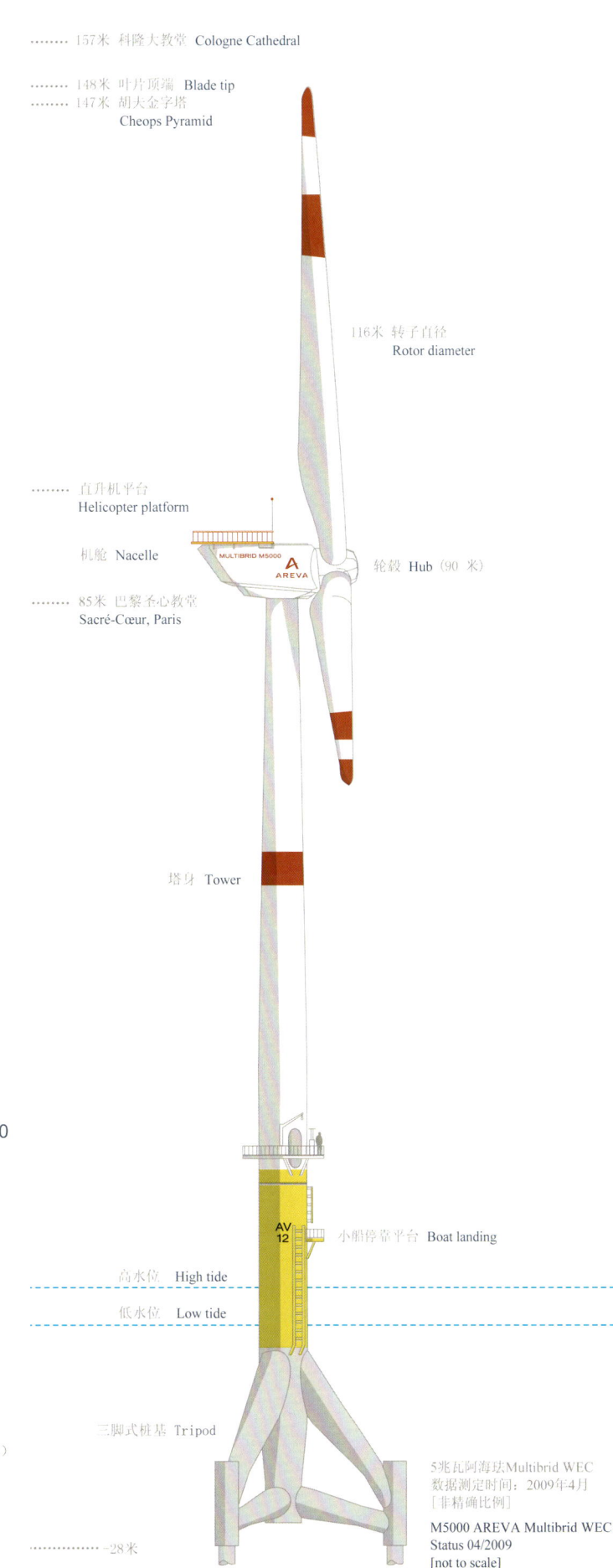

阿海珐MULTIBRID公司5兆瓦技术数据
TECHNICAL DATA AREVA MULTIBRID M5000

距海床总高 Overall height above seabed	178米
额定功率 Rated capacity	5兆瓦
速度 Speed	5.9～14.8转/分 5.9 to 14.8 rpm
初始工作风速 Cut-in wind speed	3.5米/秒（风力3级） 3,5 m/s (wind force 3)
额定风速 Rated wind speed	12.5米/秒（风力6级） 12,5 m/s (wind force 6)
停止工作风速 Cut-out wind speed	25米/秒（风力10级） 25 m/s (wind force 10)
叶片尖部速度 Blade tip speed	90米/秒（324千米/小时）
含叶轮和轮毂的发动机舱质量 Nacelle mass with rotor and hub	357.8吨
质量（基座、塔、发动机舱） Steel mass (foundation, tower, nacelle)	1390吨
基座质量 Steel mass of foundation alone	667吨

直面挑战 Facing challenges 37

步的研发。从陆上产品的效果和北海已经投入运行的这些风力发电机来看，5兆瓦级风力发电机的市场空间很大。更大功率的风力发电机一定会为风电场经营者提供上述的创新优势。

依此看，Multibrid的M5000（5兆瓦）不久会变成M6000吗？

额定功率增加是一方面，最重要的是满足用户需求。此外，我们也在考虑更大的叶轮直径和针对特殊风场的改进。

每台风力发电机再多产生一个兆瓦的电能，制造商和经营者从中得到多少经济效益？

这个问题只能针对每个风电场回答。但是，增加的输出功率能使每台风力发电机每年赚到几十万欧元。

你认为2020年之前还能安装多少台阿海珐Multibrid海上风力发电机？

计划为500台至1000台，具体情况取决于国际市场需求。

阿海珐是一家拥有多个子公司的大型集团，风能是它的新业务，是什么原因促成阿海珐公司收购了Multibrid公司，从而进入风能市场？

2006年，阿海珐集团成立可再生能源公司，2007年，集团收购了Multibrid股份有限公司51%的股份，并且在2011年之前将购买100%的股份。我们计划将无二氧化碳排放的能源方案引进全世界的能源市场。这是我们建立可再生能源公司的动机，也是我们进入风能行业的原因。2009年，我们进一步加强了对风能事业的发展，购买了德国施塔德叶轮制造商PNR公司100%的股份。

未来海上风能对集团的发展将起到什么作用？

从2009年以来，海上风能已经是我们集团战略中关键的组成部分。阿海珐集团可再生能源公司开发有风能、太阳能、生物质能和氢存储介质。我们的发展着重于海上风能行业。凭借德国的高水平设计和全球能源集团的财力，我们一定会在不久的将来，赢得更大的国际市场份额，迎来美好的发展前景。

Can we expect technical modifications to the M5000 turbines in the near future?

Technical development of the M5000 will proceed in parallel with series production at our company. Different wind-farm sites require different modifications, and we will also incorporate specific customer wishes into their versions of our high-tech product. If you're referring to the rated output of the turbine that currently generates five megawatts, then we first need to define "near future."

Where do you see the most difficult technical challenges in offshore wind energy? Is there room for improvement?

The greatest technical challenge is the maximisation of the energy output of our offshore turbines. The M5000 is already at a very high level of development, but together with our customers we are working towards further improvements in the installation and operation of our systems and will continue to do so over the entire lifetime of a given wind farm.

Do you share the opinion that offshore wind energy will be a success story similar to that of onshore wind energy during the past 20 years?

Yes, the signs point to offshore wind energy becoming every bit as much a success story in the future as wind energy on land is today. The greater energy yield from high-capacity turbines plus the considerably stronger and steadier winds at sea, in combination with ongoing cost reductions, will ensure high demand.

Assuming your assessment is correct, where will the offshore market develop most rapidly in the next decade?

We're keeping an eye on the different Euro-pean markets, and see great potential in the UK and Germany. We also expect strong market development in North America and China.

What types of turbines do you plan to launch in the coming years? In addition to series production of the 5-megawatt class, will we see even larger turbines from AREVA Multibrid?

Over the short term, we are prioritising the optimisation of the technical possibilities of the M5000 and the expansion of our production capacity. Series production for orders in hand, and further research and develop-ment, are naturally proceeding in parallel through the support of our parent company. The 5-megawatt class looks very promising, with the onshore results and the energy these turbines are already generating in the North Sea. A higher power-output class will have to offer farm operators the same innovative advantages.

… so will the Multibrid M5000 soon become an M6000?

Our thinking is following several different channels, and is aligned first and foremost with the desires of our customers. Increased rated capacity is certainly one aspect, but larger rotor diameters and modifications for specific wind sites are also on our list.

What financial benefits do manufacturers and operators get from another megawatt per turbine?

This question can only be answered on a site-per-site basis. But the additional output can add up to several hundred thousand euros earned per turbine per year.

Do you have an idea how many AREVA Multibrid offshore turbines will be standing in the sea by 2020?

We project 500 to 1,000 installed offshore turbines, depending on how international demand develops.

AREVA is a large group with many subsidiary companies. Its wind energy activities are relatively new. What motivated AREVA to acquire Multibrid and thereby enter the wind-energy market?

The AREVA Renewables Division was founded in 2006. In 2007 the group bought 51 percent of Multibrid GmbH, and will have acquired 100 percent by 2011. Our vision is to offer CO_2-free solutions to the worldwide energy market. That is the motivation behind our establishment of the Renewables Division, and that's why we got into wind energy. In 2009 we further strengthened our commitment to wind energy with the purchase of 100 percent of the rotor-blade manufacturer PNR in Stade, Germany.

What role will offshore wind energy play for the parent company in the future?

Offshore wind energy has been a key element in our group's strategy since 2009. The AREVA Renewables Division covers wind, solar, biomass and the development of hydrogen storage media. Our expectations for business growth are highest in the offshore wind field. The combination of highly qualified German engineering and the financial power of a world-wide energy group offer excellent prospects for a high international market share in the near future.

从梦想到现实
From vision to reality

用海上风能发电的想法为时已久,一些方案很奇特。例如,冈特•瓦格纳在1982年安装了一台25米长的工作叶片,并呈直角端连接了一个短的稳定叶片。这位聪明的柏林商人建议在北海上发电,用这个装置达到250千瓦的额定功率。他急切地告诉了每一个人他要建造这个额定功率为100兆瓦的装置,但他从来没通过试验阶段。

而其他方案在技术上更为可行,至少初看上去与今天的海上风机惊人地相似。在埃里•奇霍的档案中有许多引人关注的文件。上世纪80年代初,他在MAN诺伊技术公司担任飞机设计工程师,负责大型GROWIAN风机的空气动力设计。一张绘于上世纪70年代末的彩色蓝图上展现了一个用两根桩腿支撑的海上风塔,塔的上面装有一个两叶片的叶轮。更远的地平线处还能看到一些大型风机的轮廓。而在同一时期的另一张标题为"Helgoland的风能"的手绘图上,水中矗立着一座三叶片风塔,尽管它紧邻码头岸墙。

但是这些都已成为了历史。海上风能方案真正成形是在上世纪90年代后半期。当时陆上风能已经起飞。海上风能要在能源行业越来越得到重视,并日益成功,就必须经过艰苦的创业阶段,克服各种阻力。此外,第一个社会民主党-绿党联合政府于1998年执政。他们不遗余力地推动再生能源法案的工作,以实现可再生能源在各层面上的持续突破。该法案最终于2000年开始实施,并取代了自1991年生效的电力法案。新的法律为风力、太阳、水和生物发电提供了政策框架。此外,再生能源法案首次规定了海上风能发电的资费。

这一有利的环境在上世纪90年代末激励了很多工程师、风能发展商和制造厂家,他们提出了在北海和波罗的海实施的初步海上计划。1999年9月,在胡苏姆市北弗里希亚镇举办的"胡苏姆风电"博览会上,各种海上风电业务成为讨论的焦点。当时,瑞典和英国已经开始积累其海上风电场的经验,荷兰也有建造海上风电的计划。此外,从风能起源国家——丹麦传出了一个重要的、令人鼓舞的消息。丹麦人于1991年在波罗的海(Vindeby)建立了首个海上风电场,额定功率5兆瓦;第二个海工项目凯特加特于1995年开始进行,其额定功率也是5兆瓦。与此同时,其它大型项目也处在推进阶段:造型优美的米德尔格伦登项目紧邻哥本哈根海岸,该项目有20台风机,总装机容量达40兆瓦;还有北海的Horns Rev项目,计划装机容量达160兆瓦。这使各界非常惊奇,有时甚至是更多的怀疑。尽管如此,"海上风电"这个主题已在能源行业稳固地扎下根来。

The notion of generating wind power at sea has been around for quite a while. Some ideas have been strange. Like those of Günter Wagner who, in 1982, installed a 25-metre-long working blade with a shorter stabilization blade attached at a right-angle. Using this construction, intended to achieve a rated capacity of 250 kilowatts, the smart Berlin businessman proposed generating electricity on the North Sea. However, he never got past the experimental stage, although he told everyone brashly that he intended to build this construction with a rated power of 100 megawatts.

Other ideas, on the other hand, were technologically sounder. At least at first glance they were astonishingly similar to today's offshore turbines. There are remarkable documents to be found in Erich Hau's archives, an aircraft construction engineer at MAN Neue Technologien who at the beginning of the 'eighties was responsible for the aerodynamics of the large-scale GROWIAN wind turbine. You will find a coloured blueprint dating from the end of the 'seventies showing a two-bladed rotor on a tower braced with two stays on a foaming sea. The outlines of further offshore giants are to be seen on the horizon in this atmospheric illustration. In another hand-drawn illustration from around this time, with the title 'Wind Energy for Helgoland', there is a three-blader standing in the water – even if it is directly next to the quay wall.

But that's all history. Offshore wind energy only really took shape in the second half of the 'nineties. At this time, the wind-energy sector on land had already taken off. However, it had had to battle through a tough pioneering phase and a great deal of resistance to become an increasingly successful industry that was taken more and more serious-ly by the energy sector. Moreover, the first Social Democratic Party/Green Party coalition government took power in 1998. They worked painstakingly on the Renewable Energy Act, which finally came into effect in 2000 and replaced the Electricity Act that had been in force since 1991. The new law provided electricity generation from wind, sun, water and biomass with the energy-political framework that was required to give renewable energies a lasting breakthrough on all levels. Moreover, the Renewable Energy Act defined a tariff for electricity from offshore wind energy for the first time.

This positive environment inspired various engineers, wind-energy developers and manufacturers at the end of the 'nineties to suggest initial and ambitious offshore plans in the North and Baltic Seas. In September 1999, various offshore activities became the focal point of discussions at the wind-energy trade fair 'HusumWind' in the North Friesian town of Husum. The Swedes and British were beginning to gather their first experience with offshore wind farms near the coast and there were also offshore plans in the Netherlands. Moreover, an important

源自东弗里斯兰群岛

阿尔法•文图斯项目最先起源于莱尔。从这个东弗里希亚城镇开始的梦想，在10年后变成了现实。1997年，一名专注于再生能源的电气工程师、企业家英戈•德布尔（英格•德布尔）在其出生地创立了一个仅有3人的Prokon北方能源系统有限责任公司。该公司很快以各种风能项目而声名鹊起，现在，公司员工已经发展到400多人。德布尔以坚定的决心和执着的信念，接连开发了一个又一个陆上风电场。其他人或许会满足于这样的成功事业，但德布尔没有。作为船长的儿子，他想走得更远。他属于那种不断寻求新的挑战的人。还有什么比自己开发海上风电场更具挑战性呢？

开发海上风电场，英戈•德布尔和自己的员工必须从零开始。他们甚至找不到可资借鉴的北海和波罗的海地图，但他们需要通过这些地图了解详细的海底状况、水深、水流、平均潮差、海运航线和风力状况信息。因此，Prokon北方公司不得不向德国联邦海事局专门提出申请，以获准复制航海地图。为了更好、更实际地了解风电行业，这些德国的海上开拓者从莱尔出发，前往卡尔玛和欧蓝德岛之间的瑞典厄特格伦登海上风电场考察。该风电场由安然风能德国子公司建造，后被通用电气公司收购，几年后，又转让给大瀑布电力公司。经过无数次考察、咨询，并对航海地图进行大量分析，德布尔和同伴们最终选择了一片海域，该海域就在东弗里希亚海岸的正方前。规划的风电场将建立在波尔坎岛的北边，位于两条繁忙的国际海运航线之间，北边是通往德国湾的西线，南边是泰尔斯海灵岛——德国湾航线。与陆上风电开发不同，这些海上风能开拓者没有这片海域精确可用的实际风力状况数据。德国联邦海事局只有从灯塔船上测得的水面上的风力测量数据，风电专家不得不根据相应的高度进行推算。然而，他们对这个波尔坎岛附近的风场预测得相当准确，这一点在后来的调查平台FINO 1上得到证实。该平台于2003年开始测量风力。风力测量架显示今天阿尔法•文图斯风电场边上100米高度的风速平均值略大于10米/秒。相比之下，德国大陆理想的沿海区域的风速大约只有7米/秒。

"在12海里区域之外规划这样的项目，我们是第一家"，45岁的德布尔深深地吸了一口烟说道。"我们研究了整个沿海地形和浅滩海地区并得出结论，分道通航区南部的任何计划都不可行"。

该项目距离波尔坎岛45公里。他们何时选定这个地方并将之命名为"波尔坎岛西项目"，德布尔对此一直守口如瓶。然而，这一定发生在1999年9月底以前。因为9月他第一次去了汉堡德国联邦海事局，在那里，他向负责海洋管理的M5部门领导克里斯琴•达尔凯律师提交了他的项目草案。那时，达尔凯刚从沃泽伯格"水域和航运管理局南部处"来到德国联邦海事局，达尔凯此前已是负责处理德国专属经济区（EEZ）内法律问题和海上法律事务部门的领导。

当联合国海洋法公约于1995年开始生效时，根据国际法，专属经济区仅是一个国际公认的航海区域。此后这使得包括德国在内的与之毗连的国家决定对其进行经济开发。专属经济区从12海里区域扩展到200海里。从历史角度来看，专属经济区极大扩展了海上影响力的范围。20世纪初，专属经济区只有3海里区域，相当于加农炮的射程。1982年，根据海洋法公约，专属经济区扩大到12海里。目前，人

stimulus was provided particularly from the motherland of wind energy – Denmark. The Danes had already set up the very first offshore wind farm in the Baltic Sea (Vindeby) in 1991 with a rated power of five megawatts; Tunø Knob (Kattegatt), the second offshore project, followed in 1995, likewise with a rated capacity of five megawatts. And at the same time, other larger projects were in their advanced stages: the aesthetically pleasing project, Middelgrunden, with its 20 wind turbines and a total of 40 megawatts directly off Copenhagen as well as Horns Rev with a planned capacity of 160 megawatts in the North Sea. There was great astonishment in the air, sometimes even greater scepticism. Nevertheless, the subject of 'offshore' was becoming firmly engrained into the minds of the sector.

It all began in East Friesland

If you are searching for the origins of alpha ventus you will first find yourself in Leer. It all began in this East Friesian town – everything that was to actually become reality ten years later. In 1997, Ingo de Buhr, electrical engineer and enthusiastic entrepreneur in all matters involving renewable energies, founded the company Prokon Nord Energiesysteme GmbH in his birthplace, with three employees. It quickly made a name for itself with various wind energy projects. The company now has over 400 employees. His determination and persistence enabled de Buhr to develop one wind farm after the other on land. Others would have been satisfied with this successful business, but not de Buhr: the son of a ship's captain wanted to go further. He's one of those people who is constantly looking for new challenges. In fact he probably needs them. What could have been more obvious than to start developing his own offshore wind farm at sea?

To do so, Ingo de Buhr and his employees had to start from scratch. There weren't even publicly available maps of the North and Baltic Seas to fall back on, which would have provided detailed information on the seabed conditions, water depths, currents, mean tidal ranges, shipping routes and wind conditions. Therefore, Prokon Nord had to make a special application to the German Federal Maritime and Hydrographic Agency (BSH) for permission to make copies of the nautical maps. In order to gain a better and more practical understanding of the subject matter, these German offshore pioneers travelled from Leer to the Swedish offshore wind farm Utgrunden between Kalmar and the island Oland. The project was built by the German subsidiary of Enron Wind, later acquired by General Electric. Some years later the wind farm was handed over to the energy company Vattenfall. Then, after numerous visits, consultations and extensive analysis of the nautical maps, de Buhr and his fellow pioneers finally chose a section of the sea that was, in fact, more or less directly in front of their East Friesian front door. The planned wind farm was to be set up to the north of the island of Borkum, between two busy international maritime shipping routes: to the north, the German Bight Western Approach and to the south, Terschelling-German Bight. In contrast to onshore developments, these offshore wind energy pathfinders had no exact, useable data on the real wind conditions in this area. The BSH merely had wind measurements available from lightships measured directly above the water surface, which the wind experts then had to extrapolate to the respective heights. However, they were fairly accurate with their optimistic predictions for the site off Borkum, as was found later on the research platform FINO 1, which started measuring the winds in 2003. The wind measurement-mast registered an average

类对海上进行开发的结果是将专属经济区，其范围达200海里，纳入海图。这一海上区域也许不是主权国家领土的一部分；然而，国家对其拥有许多开发权，如传统上的捕鱼、采矿以及石油和天然气的开采，最近还包括了风电开发。1995年1月1日，德意志联邦共和国宣布，北海的28600平方公里和波罗的海的4500平方公里为其专属经济区。然而，只有少数人能在世纪之交的时候想到原来是一片蓝色的专属经济区现在会变成什么样子，最初只是一片蓝色的专属经济区，在短短的15年内就规划了30多个海上风能项目，这些项目的分布复杂，很有几分表现主义的特质。

达尔凯或许也没想到。不过，他刚把办公室安置在能看到易北河的地方，从挪威穿过北海的欧洲燃气管线II也在法律上确定下来，同时越来越多的海上风能项目申请书堆满了他的办公桌。对这种项目激增，德国联邦海事局毫无准备。

不仅北海上有众多的计划，波罗的海也是如此。最先要说的是波罗的海I和Kriegers Flak项目。早在1997年，德国梅克伦堡——西波美拉尼亚州政府的一个跨部工作组就对位于Fischland-Dar-Zingst半岛北部12海里区域内的波罗的海I项目进行了初步研究。作为德国近海的风电项目，其审批过程非常漫长复杂，已成为一个典型案例。该项目需要进行综合环境分析，梅克伦堡——西波美拉尼亚州要对其进行空间规划，还要进行联邦排放物管制条例的调查，几乎花费了10年时间，才在2006年3月拿到全部许可证。Kriegers Flak项目也在专属经济区，其通过项目审批的速度更快些。2005年4月，德国联邦海事局批准了博尔格伦德的Offshore Ostsee Wind（OOW AG）公司提交的规划方案，准予其在波罗的海专属经济区内建造风电场和铺设电缆线路。

新的海上开发权诉求

从上世纪90年代后期开始，公用事业律师达尔凯收到的要求开发北海和波罗的海专属经济区的申请越来越多。然而，当时在德国，在他权限内处理这种申请没有经验可借鉴。因为在这个领域没有现成的法律途径，更不用说专属经济区的空间规划战略，根本没有可用的批准程序的先例。在公海利用风能还从未进行过。在12海里的区域内运用的法律要求和义务与专属经济区没有关系。这意味着专属经济区的边界从法律上已被界定并且受到国际法的制约，但正如达尔凯所说，在上世纪90年代末期，在这些边界范围内的专属经济区几乎没有法定管辖权，因为直到那时，还没有人对海床之上确定的区域要求专属的权利。凡是没有开发利用特定区域，其它诸如捕鱼、航运、军事、航空之类利益也就得不到保护，在这里重要的是自然保护，尤其是保护海鸟和鼠海豚。

确切地说，达尔凯面对的这种特定区域的开发（即利用海上风的开发）始于1999年夏末。然而他没有逃避或拖延，而是立刻行动，最先制定了未来审批程序的基本原则。"他反应很快"，这是英戈•德布尔对这位打破常规和务实的德国联邦海事局公务员的称赞，因为这些问题最初几乎都由达尔凯独自处理。这样，达尔凯逐渐建立这些公海海域的完整监管模式。然而，回顾过去，他对由于时间仓促和行动压力，没能一气呵成制定并实施完整的、条理清晰的法律体系而感到惋

wind speed of just over ten metres per second at a height of 100 metres on the edge of what is today the alpha ventus test field. As a comparison, good coastal locations on the German mainland only get around seven metres per second.

"We were the first to plan such a project outside the 12-nautical-mile zone" says the mid-forty year-old de Buhr drawing deeply on his cigarette. "We had looked at the whole coastal landscape and the Wadden Sea region and came to the conclusion that any plans south of the Traffic Separation Zone were not feasible."

It remains his personal secret when exactly they decided on the location and the name they gave it of 'Borkum West', 45 kilometres off Borkum. However, this must have been before the end of September 1999, because it was in this month that he went for the first time to the Hamburg Federal Maritime and Hydrographic Agency (BSH) where he presented his draft project plans to lawyer Christian Dahlke, Head of Unit 'M5 – Management of the Oceans. At the time he had just moved from the 'Water and Shipping Directorate, South' in Würzburg to the BSH. Dahlke had become head of a unit that handles le-gal questions and maritime law matters within the German Exclusive Economic Zone (EEZ).

The EEZ only became an internationally-recognized nautical area under international law when the UN Convention on the Law of the Sea came into force in 1995. This has since enabled the respective countries bordering it, including Germany, to determine its economic exploitation. The EEZ stretches from the 12-nautical-mile zone to 200 nautical miles out at sea. Seen from a historical perspective, the EEZ is a huge extension of maritime spheres of influence. In the early 20th century there was the 3-nautical-mile zone, which corresponded to the range of a cannon ball. In 1982 the 12-nautical-mile zone was included under the Convention on the Law of the Sea. The end, for now, of civilization's spread onto the seas is the inclusion of the EEZ into the sea charts, with its range of over 200 nautical miles. This maritime area may not be a part of the sovereign state; however, the respective coastal country has numerous rights to its exploitation, traditionally for fishing and mining as well as for oil and gas exploration. Most recently, this has come to include the generation of electricity from wind power. The Federal Republic of Germany declared its EEZ in the North and Baltic Sea on 1st January, 1995: 28,600 square kilometres of the North Sea and 4,500 square kilometres of the Baltic Sea. Only a few, however, could have imagined at the turn of the century that what was initially a plain blue nautical chart of the EEZ would now, within only 15 years, display more than 30 planned offshore wind energy projects in a complex arrangement with an almost expressionist feel.

Dahlke probably didn't either. Nevertheless, he had only just finished setting up his office with a view over the River Elbe, and the gas pipeline Europipe II from Norway across the North Sea had just been legally finalized, when more and more applications for offshore wind energy projects started flooding onto his desk. The Agency was just not prepared for this rush.

There were busy plans not only for the North Sea, but also for the Baltic. Deserving of first mention here are the projects Baltic I and Kriegers Flak. As early as 1997, an inter-ministerial Working group of the German Federal State government of Mecklenburg-Western Pomerania was working on preliminary studies for the Baltic I site, which is located within the 12-nautical-mile zone to the north of the Fischland-Darß-Zingst peninsula. This project is a prime example of how long-winded and multi-faceted a licencing process for an offshore wind

安装在布伦斯比特尔工业区的5兆瓦瑞能样机，2004年11月上线运营。
The 5M REpower prototype was installed in the Brunsbüttel industrial zone and went online in November 2004.

惜。这个不足尤其影响了并网连接的所有事宜，包括电缆线路、传输线通道和并网节点。"风电场审批和风电场并网连接没有合并到一个程序完全是件愚蠢的事情。"此外，从来没有按照公共利益建立一个专属经济区的总体规划，以规定单一公司的开发权。这就是为什么达尔凯不再像以前那样自认聪明了。"在既不知道发展商计划在哪里开发项目，也不知道在与陆上电网连接时会发生什么问题的情况下，就开发基础设施，这确实不是明智之举。"

现在的形势不同了。达尔凯坚持认为，"电网运营人、电力传输部门和大瀑布电力公司应当在联邦网络局的支持下制定总体规划"。尽管开发海上电网并将其延伸到陆上的问题没有得到解决，但2009年秋天生效的德国专属经济区空间规划却是实现可持续的空间开发道路上一个重要里程碑，这个规划目的是最终系统地使该区域的社会经济要求与生态功能相适应。"

开发这片海域的申请显然从来没有停止过。这听起来似乎不可信，但却是真实的："一些专属经济区的开发申请相当密集，我们为第21座或第22座风电场的风力发电机出让了大约占50或100米的实际空间，这两个风电场很可能于下一个十年或再下一个十年开建，"达尔凯补充说。每一个海工项目的许可证，他会收到4份新的项目申请。"你必须付出高昂的代价"，他开玩笑的同时又严肃地声明："海就是海。海上开发不单单是陆上开发的延伸。因此，不应出现与海事无关的运营。在海上没有开设快餐店之类所需要的空间。基本上，人类对于大海来说只是客人。放置在海上的任何东西，之后也必须清理干净。"

这位德国联邦海事局执照审领负责人对自然保护区很重视。"早在2002年，我们提供了一份环境研究的标准程序。这为审批过程中有关风机生态影响的争论提供了一个完整而又切实的基础，因而中止了许多讨论，"达尔凯高兴地说。自然保护是一个非常复杂的问题，为此他在过去的几年里进行了许多研究。以鸟类学为例，"鸟类的行为太让人着迷了"，这位律师谈起这些长有两个翅膀的动物时非常兴奋，即兴讲述了鸟类繁殖和飞行的方式。

他还清楚地记得2001至2003年的首次申请大会。当时，海上环境问题导致了无休止的争论。这位律师回忆说："他们从早上一直争论到深夜"。自2005年9月以来，大约有三分之一的专属经济区成为自然保护区。德国联邦海事局驳回了2个波罗的海的项目，从而证明专属经济区的审批程序并不是"走过场"。未批准的原因是由于它们的位置很可能会威胁到黑色海番鸭、丝绒海番鸭和绒鸭种群，它们受欧洲鸟类和栖息地条例的保护。风电场的建造可能会惊扰这些鸟类并使之丧失栖息地。

最初，达尔凯对海工项目审批程序只是制定了一个草案，随后在法律内容程序等方面逐步完善。这位德国联邦海事局工作人员强调说："我们编制的是一种全新的申请程序"。不过，达尔凯经常成为公众抨击的对象：甚至还没等第1个申请程序完成，他不得不回应批评尤其是来自自然保护组织的批评，说他个人同意海洋的完全工业化。尽管达尔凯坚持在审批程序内进行特定的环境影响评估，但抨击还是纷至沓来。环境影响评估将最大可能地证明海上风电场在其规划位置

farm close to the German coastline can be. It required comprehensive environmental analysis, a spatial planning process from the state of Mecklenburg-Western Pomerania and a Federal Emissions Control Ordinance investigation. It took therefore almost a decade until all the licences were granted in March 2006. The project application for Kriegers Flak, situated in the EEZ, crossed the finishing line somewhat more quickly: in April 2005 the BSH granted the applicant, the Offshore Ostsee Wind AG (OOW AG) from Börgerende, a licence for their planned project within the EEZ in the Baltic Sea, approving the wind farm and the cable route.

New exploitation claims at sea

Since the late 1990s, the public service lawyer Dahlke was increasingly confronted with massive applications to exploit the EEZ, both in the North Sea and also the Baltic Sea. However, at the time there was no experience at all in Germany with such requests within his authority for him to fall back on. There was no well-trodden legal pathway, let alone an (EEZ) spatial planning strategy, and no usable precedents for a licencing process at all in this area. Harvesting wind energy on the high seas was simply virgin territory. The legal requirements and obligations that are valid within the twelve-nautical-mile zone had no relevance for the EEZ. This meant that the borders of the EEZ had been legally recognized and were binding under international law, but as Dahlke puts it, at the end of the 'nineties within these borders the EEZ was more or less without legal jurisdiction because up until then no-one had made 'exclusive' claims to any definite area above the seabed. And where there is no utilization of any specific area, there is no defence either of other interests such as fishing, shipping, military, aviation – and crucially here, nature conservation, which in particular should protect sea birds and harbour porpoises.

It was precisely this exploitation of specific locations, namely with offshore wind turbines, with which Dahlke was confronted starting in late summer 1999. Nevertheless, instead of dodging the issue or putting it off, he did not waste a minute and worded the first basic principles for a future licencing process. "He reacted quickly", is Ingo de Buhr's praise for the unconventional and pragmatic action of the BSH civil servant who initially handled these questions almost on his own within his Agency. In this way, Dahlke created a sound regulatory framework for these open sea areas step by step, which until then had not been regulated. However, in retrospect he regrets that due to a permanent lack of time and the pressure to act, he never developed and put into place a legally sound, coherent juridical framework in one go. This shortcoming particularly affects all matters involving the grid connection – cable routes, transmission line corridors and grid nodes. "It's simply an awkward fact that the licence for a wind farm and the wind-farm grid connection have not been bundled together into a single procedure." Moreover, there has never been an "EEZ master plan" that regulates individual companies' claims to exploitation in accordance with the common interest. That's why Dahlke does not pretend to be any wiser now than before. "It would not have been particularly clever to develop an infrastructure without knowing where the developers intended to locate their projects and what was going to happen with the electricity grid on land."

It's a different matter nowadays. "The grid operators, transpower and Vattenfall, should now draw up a master plan with the support of the Federal Network Agency", Dahlke insists. Notwithstanding this unre-

对环境来说是否真正安全。

当达尔凯在汉堡忙于研究和改编德国海上设施条例、反复阅读特别是海上空间规划文件时，英戈·德布尔正在莱尔做准备工作。他委托德国风能研究所进行海上风能评估，委托德国汉堡的德国劳氏船级社作航运风险分析，并与渔民及其协会组织作大量的深入讨论。同时，他的同事弗雷尔克·南宁加作为生物学家多次进行了海上哺乳动物和鸟类的统计。此外，阿尔弗莱德-威根纳极地和海洋研究所对波尔坎岛西12平方公里项目区域的沙质海床上（海底生物栖息地）的鱼类或其他生物进行了调查。Prokon北方公司还与德国下萨克森州的有关管理机构一起合作，该机构负责规划连接大陆的急需电缆线路。2001年秋天，并网问题仍旧没有解决。不过，在审批大会深入审阅有关文件并作出结论之后，德国联邦海事局于2001年11月9日这个具有历史意义的日子，最终批准了Prokon北方公司的第一个项目：波尔坎岛西风电场。

这以后不久，2002年1月，他们又从柏林得到了一个好消息。社会民主党-绿党联合政府正式通过"关于海上风能的使用"海上战略文件，该战略文件随后受到继任政府的承认。从本质上讲，此文件在今天仍有法律效力。文件在以"目标"为标题的章节中阐明："以目前的条件和可用区域，在初始阶段（初期建造阶段），即到2006年，至少能从海上风能中获取500兆瓦的装机容量，在中期阶段，也就是到2010年，装机容量可达2000至3000兆瓦。远期来看，即到2025年或2030年，当经济可行性达到时，在沿海水域和专属经济区也可能获得大约20000到25000兆瓦的装机容量。为此，海上风电场投资人和电力行业应为如此大量的海上电力运输（足够的电缆容量，与大陆电网连接；如果必需，在陆上增加并网能力）创造先决条件。"

但是事情根本没有像预期的那样。事实上，Prokon北方公司的东弗里希亚项目要在2003年开始装配海上风机。2002年4月30日，虽然英戈·德布尔收到了威悉河-埃姆斯河地区政府颁发的连接海岸的电缆布线国家规划声明，但开始时，沿岸居民反对的呼声很高。波尔坎岛的居民和渔民控告德国联邦海事局颁发建设许可证。然而，由于证据不确凿，他们的控告被行政仲裁委员会驳回。

其它方面的进展也很艰难。直到2004年1月，解除在下萨克森州浅滩海地区施工禁令的申请才被批准，于是启动所需要的电缆线路。与此同时还对该敏感区域的自然保护区进行了分析。最终，Prokon北方公司在同年11月得到执照，铺设穿越浅滩海的电缆。

整个过程经历了马拉松式的问询和审批，花费了大量的时间和金钱。同期向德国联邦海事局提交申请的其它海上开发项目也遇到了类似的情况。这种在陆上不能实现的特大型项目的前景令许多人深受鼓舞。德国机械设备制造业联合会（VDMA）委托进行的一项研究预测，海上风能领域的投资预算为500亿欧元。"许多中小型项目开发商蜂拥而至，他们相信自己能运营80台或更多风机的风电场"。诺伯特·吉斯在反思当时规划项目的经济可行性时说道，他现在是瑞能系统公司海上项目部总监，"一座装有80台风机的海上风电场相当于大约800兆瓦火力发电场所要求的投资。这个事实被低估，正像海工项目管理的困难被低估一样。""项目规模对融资有深远的影响，这就

solved matter of developing the offshore grid and extending it onshore, the spatial plan that came into effect for the German EEZ in the autumn of 2009 was a milestone on the way to a "sustainable spatial development, in order to finally – and also systematically – accommodate all socio-economic claims to the area with the ecological functions".
And the applications to exploit this area at sea apparently never cease. It may sound incredible but it is true: "It's getting quite crowded in some areas of the EEZ… we end up bartering about 50 or 100 metres of virtual space for wind turbines in the 21st or 22nd wind farm, which will hopefully get built in the next decade – or the one after next", admits Dahlke. For every offshore licence granted he receives four new project applications. "That's the high price you have to pay", he jokes and in the same breath clarifies soberly: "The sea will remain the sea. Offshore exploitation is not simply the extension of exploitation on land. Therefore, there should be no operations at sea that are not maritime ones. There's no room for fast-food restaurants or the like on the open sea. Basically, the sea is a place where human beings are only guests anyway. If we put anything there then we also have to clean it up."
The head of the BSH licencing procedures takes nature conservation very seriously. "As early as 2002 we presented a standard procedure for environmental studies. This gave the ecological debate on the impact of wind turbines a sound and factual base within the framework of the licencing process and thus cut short many of the discussions", Dahlke is pleased to say. In order to understand the complex subject matter he has learned a lot over the years about many of the nature protection issues, for example ornithology. "It's fantastic, what birds can do", enthuses the lawyer about the world of these two-winged creatures and gives an impromptu talk on breeding and flying patterns.
He can still remember well the first application conferences in the years 2001 to 2003, when the subject of the marine environment led to never-ending discussions. The lawyer looks back and says: "They ended up in a war of words that lasted from the morning until late in the evening". The fact that the licencing procedures for the EEZ, around a third of which has been a nature reserve since September 2005, were not just for 'show' was proven when the BSH rejected two projects in the Baltic Sea. They failed because ornithological studies ascertained that the project locations 'Adlergrund' and 'Pommersche Bucht' would have threatened stocks of black scoters, velvet scoters and eider ducks, all protected by the EU Birds and Habitats Directive. The birds would have reacted sensitively to the construction of the wind farms, the consequence of which could have been the loss of their habitat.
Dahlke quickly became 'lord' of the offshore licencing procedures which he established, initially improvising and then developed further, step by step – in legal, content and in particular procedural terms. "We developed a completely new application process", emphasizes the BSH man. Nevertheless, it was not uncommon for Dahlke to be the subject of public attacks: even before the first application pro-cess had even been completed he had had to fend off criticism, in particular from nature conservation organizations, suggesting that he would personally approve a complete industrialization of the sea. The attacks came although Dahlke had insisted on a specific environmental impact assessment within the licencing processes, which would provide the best possible proof of whether an offshore wind farm is really environmentally safe at the site where it is planned.
While Dahlke was fighting with the paperwork in Hamburg, studying and reworking the German Marine Facilities Ordinance and opening and closing the maritime spatial planning files, Ingo de Buhr was doing

2004年11月第一台5兆瓦样机与电网连接。两年后在不来梅港附近的三脚式桩基上安装了第二台5兆瓦风机。
In December 2004 the first prototype of the M5000 was connected to the grid. Two years later the second machine of this type was installed on a tripod near Bremerhaven.

使得许多中小型开发企业要么与有实力的伙伴进行战略合作，要么将自己连同项目一起出售给大型能源公司。"长期担任VDMA风机生产商协会主席的吉斯认为原因很明显："海上风能项目不仅是陆上活动的延伸，还是一种新型可再生能源。""风电行业因此面监着模式转换。在早期，小型分散的私人风机业主和运营商在这个领域一枝独秀，而现在是大型公司包括传统的能源供应商千方百计想挤进风能领域。德国风能协会（BWE）必须适应这种新形势。"吉斯继续说。然而，风能行业只会慢慢地认识到这一点。

无论过去和现在，海上风电对开发商、项目经理人、运营商和协会以及风机制造商和供应商都提出了新的要求。回顾2003年至2005年那段时间，初期的发展很困难，特别是对制造商来说更是不易。风机制造商Enercon、瑞能和Multibrid共同努力安装它们的第一台5兆瓦样机。然而，有影响力的客户在哪里？那些将海上风能视为新的商机并已经为海上风电安装准备好后勤保障的合作伙伴在哪里？此外还有一个关键问题仍悬而未决。哪些风能项目更易实现？是那些在新生产线的规划和融资上有经济可行性的项目，还是那些能带来稳定的多兆瓦风机订单的项目？

在此期间，丹麦最先开拓出市场，荷兰、瑞典、英国和德国的海

his homework in Leer. He started doing what all other project developers were also doing after him. He commissioned an Offshore Wind Resource Assessment from the German Wind Energy Institute (DEWI), commissioned Hamburg-based Germanischer Lloyd with a Shipping Risk Analysis and had numerous in-depth discussions with fishermen and their associations. At the same time his Prokon Nord colleague, biologist Freerk Nanninga, conducted numerous counts of sea mammals and birds. Moreover, the Alfred-Wegener-Institut investigated the situation of the fish and other beings living on and in the sandy seabed (benthos habitat) of the twelve-square-kilometre project area of Borkum West. As well as this, Prokon Nord worked with the respective authorities of the German Federal State of Lower Saxony, who had to arrange for the urgently necessary cable route to the mainland. In the autumn of 2001 the grid connection issue was still unresolved. Nevertheless, following the conclusion of the Application Conference in which an in-depth examination of the documents had been presented, on the historic day of 9th November (also for other reasons) the BSH finally granted the pioneers from Prokon Nord construction approval for the first-ever project of all: Borkum West.
Shortly after this, in January 2002 they benefited from a tailwind from Berlin. The Social Democrats – Green Party coalition government officially adopted an offshore strategy paper 'On the use of wind ener-

gy at sea', which was later confirmed and received widespread approval by subsequent governments. Essentially it is still valid today. Under the chapter heading of title 'Objectives' it states that: "under the current conditions and in the areas that will be presumably available in the initial phase (for the initial construction stage), from today's perspective a total of at least 500 megawatts of installed capacity can be achieved from wind energy exploitation at sea by 2006, and in the medium-term, 2,000 to 3,000 megawatts by 2010. In the long term this will mean that, by 2025 or 2030, when economical feasibility has been achieved, about 20,000 to 25,000 megawatts of installed capacity will be possible (coastal waters and EEZ). To do this, it is necessary that investors in offshore wind farms and the electricity industry create the preconditions for the transport of such amounts of offshore-generated electricity (sufficient sea cable capacities, connection to the mainland grid, if necessary creation of additional grid capacities on land)".

But things did not turn out at all as expected. In fact, the East Friesians at Prokon Nord wanted to start assembling the offshore turbines in 2003. However, although Ingo de Buhr received a positive State Planning Declaration for the cable route to the coast from the Weser-Ems regional government on 30th April 2002, there was initially a great amount of opposition on the coast. The island community of Borkum and some fishermen filed a complaint against the building approval issued by the BSH. This was, however, later rejected by an administrative tribunal due to insubstantiality.

It was also hard going in other ways. It wasn't until January 2004 that the application to lift the construction ban in Lower Saxony's Wadden Sea region was approved, thus opening up the desired cable route. At the same time there were accompanying nature-conservation analyses of this sensitive area. Prokon Nord finally received the licence in November of the same year to lay a cable across the Wadden Sea.

It had been a marathon of consultation and consent and had taken a lot of time and cost a lot of money. It was a similar situation for other offshore project developments that had, in the meantime, submitted their applications to the BSH. Many had been inspired by the prospects of very large projects that could not have been implemented on land. A study commissioned by the German Engineering Association (VDMA) predicted investments in the offshore wind energy sector of about 50 billion euros. "Numerous SME (small and medium-sized enterprise) project developers had rushed in, believing that they could operate farms themselves with 80 and more turbines", reflects Norbert Giese, today Director of REpower Systems AG's Offshore business unit, on the economic feasibility of the planned projects of the time. "However, an offshore wind farm with 80 turbines corresponds approximately to the volume of investment required for an 800-megawatt coal-fired

左图：不适合有眩晕症的人：一个船员站在载人平台上离开了自升式平台。
Photo left: Not ideal for people with vertigo: a crew member leaves the jack-up barge with the cherry picker.

power station. This fact was underestimated, likewise the challenge of project management at sea. "The size of the projects has far-reaching consequences for financing; there is a reason why many SME developers either got large strategic partners on board, or went with their offshore plans to the big players in the energy sector. If you ask Giese, long-time Chairman of the wind-turbine manufacturer section of VDMA, the reasons are clear: "Offshore is not just an extension of onshore activities. It is a new form of renewable energy of its own." The wind-energy sector was thus faced with a paradigm shift. While in the early stages in particular, small, private and decentralized owners and operators of wind turbines had dominated the scene, it was now the large corporations which were pushing their way into the offshore wind-energy sector, including the classic energy providers. The German Wind Energy Association (BWE) had to adapt to this new situation, continues Giese. However, this took time and the wind-energy sector only slowly realized this.

Offshore wind power placed and still places new demands, not only on the developers, project managers, operators and associations, but also on the manufacturers and suppliers of offshore turbines. It can be seen how difficult the start into this phase was, especially for the manufacturers, by looking in particular at the years 2003 to 2005. The wind turbine manufacturers Enercon, REpower and Multibrid had started to make concerted efforts to get their first 5-megawatt prototypes installed. However, where were the influential customers? And where were the partners in the maritime industry who regarded offshore wind energy as a new business opportunity, having developed and made available the respective logistics for wind-power installations at sea? Moreover, the key question remained unanswered. Which offshore projects at all were close to realisation: those that would allow for economically-viable planning and financing of the new production lines – or those that would result in firm orders for multi-megawatt turbines?

While during this period the first markets had developed in Denmark, the Netherlands, Sweden and England, the German offshore scene had got stuck half-way. There was a clear lack of small, well-defined projects to enter the market. Instead the offshore developers were plagued with endless discussions about the lack of grid connections and their potential financing. They had been discussing the laying of a cable through the Wadden Sea with nature conservationists and tourism managers. They had argued with the experts from the shipping industry and the Navy about possible collision risks for tankers, freighters and submarines. And they had quite frequently and repeatedly been turned away by banks and insurance companies with their plans. Ap-

约尔根·蒂勒（左）在第四次海事会议上提出德国建立试验风电场。克里斯蒂安·达尔克（右）为海上风能电站建立了审批流程。
At the 4th Maritime Conference, Jörgen Thiele (left) called for a German wind energy test field. Christian Dahlke (right) developed an approval procedure for offshore wind farms.

工项目则半途而废。市场明显缺少小型、规划完善的项目。而开发商深受无休止的有关缺少并联电网和资金的争论的影响。他们一直与自然保护主义者和旅游管理人员就穿过浅滩铺设电缆的事宜进行讨论，与航运业界专家和海军就油轮、货船和潜艇可能碰撞的风险进行辩论。他们的计划多次被银行和保险公司拒绝。很显然，金融部门认为海上风能风险比投资巴哈马群岛的对冲基金风险更大。更糟的是，当时用于海上风能发电的EEG入网资费并不比岸上风能高多少，随后的基础设施规划加速法案还没有提上日程。此外，钢材、铜和其它原料价格不断上涨。这种情况已偏离了预定路线，而且政客们也犹豫不决。

政治车轮缓慢前行

2005年1月底，德国总理格哈德·施罗德在不来梅第四届国家海洋会议开幕演说中没有提到海上风能，这让来自风能行业的大约50名代表灰心丧气。这是对海上风能的轻视还是一次疏忽？尽管如此，海上风能界还是在海洋会议上第一次举行了一个"海上风能"专题讨论会。为了使这个讨论会顺利进行，石荷州经济部公务员弗里茨·卢克和德国海洋技术协会（GMT）的负责人约阿希姆·施瓦茨博士事先做了许多工作。在这次讨论会上，什未林机械制造公司的总经理约尔根·蒂勒发表了主题演讲。在演讲的最后，他提议在深海水域建立一个试验风电场，该提议经过所有与会者讨论后得到一致同意。

为了将这个小组会议上讨论的结果有效地反映在下午进行的闭幕会议上，帕舍达格（德联邦环境部水电、风能和可再生能源并网负责人）和延斯·埃克霍夫（负责建设、环境和运输的不来梅州议员，及这次活动的主持者）草拟了海上风能行业最重要的要求。这位不来梅州议员用

parently, the financial sector regarded the risk of offshore wind energy as greater than investing in hedge funds on the Bahamas. To make matters worse, at the time the EEG feed-in tariff for electricity from offshore wind energy was not much higher than that for onshore wind, and the subsequent Infrastructure Planning Acceleration Act was not yet on the agenda. Moreover, the prices for steel, copper and other raw materials were rising continually. The situation had gone off track and the politicians were dithering.

The wheel of politics grind slowly

German Chancellor Gerhard Schröder did not mention offshore wind once during his opening speech at the 4th National Maritime Conference in Bremen in late January 2005. The chins of some 50 delegates from the wind-energy sector dropped. Was this an affront to offshore wind energy – or simply an oversight? In spite of this 'faux pas' by the Chancellor, the offshore wind energy community held a separate workshop for the first time on 'Offshore Wind Energy' at the Maritime Conference. In particular, Fritz Lücke, a civil servant from the Schleswig-Holstein Ministry of Economics and Dr.-Ing. Joachim Schwarz, Director of the German Association for Marine Technology (GMT), had put in a lot of effort beforehand to get the workshop going. The keynote speech for the workshop was given by Jörgen Thiele, MD of the Schwerin Maschinenbau (machine toolmaker) company. At the end of his speech Thiele called for a German wind-energy test field in deep waters and received unanimous agreement in the subsequent discussion from the participants of the workshop.

In order to get the results from the small working group effectively represented in the large final meeting organized for that afternoon, Udo Paschedag, Unit Head at the Federal Ministry for the Environment with responsibility for hydropower, wind energy and grid integration of renewable energies, and Jens Eckhoff, Bremen State Senator for Construction, Environment and Transport and host of the event, got together in a back room of the Bremen Congress Centre. In order to rescue what they could they drafted the most important demands of the offshore wind-energy sector. The Bremen Senator wrote down in keywords the essential requirements: 1. Offshore test field; 2. Easier financing; 3. Simplified licencing procedures; 4. Grid connection and extension and 5. Research and development.

These notes provided the mental framework for the rhetorical counter-attack, which Jens Eckhoff then delivered in front of the large audience of around 800 representatives from shipyards, shipping companies and port operators. "I was very clear in what I said", remembers Eckhoff. He unflinchingly criticized the Chancellor for not treating offshore seriously. "It is, however, a central task for the Federal Government to coordinate offshore developments", demanded Eckhoff. "That's why a situation just cannot be accepted where German wind- turbine manufacturers are not able to demonstrate in the German EEZ what they can really do." The Senator from Bremen insistently emphasized the importance offshore wind energy will have for Germany in general and for energy supplies in particular. The statement of the Bremen senator touched a nerve. The Chancellor's Coordinator of Maritime Policy, Georg Wilhelm Adamowitsch, obviously felt that his toes had been trodden on. He reacted spontaneously to the criticism and rushed to a microphone. "What is the wind-energy sector complaining about?" he asked around abruptly. He completely dismissed the demands made by the CDU state politician and pointed out supposed shortcomings of the

gy at sea', which was later confirmed and received widespread approval by subsequent governments. Essentially it is still valid today. Under the chapter heading of title 'Objectives' it states that: "under the current conditions and in the areas that will be presumably available in the initial phase (for the initial construction stage), from today's perspective a total of at least 500 megawatts of installed capacity can be achieved from wind energy exploitation at sea by 2006, and in the medium-term, 2,000 to 3,000 megawatts by 2010. In the long term this will mean that, by 2025 or 2030, when economical feasibility has been achieved, about 20,000 to 25,000 megawatts of installed capacity will be possible (coastal waters and EEZ). To do this, it is necessary that investors in offshore wind farms and the electricity industry create the preconditions for the transport of such amounts of offshore-generated electricity (sufficient sea cable capacities, connection to the mainland grid, if necessary creation of additional grid capacities on land)".

But things did not turn out at all as expected. In fact, the East Friesians at Prokon Nord wanted to start assembling the offshore turbines in 2003. However, although Ingo de Buhr received a positive State Planning Declaration for the cable route to the coast from the Weser-Ems regional government on 30th April 2002, there was initially a great amount of opposition on the coast. The island community of Borkum and some fishermen filed a complaint against the building approval issued by the BSH. This was, however, later rejected by an administrative tribunal due to insubstantiality.

It was also hard going in other ways. It wasn't until January 2004 that the application to lift the construction ban in Lower Saxony's Wadden Sea region was approved, thus opening up the desired cable route. At the same time there were accompanying nature-conservation analyses of this sensitive area. Prokon Nord finally received the licence in November of the same year to lay a cable across the Wadden Sea.

It had been a marathon of consultation and consent and had taken a lot of time and cost a lot of money. It was a similar situation for other offshore project developments that had, in the meantime, submitted their applications to the BSH. Many had been inspired by the prospects of very large projects that could not have been implemented on land. A study commissioned by the German Engineering Association (VDMA) predicted investments in the offshore wind energy sector of about 50 billion euros. "Numerous SME (small and medium-sized enterprise) project developers had rushed in, believing that they could operate farms themselves with 80 and more turbines", reflects Norbert Giese, today Director of REpower Systems AG's Offshore business unit, on the economic feasibility of the planned projects of the time. "However, an offshore wind farm with 80 turbines corresponds approximately to the volume of investment required for an 800-megawatt coal-fired

左图：不适合有眩晕症的人：一个船员站在载人平台上离开了自升式平台。
Photo left: Not ideal for people with vertigo: a crew member leaves the jack-up barge with the cherry picker.

关键字记下了几项要求：1.海上试验风电场；2.放宽融资；3.简化审批程序；4.电网连接与扩展；5.研发。

然后，延斯•埃克霍夫当着来自船厂、轮船公司和港口经营者的大约800名代表的面，公布了这些要求。"我非常清楚我所说的"，埃克霍夫回忆说。他坚决批评了格哈德•施罗德没有认真对待海上风能。"无论如何，协调开发海上风能是联邦政府的一个中心任务"，埃克霍夫要求。"德国风机制造商在德国专属经济区（EEZ）不能证明其能力，这是不可接受的。"来自不来梅的这位议员坚持强调海上风能对上至德国国家下至能源供应商的重要意义。他的陈述触及了施罗德总理的海事政策协调员格奥尔格•威廉•阿达莫维奇的敏感神经。他本能地对批评作出反应，奔向麦克风，"风能行业在抱怨什么？"他突然问四周。他完全不理会CDU州政治家提出的要求，指出风能行业的缺点。

那是2005年1月底的事，时间在飞快流逝。虽然德国联邦海事局于2001年下半年已经授予专属经济区第一个海上风电场许可证，但是这个项目还是被搁置了。开发商一直忙于做计划，但新的问题不断出现，而政府也没有明确的解决方案。难道几年前掀起的海上风能的热潮就这样灰飞烟灭了吗？特别是中小型企业的失望情绪在逐步加剧，因为他们担心的项目会在开发阶段受阻。

德国海上风能的主要利益相关方感觉他们的机会日渐减少。业内传言四起：银行和保险公司不想合作；风机制造商也无法参与；电网经营者准备不足且原料价格猛烈上涨。德国风能协会（BWE）一直在争取更多的支持。在幕后，创办于2001年的德国风能论坛及其执行委员会委员约尔格•库比尔正在与政治决策者进行艰苦的讨论。是这位前任汉堡环境事务议员约尔格•库比尔第一个认识到，海上风能可以用于"工业发电"，他再次强调这一点。仅中小型企业（SME）主导不了这个领域的发展。"没有大型能源公司的参与，这件事不会有成效"，库比尔确信。在他担任议员期间，他是汉堡市政电力事业管理委员会（HEW）的主席，该主席职位后来由大瀑布电力公司接替。"我十分熟悉大型能源企业的体制和他们思考的习惯"，他说。"他们不像小型公司那样灵活，他们需要知道自己的长期目标大致是什么样子。"

但是，在2005年春天，正在兴起的海上风能行业所专注的不是长期的目标。在几年的等待之后，他们需要在短期内见到成效。帕舍达格对那段时间的评价是，"如果在那段时间我们继续犹豫不决，那么德国可能到2020年也不会有海上风能"。当时，每一个人都在拼命寻找解决方案。

与此同时,柏林的一些部门对海上风能的争论达到顶峰。即便社会民主党-绿党联合政府对实现一万兆瓦功率的海上战略目标雄心勃勃，但是这个目标如何实现还受到来自经济部和环境部的强烈反对。之前，阿达莫维奇坚决反对环境、自然保护和核安全部门派代表出席第四届海洋会议的第一次海上风能专题讨论会，单单这个事实就足以证明了这一点。

在这个值得纪念的不来梅事件之后，在柏林联邦环境部，帕舍达格办公室里的电话响个不停。大家都想知道下一步会怎么样。没有一个制造商敢迈步向前。"经济事务部对海上风能开发不太有兴趣，所

wind-energy industry.

That was the end of January 2005. Time was running out. Although the first licences for offshore wind farms in the EEZ had already been granted by the BSH in the second half of 2001, the projects were stuck. Developers may have been busily making plans; however new issues kept cropping up for which politics and administrators had no definite solutions. Was the offshore euphoria that had been ignited only a few years before going to end up in a puff of smoke before a single wind farm had been installed in German waters? Disappointment was spreading, especially amongst the SME offshore developers as they feared that their projects would get stuck in the development phase – if they went anywhere at all.

The German offshore wind-energy stakeholders saw their chances dwindling. There were rumours going around in the business. The banks and insurance companies did not want to play along; the turbine manufacturers just couldn't; the grid operators were not ready and costs were soaring due to increasing raw material prices. The German Wind Energy Association [BWE] was rallying for more support. And behind the scenes the Offshore Wind Energy Forum, founded in 2001, and its Member of the Executive Board Jörg Kuhbier were having painstaking discussions with political decision-makers. The former Hamburg Senator for the Environment was the first to recognize that offshore wind energy, as he emphasizes it, is "industrial electricity generation". This was an area that could not be mastered by SMEs from the renewable energy sector alone. "Without commitment from the large energy companies it's not going to work", Kuhbier was convinced. During his time as Senator he was also Chairman of the Supervisory Board of the Hamburg municipal electricity utility (HEW), later taken over by Vattenfall. "I am thoroughly familiar with large energy producers' structures and the way they think", he says. "They are not as flexible as the smaller companies and they need to know what the long-term targets are going to look like."

However, it was not the long-term that the burgeoning offshore sector was looking at in the spring of 2005. After a few years of waiting they needed short-term perspectives. "If we had continued to hang around at the time, then we probably would not have had any offshore wind energy by 2020 in Germany", is Udo Paschedag's retrospective assessment of that period, a time when everyone was desperately looking for solutions.

In the meantime, the confrontation regarding offshore wind energy was coming to a head within the federal ministries in Berlin. Even if the SDP / Green federal government coalition had come up with ambitious ideas of setting up 10,000 megawatts of power as their offshore strategic target, the ideas on how this could be implemented were almost diametrically opposite in the Economics Ministry and the Environment Ministry. Simply the fact that Adamowitsch had previously categorically rejected the Federal Ministry for the Environment, Nature Conservation and Nuclear Safety being represented with its own staff during the first workshop for Offshore Wind Energy at the 4th Maritime Conference clearly demonstrates this.

After this memorable event in Bremen the telephone in Udo Paschedag's office in the Federal Environment Ministry in Berlin didn't stop ringing. Everyone was wondering what would happen next. None of the manufacturers was daring to push their way forward. "The Ministry of Economic Affairs was just not interested in offshore development. Every step was a hard one to take", says Paschedag. "We tried again and again to put the subject of offshore wind energy onto the po-

以当时是举步维艰。"帕舍达格说。"虽然我们再三尝试把海上风能提到政治议事日程上来，但还是毫无结果。"

就像帕舍达格所说，在2005年上半年，极需一个"能够打破僵局的人"。在不来梅讨论会期间，制造商都说他们需要一个试验风电场，就连德国风机市场领导者Enercon公司创始人及所有人阿洛伊斯•沃本也支持这个观点。"我们都需要它"，据报道他这样说。然而，尽管此观点在行业内一致认可，但还有一个决定性的问题没有明确：谁来做它？不过帕舍达格确信，只有共同努力才会有助于实现目标。这中间需要银行、保险公司、制造商、部件供应商、能源公司、电网经营者等机构共同承担风险，还需要项目发展商协同工作，以便所需的风电场尽快建成运转。"在美国，很多事情都可以通过相应的基金会运作，这件事为什么不这样做呢？"，帕舍达格突然冒出这样一个念头。

汉堡智囊团：小组内的团结

星星之火，可以燎原。2005年2月一个灰暗沉闷的日子，在位于汉堡市中心凯悦饭店别致的咖啡馆里，帕舍达格召集风能支持者进行了第一次聚会。所有到场的人员都对他的意见很感兴趣，并表示积极支持。他们是来自瑞能风机制造公司的马丁•斯基巴博士、Enercon公司的安德烈亚•杜泽、KGW铁塔制造厂的约尔根•蒂勒（兼Schwerin Mecklenburg工商会所的主席）、德国WindGuard股份有限公司的延斯•埃克霍夫、约尔格•库比尔和克努特•雷费尔特博士、德国海洋技术协会的约阿希姆•施瓦茨博士、德国F+Z Baugesellschaft mbH建筑公司的汉斯•卡勒博士和VDMA的托尔斯滕•赫丹。

帕舍达格在回忆这次有意义的聚会时，他一边喝茶一边说："银行界没有人参加这次聚会"。在对建立基金会这一想法进行讨论并表决之前，帕舍达格告诉大家，他那时的老板联邦环境部长于尔根•特里廷曾许诺支持这一提议。随后大家对其中的利弊进行了讨论，并最终达成一致意见。在帕舍达格的提议下，会议决定由著名的基金会专家马丁•舒尔特教授负责制定基金会的框架、工作范围和目标。与此同时，VDMA的电力系统分会连同海上风能专家约翰内斯•席尔一起搜集"海上风能风电场"的选择标准。最终，席尔提出了建设试验风电场所需要的33条标准。

然而，对建立海上风能风电场来说，更重要的还包括经济可行性和基础设施。据席尔写道："为了建立电网设施，联邦政府需要协调供电公司、运营商和制造商以及联邦政府、州和市政当局的审批机构，为实施电缆铺设、电网连接和筹措资金提供帮助。而且VDMA动力系统公司希望"风机制造商和基金会在德国建立一个试验风电场，或者至少建立一个生产流程。试验风电场的大部分风机、基础部件、铺设电缆和后勤保障都来自国内，这样德国就能够开始批量生产海上风机、基础设施、电缆，实施安装并进行技术服务和维护"。按照席尔的提议，在20海里至25海里以内应建立一个维修港，位置最好在北海专属经济区内。

此外，在开始选择合适的项目之前，海上风能基金会应具备合法

litical agenda, but at the end of the day it was in vain."

In the first half of 2005 an "icebreaker" was desperately needed, as Paschedag puts it. All the manufacturers had said during the workshop in Bremen that they would need a test field. Even Aloys Wobben, founder and owner of the German wind-turbine market leader Enercon welcomed the idea. "That's just what we all need", is what he reportedly said. Nevertheless, in spite of this broad agreement in the industry there was one decisive question left unanswered: who's going to do it? At least Paschedag was absolutely sure that only a concerted effort would help. Some kind of organization would be needed so that the risk was spread fairly over several shoulders – the banks, insurers, manufacturers, component suppliers, energy companies, grid operators and not least the project developers should all work together to get the desired test field going. What was to be done? Suddenly the idea of a foundation cropped up. "They create foundations in the USA for anything and everything, so why not for the German offshore industry as well?", was what went through Paschedag's mind.

Hamburg think-tank: unity within a small group

The embers were beginning to flicker into a flame. In the discreetly chic, hanseatic café of the Hyatt Hotel in Hamburg's city centre, on a grey and dreary day in February 2005 an illustrious group of wind energy supporters that Paschedag had brought together met for the first time. All those present were immediately keen on his idea and said they wanted to actively support it. They were Dr. Martin Skiba from turbine manufacturer REpower; Andreas Düser from Enercon; Jör-gen Thiele from the tower manufacturer KGW and President of the Schwerin Mecklenburg Chamber of Industry and Commerce (IHK); Jens Eckhoff and Jörg Kuhbier, as well as Dr. Knud Rehfeldt from German company WindGuard GmbH; Dr.-Ing. Joachim Schwarz from the German Association for Maritime Technology (GMT), Dr. Hans Kahle from construction company F+Z Baugesellschaft mbH and Thorsten Herdan from VDMA.

"The bankers were missing." Paschedag drinks a cup of tea while he recalls this noteworthy meeting. Before the pros and cons of the foundation idea were discussed, Paschedag told the informal group that his boss at that time, the Federal Minister for the Environment, Jürgen Trittin, had personally promised him support for the initiative. Then the participants discussed the advantages and disadvantages and at the end of the day they all agreed. Taking up a suggestion by Udo Paschedag, they decided that Professor Martin Schulte, the renowned expert on foundations, should be commissioned to create a suitable concept for the structure, content and objectives of the foundation. In the meantime, the Power Systems section of German industry federation VDMA, with its offshore expert Johannes Schiel had started collating a list of criteria for the choice of a suitable, as it was called then, 'Offshore Wind Energy Test and Demonstration Field'. Schiel put together an impressive list of 33 criteria that such a test field should ideally fulfil.

The important aspects were, amongst others, economic viability and availability of infrastructure. Schiel wrote: "In order to enable the operator to set up the grid infrastructure, the Federal Government needs to act as a mediator for the implementation and financing of the cable route and grid connection and talk to the power supply companies, operators and manufacturers as well as to the licencing authorities in the federal government, states and municipalities." Moreover,

英戈·德布尔（Prokon北方公司）甘于冒险，他成功推动了施塔德港的改建，使之成为行业的中心。今天，5兆瓦的风机叶片是在原先的铸铝车间生产的。
Willing to take high risks, Ingo de Buhr (Prokon Nord) pushed forward the successful redevelopment of Stade as an industrial centre. Today the M5000 rotor blades are made where previously aluminium was cast.

的手续。他们必须在实施之前做好一切准备,而不至于刚一启动就面临不必要的风险。

德累斯顿科技大学法律系的马丁•舒尔特教授立即接受了这一任务,就成立"海上风能基金会"准备了一份27页的法律分析,并在四月份举办的汉诺威展览会上将其主张向与会风能界人士作了介绍。帕舍达格在回顾当时的情景时说:"大家对草案进行了热烈的讨论,大多数人最后都表示了赞同"。

为此成立了一个筹备工作组,在随后的几个星期内,该筹备工作组多次聚集在一起对基金会、试验风电场和基本设施运营商之间将来的内部关系进行了研究讨论。基金会的组织结构获得广泛的支持,并且其资金在原则上获得德国联邦政府环境部的批准,之后的关键问题是选择一个合适的项目,并为其申请许可证。他们手头有几个备选项目。

克努特•雷费尔特博士是德国WindGuard咨询公司的CEO,他受筹备工作组的委托,对项目进行基本评估,选择一个最适合的项目。帕舍达格表示,一些项目开发商如Husum OSB Butendiek & Co.KG公司就拒绝了他们,当时该公司正在推广从陆地到海洋的"民用风力场"概念,并规划了一个距Sylt岛30公里的风电场项目,该项目将安装80台风机,每台风机的功率为3兆瓦。克努特•雷费尔特回忆时说"这是个错误"。而OSB Butendiek股份有限公司的总经理沃尔夫冈•保尔森的看法颇有不同,他认为:"尽管我们很感兴趣,但我们的项目不一定会被基金会选中。我们的项目地址在自然保护区内,所以我不相信他们会选择我们的项目。"事实上,这个项目本身就存在众多的反对者,特别是自然保护组织和联邦政府自然保护局,因为他们的目的就是阻止海上风电项目建立在重要的鸟类保护区。

雷费尔特在2005年6月撰写的报告确认波罗的海地区不太会受到政府和行业的认可。这意味着只有4个项目可供选择,并且其中的2个项目还处于12海里区域内。由于面临下萨克森州浅滩海域未能解决的问题,以及岛上居民因电网连接提出诉讼的威胁,项目获取许可证的过程会相当困难。这将会危及到基金会一个重要目标的实现,即获得德国广大民众对海上风能的广泛接受。在另有两个项目开发商投标之后,从中最终选择了首先从德国联邦海事局获得许可证的项目:波尔坎岛西项目。其位置、风机数量和电网连接都进展良好,这是选择这一位于波尔坎岛北部项目的全部理由。

最后时刻终于来临,2005年7月,发起者们设立德国海上风能基金会。7月26日,该基金会作为非盈利机构获得下萨克森州基金会管理部门的正式承认。延斯•埃克霍夫当选了第一任主席,VDMA电力系统部门的总经理当选为副主席。董事会由约尔格•库比尔、约尔根•蒂勒和克努特•雷费尔特博士组成。雷费尔特研究过很多风能报告,蒂勒则一直在Mecklenburg-西滨海省推广海上风能,并参与在Rostock创建海上科技项目,该项目特别推动波罗的海的海上风能项目。蒂勒作为Mecklenburg地区的商会主席,一直反复强调海上风能对德国北方州和德国总体经济的工业和政治意义。作为铁三角中的第三人,约尔格•库比尔对此有相同的看法,他批评机械制造商说:"如果我们放弃在风力发电领域的技术领先地位,那就太愚蠢了"。他是一个非常善于

VDMA Power Systems wanted "turbine manufacturers and foundation suppliers to set up a test field in Germany – or at least to set up a manufacturing process. A large proportion of the turbines, foundation components, cabling and logistics for the test field were to be sourced domestically, putting Germany in a position to enter serial production of the offshore turbines, foundation structures, cables, installation and maintenance technologies and components." According to Schiel a further important criterion was a service port available within 20 to 25 nautical miles. Moreover, it should preferably be a project located within the North Sea EEZ.

However, before anyone could start choosing a suitable project at all, the idea of creating the offshore wind foundation needed to take legal shape. They had to make sure that they walked before they ran, so as not to risk stumbling right from the start.

Prof. Martin Schulte from the Faculty of Law at the Dresden University of Technology immediately accepted the task and prepared a 27-page legal analysis on the formation of an 'offshore test field foundation'. At the Hanover Fair in April the lawyer presented his ideas to the wind-energy community gathered there. "There was a lively discussion about the draft", Paschedag looks back, "At the end, however, there was an overwhelming majority in the plenum which agreed to it."

The idea had thus now been introduced to the wind-energy sector. A task force was created, which met several times in the subsequent weeks. The main task was to look into the future internal structure between the Foundation, potential operators of the test field and the infrastructure. After the organizational form of the Foundation had received widespread support and funding had been agreed in principle by the German Federal Environment Ministry (BMU), the decisive question was which one of the already-permitted offshore projects should be selected for acquiring the licence. There were several projects at their disposal.

Dr. Knud Rehfeldt, CEO of consulting company Deutsche WindGuard GmbH was commissioned by the task force to carry out a brief evaluation to find the most suitable project. According to Paschedag some of the project developers, amongst them the Husum OSB Butendiek GmbH & Co. KG, which was promoting the idea of a 'people's wind farm' from land onto the sea and was planning a project 30 kilometres off the island of Sylt with 80 turbines each rated with three megawatts, turned them down immediately. "A mistake", as Knud Rehfeldt says in retrospect. Wolfgang Paulsen, MD of OSB Butendiek saw the situation somewhat differently. "I doubt, even if we had shown a great degree of interest, that we would have been a serious candidate for the Foundation. I don't believe that they would have got involved in our site that was in a nature conservation area." And there were, in fact, numerous opponents of the North Friesian project, especially amongst the nature conservation associations and also the German Federal Agency for Nature Conservation (BfN). They aimed to hold back the dawn of the German offshore era – above all in an area that is important for bird protection.

The report written by Rehfeldt in June 2005 confirmed that the locations in the Baltic Sea would appear to be less suitable for gaining a high degree of acceptance from politicians and industry. This meant that there were only four projects left on the shortlist. However, two of these projects were within the 12-nautical-mile zone, where the licencing process would prove to be very difficult due to unresolved issues regarding the Lower Saxony Wadden Sea region and the threat of law-

协调的人，这有利于基金会的工作，无论是对内还是对外。

帕舍达格则在幕后进行策划。埃克霍夫回忆说："他问我是否愿意担任基金会主席职务"。埃克霍夫直接参与了基金会的创建工作，并且长期以来被公认为风能方面的专家。作为保守党内一个相当年轻的政治家，他一直支持风能项目。早在1997年，他就是不来梅保守党的环境事务发言人和该地区风能行业的主要联系人。不来梅州议会决定将位于威悉河地区的Hanseatic作为风能中心。"因此，我们支持不来梅港成为海上风能中心，对于不来梅港来说，这是招商引资的极好机会"。埃克霍夫很高兴有许多相当成功的公司如Multibrid和瑞能公司把他们的制造厂设立在这个地方。这也是为什么他对那些因为要保护环境而阻拦扩建不来梅港的政治家缺乏耐心的原因。埃克霍夫以毋庸置疑的口吻说："仅以保护环境为由关闭核电站是不可能的"。现在，埃克霍夫已离开政坛，在房地产行业工作。作为保守党人士，他明确地支持风能，并代表基金会对外沟通。而在建立基金会之前和之后的困难时期，帕舍达格和约尔格·库比尔则发挥着主要推动作用。库比尔微笑着谈起一开始的情形，他说，"启动基金会的那些会议就像家长夜校一样。"于尔根·特里廷说："我们也不得不考虑联邦经济部偏见所带来的影响，因为那时候该部的领导人是沃尔夫冈·克莱门特，在他的头脑里只有煤炭能源，没有可再生能源，并且认为海上风能只是他的同事于尔根·特里廷的无稽之谈"。然而基金会的发起者们以及在联邦环境部内的支持者，特别是帕舍达格和他那些最亲密的同事们，比如托尔斯滕·法尔克和吉多·武斯特利希博士不受那些偏见的影响，但是海上风能项目也不会很容易就能获得准许。董事会向环境部申请，允许他们以7月正式成立的基金会的名义购买海上风电场。当时似乎社会民主党-绿党联盟正在濒于破裂，政府部门对基金会的目的有很大怀疑。说服他人加入是一项非常艰苦的工作，然而帕舍达格最终还是说服了联邦环境部预算局批准了该项目的购买资金。2005年9月2日，也就是在德国大选之前，基金会共获得500万欧元的资金。9月6日，在有环境部长特里廷出席的情况下，基金会主席延斯·埃克霍夫在柏林勃兰登堡科学院公开声明了基金会的目标："基金会的目标是通过对德国北海和波罗的海的风能的研究和开发，加强环境和气候保护"。埃克霍夫着重强调了四个核心领域：

1.通过海上风能的技术研究、开发和创新把电能传输给终端消费者。

2.进行海上风机（包括并网连接）在安装、运营和拆装过程中对海上环境影响的生态研究，以及海上风机技术和系统的生态优化研究。

3.加强海上风电公用设备的适用性和经济可行性研究，从而进一步改善环境，保护气候。

4.促进研究机构，商业公司及其它公私机构之间的海上风能知识交流。

在此期间，基金会一直在协商并准备签署波尔坎岛西项目。项目发展商Prokon北方公司毫不犹豫地接受了基金会的报价，作价500万欧元出售了对项目的所有权。针对波尔坎岛西项目的谈判，库比尔说："英戈·德布尔很公道，他并不想单独控制海上风电场，而只想从

suits from the island communities due to the grid connection. This would have endangered one of the most important goals of the Foundation, i.e. widespread acceptance among the German general public for the start into offshore wind energy. After two more project developers had tendered, the choice finally went to the project which had received the first licence of all from the BSH: Borkum West. The location, the number of turbines and the grid connection – already in a fairly advanced stage – were all reasons for selecting the project to the north of Borkum.

So the time had come early in July 2005: the initiators set up the German Offshore Wind Energy Foundation. It was officially recognized by the Lower Saxony Foundation Authority on the 26th July as a not-for-profit foundation. The initiators elected Jens Eckhoff as the first President and Thorsten Herdan, MD of the VDMA Power Systems section as Vice President. The Board was made up of Jörg Kuhbier, Jörgen Thiele and Dr. Knud Rehfeldt. While Rehfeldt had a good reputation as someone who knows a lot about wind reports, Thiele had been working hard to promote offshore wind energy in Mecklenburg-Western Pomerania and was involved in the creation of the Offshore Technology Project (OTP) in Rostock. In particular the OTP intended to move forward the offshore plans in the Baltic Sea. As President of the Chamber of Commerce (IHK) in Mecklenburg, Thiele emphasized again and again the industrial-political significance of offshore wind energy especially for the federal states in the north of Germany and for Germany's economy in general. "It would be foolhardy if we were to give up the leading technological role in the field of wind energy", criticized the machine constructor. Jörg Kuhbier, as third person in the trio, saw things similarly; his role as skilled moderator was beneficial to the work of the Foundation, both internally as well as to the outside world. In the meantime, Udo Paschedag was pulling the strings behind the scenes. "He was the one who asked me whether I wanted to accept the position of Foundation President", recalls Eckhoff, who was directly involved in the work to set up the Foundation and who had been a recognized expert in wind energy for a long time. As a very young politician in the CDU he had stood up early on for the subject of offshore energy. Already in 1997, when he was Environmental Spokesperson for the Bremen CDU (conservative party) and the main contact person in the region for the wind-energy sector, the Bremen State Parliament had decided that this Hanseatic city on the Weser should become a centre for wind energy. "Therefore, we deliberately went on to promote Bremerhaven as the place for offshore wind energy. It was a fantastic opportunity for Bremerhaven to attract new jobs". Eckhoff is pleased that numerous companies which are nowadays very successful have located their manufacturing plants there, in particular Multibrid and REpower. That's why he has less patience for the politicians who wanted to "protect the frogs" and prevent the enlargement of the port in Bremerhaven. "With such an attitude you won't be able to shut down any nuclear power stations", says Eckhoff in no uncertain fashion. He has left active politics and works now in the real-estate business. While Eckhoff, as a CDU man with a clear commitment to wind energy, represented the Foundation to the outside world, it was Udo Paschedag and Jörg Kuhbier who were the driving forces in building up the Foundation in this difficult period immediately before and after its launch. The meetings to get the Foundation going were a bit like the parents' evenings at school", Kuhbier remembers the beginnings with a smile. "We also had to deal with the prejudices of the Federal Ministry of Economics, which was led at the time by Wolfgang Clement. He

试验风电场的管理经验中受益"。这种情形的一种解释是：由于项目所有权的出售，使得中型企业可以进一步开发5兆瓦海上风机。2003年12月，Prokon北方公司将Pfleiderer公司的Multibrid公司兼并后，成为进入风电制造业唯一的开发商，而且很快获得成功。早在2004年秋，由马丁·伦霍夫率领的工程小组就在不来梅Weddewarden开始了5兆瓦样机的项目，此后一直在进行全面的试验。在这点上，基金会的出价收购来的正是时候。"把试验风电场的投资权转给那些等待中的潜在客户是一个好主意"，英戈·德布尔说。

基金会成功调解

如果你认为今后的道路一帆风顺，那就大错特错了。就像英戈·德布尔所担心的那样，风机制造商们拿到项目后就有所放松，这就是为什么失败比预期来得更快的原因。他希望三家风机制造商Enercon、瑞能和Multibrid都租用基金会的风电场，然后建造和运行四台5兆瓦风机。但是，瑞能和Multibrid还没开始时，Enercon在Hoorsiel安装海上风机就已经失败了，并不顾最初的协议退出这个项目。Enercon首席执行官阿洛伊斯·沃本给出的原因是，"从长远考虑，我们决定不参与海上风能开发，以便不影响公司在国际市场的快速发展。"

奥里奇的断然拒绝在基金会引起了震动。在此期间，至少库比尔公司为获得风电场并网做出的努力取得了成功。作为独立的调解方，基金会有能力说服下萨克森联邦州、诺得尼岛居民及波尔坎岛北部几个海工项目的开发商，共享穿过诺得尼岛的电缆线路是一个好主意。联邦德国环境部时任秘书马蒂亚斯·马赫尼希在项目准备阶段一直提供支持。他邀请持争议的各方来到德国环境部，并按帕谢达格的说法对他们提出警告。"马赫尼希明确指出，如果他们不立即停止下来，他们的意见不合就会对德国整个海上风能开发产生不利影响。"在一条公用电缆线路最终获得同意之后，开发商就能够说服能源供应商EWE公司、意昂公司和大瀑布电力公司承担起电网连接的规划和施工。尽管他们多次努力为风电场寻找新的合作伙伴，但都没有成功（西门子公司也拒绝了），最终三家能源供应商填补了空缺。2006年4月，三家公司的经理与德国总理默克尔在其柏林办公室达成一致意见，尽快建立并运行海上试验风电场。几个月后，德国海上风能基金会和DOTI签订了20年期限的租约，DOTI由供应商意昂公司、EWE和大瀑布电力公司联合组建。用基金会副主席兼德国VDMA能源主席托尔斯滕·赫丹的话来说，我们要用德国的试验证明，5兆瓦或更大的风机能在深达40米且距离海岸40公里以上的水域实现经济运行，这个基础终于打下了。"通过阿尔法·文图斯风电场，德国海上风电技术将成为一个重要的出口项目。"

only had coal power on his mind but not renewable energies and regarded offshore power as merely the ramblings of his colleague, Jürgen Trittin. "Nevertheless, the initiators of the Foundation and its proponents in the BMU, in particular Udo Paschedag and his closest co-workers, Thor-sten Falk and Dr. Guido Wustlich, were not put off by the prophets of doom. However, it was not easy to get a grant. The Board-to-be applied to the BMU for a grant to purchase licence rights for the offshore test field in the name of the Foundation that had been officially set up in July. At the time it seemed the SDP/Green Party coalition was coming to an end, and there was a great degree of scepticism within the ministries towards the intentions of the Foundation. It was tough work convincing anyone to join in. But Paschedag did find people, from the employees of the BMU budget department amongst other groups, who ended up approving the funds for purchasing the rights to the project. Before the German general election in the autumn of 2005, on the 2nd September amounts to the sum of five million euros were released to form the Foundation's capital. On 6th September, President of the Foundation Jens Eckhoff publicly presented the intentions of the Foundation at the Berlin-Brandenburg Academy of Sciences, in the presence of Environment Minister Trittin. "The goal of the Foundation is to promote environmental and climate protection through improved research and development of wind energy in the German North and Baltic Seas. Eckhoff emphasized four core areas to be promoted:

1. Technological research, development and innovation in offshore wind energy – taking into account the transport of the energy to the end consumer.
2. Accompanying ecological research on the impact on the marine environment of the construction, operation and removal of offshore wind turbines, including their cable connection to the grid as well as research into ecological optimization of turbine technology and the turbine systems for offshore wind energy.
3. Research into the suitability and economic feasibility of public instruments for promoting offshore wind energy with regard to improved environmental and climate protection.
4. Exchange of knowledge about offshore wind energy between the scientific and business communities, as well as other public or private institutions.

At this point in time, the Borkum West deal had been negotiated and was ready for signing. The project developers Prokon Nord took up the offer from the Foundation without any great hesitation. They sold their rights to this project for five million euros. "Ingo de Buhr dealt with us very fairly", says Kuhbier about the negotiations. "At the time he was happy not to have to master the offshore experiments alone and simply wanted to benefit from the experiences in the test field."

An interpretation of the situation that the Prokon Nord CEO does not wish to contradict: thanks to the sale of the project rights, the middle-sized enterprise could now concentrate on further developing their own offshore turbine, the M5000. When Prokon Nord took over the company Multibrid from Pfleiderer AG in December 2003 it became the only developer in the industry brave enough to enter the manufacturing business. It was a daring enterprise that was soon to demonstrate visible success. The small team of engineers gathered around Martin Lehnhoff was able to start up the prototype of the M5000 in Bremerhaven-Weddewarden as early as the autumn of 2004 and since then has been carrying out in-depth tests. In this respect, the offer from the Foundation came at just the right time. "It was a good idea to pass on the investments for the test field to the potential customers-in-waiting", says

Ingo de Buhr.

Successful moderation by the Foundation

Anyone who believed that it was to be all easy going from now on was making a huge mistake. As Ingo de Buhr had already feared, the wind-turbine manufacturers ignored these efforts and this is why the original idea failed more quickly than expected. The idea was that each of the three turbine manufacturers, Enercon, REpower and Multibrid would lease their share of the test field from the Foundation and then build and operate four of their 5-megawatt turbines. Whereas REpower and Multibrid waited in the starting blocks, Enercon, however, withdrew in spite of the original agreement after their experience with a failed offshore turbine foundation off Hooksiel. The reason given was that Enercon CEO Aloys Wobben "decided for strategic reasons against offshore energy", so as not to endanger the rapid development of his company on the international stage.

The rebuff from Aurich caused a stir within the Foundation. But at least the efforts of Kuhbier and Co. to get the grid connections for the planned test field were rewarded during this turbulent phase. As independent moderator, the Foundation was able to convince both the Federal state of Lower Saxony, the island community of Norderney and also the developers of several offshore projects north of Borkum that a shared cable line across Norderney would be a good idea. There had been support in the run-up from Matthias Machnig, the State Secretary of the time in the BMU. He invited the squabbling parties to the BMU and "read them the Riot Act", as Paschedag puts it.

"Machnig made it unmistakably clear to all those involved that their disagreements would have negative consequences on the whole offshore development in Germany if they didn't stop as soon as possible. After a common cable route had finally been agreed, the offshore developers were able to convince the energy supply companies EWE, E.ON and Vattenfall to take on the planning and construction of this grid connection. Since the search for new cooperation partners for the test field failed in spite of numerous attempts to attract other wind-turbine producers – Siemens amongst others also refused – the three energy suppliers eventually filled the gap. In April 2006, their managers agreed with German Chancellor Angela Merkel at an energy summit in her offices in Berlin to set up and run an offshore test field as soon as possible. A few months later, the lease agreement for a duration of 20 years had been finalized between the German Offshore Wind Energy Foundation and DOTI (Deutsche Offshore-Testfeld und Infra-struktur GmbH & Co. KG), which had been founded by the suppliers E.ON, EWE and Vattenfall. In the words of Thorsten Herdan, Vice President of the Foundation and Chairman of the VDMA Power Systems section, the basis had finally been laid to demonstrate with the test field in Germany that wind turbines with five megawatts and more could be run economically in water depths of up to 40 metres and more than 40 kilometres off the coast: "With the help of alpha ventus, German offshore technology can become a major export industry."

工业与政治的对话
Dialogue between industry and politics

访海上风能基金会董事会成员克努特·雷费尔特博士
BOARD MEMBER OF THE OFFSHORE WIND ENERGY FOUNDATION

克努特·雷费尔特
Dr. Knud Rehfeldt

克努特·雷费尔特博士在不来梅获得风机控制博士学位，1995年至2001年，在德国风能研究所（DEWI）工作，在此期间于潘普洛纳建立了德国风能研究所西班牙办事处。自2001年开始担任德国WindGuard公司总经理，雇员约70人，主要为风能行业提供国际化的服务。

雷费尔特先生，为什么要建立海上风能基金会？

在2005年海事会议期间，有几个德国的风机制造商表示希望在公海建立一个试验风电场，他们聚集在一起，共同讨论如何建立风电场。一般来说，建立风电场所面临的首要问题是"如何获取项目所有权以及什么样的机构能运营这样的试验风电场"。一开始，大家对组织结构上的看法迥然不同，看法也在不断改变。直到讨论将要结束时，大家才一致认为要获取海上风能项目,非营利的基金会是最佳解决方案。

风机制造商为什么不自己解决风电场的问题？

这些制造商包括Enercon公司、瑞能公司和阿海珐Multibrid公司（当时是Multibrid公司）。事实上这些制造商都想联合起来建立一个风电场。然而经验表明，成立一个由三家互有竞争的公司所组成的机构，始终是件很困难的事情，这也是为什么大家都期待一个独立的机构，但是这样的机构在此之前还不存在。海上风能基金会填补了这个空白，基金会将代表不同利益的参与者聚集在一起，按照大家共同的利益落实风电场的建设。

基金会的任务只是获得一个试验风电场吗？

完全不是这样。基金会的任务不仅是要获得一块试验风电场，并将其交给运营者，我们还要推动海上风能的发展。更为重要的是，基金会的主要目的是传播技术，通过设立风电场，将阿尔

Dr. Knud Rehfeldt received a PhD in Bremen in the field of wind turbine control. Between 1995 and 2001 he worked at the German Wind Energy Institute (DEWI), during which time he established the DEWI Spanish office in Pamplona. Since 2001 he has been Managing Director of Deutsche WindGuard, an inter-national service provider to the wind-energy industry with some 70 employees.

Mr. Rehfeldt, why was the Offshore Wind Energy Foundation established?

During the Maritime Conference 2005 several German wind-turbine manufacturers expres-sed their desire to set up a test field on the open sea. All the protagonists came together in a large group to discuss how such a test field could be realized. The first questions were, broadly speaking, "How do we obtain the project rights?" and "What sort of organization would be necessary at all to be able to operate such a test field?" At first there were very differing ideas about the possible and neces-sary structures, as so many variations were available. At the end of the discussion process it appeared that a non-profit-making foundation would be the best solution to be able to acquire the rights for an offshore project.

Why didn't the turbine manufacturers try to tackle the test field themselves?

The manufacturers – that is, Enercon, REpower and AREVA Multibrid, at the time still named Multibrid, had in fact wanted to get together with a field and set up their turbines there. However, experience has shown that it is always difficult to set up an organization comprising three competing companies, and that's why everyone was looking for an independent body – which didn't yet exist. We were able to fill this gap with the Offshore Wind Energy Foun-dation and get all partici-pants, with their respective interests, around the same table to implement the test field in everyone's common interest.

法·文图斯项目积累的经验告诉同行。为此基金会首要的任务是要加强本行业与政府的沟通。

这样做的主要目的就是要有益于公共利益，这也是基金会始终追求的目标。

为什么德国第一个海上风电场要建立在离海岸那么远的地方？

如果在近海建立海上风电场，会由于许多原因难以获批。目前有4个近海项目计划，但是由于这种困难的审批状况，在专属经济区内的许多海工项目大批上马之前，它们大概都无法实现并网。目前看来，在近海区域不会有更多的计划。现在，事情就停下来了，这样可以避免与自然保护主义者、渔业和旅游业之间发生冲突。当然，

Is the task of the Foundation simply to acquire a test field?

No, not at all. The Foundation not only has the task of acquiring a test field and passing it on to an operator, but also intends to take the initiative in promoting the development of offshore wind power. What's more, the Foundation is pursuing the important goal of passing on know-how. It's not just about setting up a test field but also about passing on the experience gathered from realizing alpha ventus wherever possible to all protagonists in the offshore wind-energy industry. On top of this comes the task of intensifying the dialogue between the sector and politics.

The overarching idea of all these activities is the benefit to the public interest, which the Foundation consistently pursues. It does not intend to make any money out of the test field. That was not the original aim and will not be in future, either.

Why did the first German offshore wind-farm need to be set up so far away from the coast?

In Germany we find ourselves in the situation that offshore farms near the coast will encounter serious problems in receiving a licence, for numerous reasons. There are four projects planned near the coast; however they will probably not get connected to the grid due to this difficult approval situation until after numerous offshore projects in the Exclusive Economic Zone have come onstream. And at the moment it appears that there will be no further plans for sites near the coast. For now that spells an end to the matter and this avoids any potential for conflict with the nature

从梦想到现实 From vision to reality

海上风能从近海区域开始，然后再慢慢向深水区域发展是比较理想的。

是什么促使您为海上风能基金会工作？

自1989年以来我就在风能行业工作，对陆上风能非常熟悉。对于我来说，问题是"我们将来如何达到德国联邦政府气候政策的目标？"。风能肯定是未来混合能源中极其重要的一部分，无论是陆上还是海上都要充分加以利用。我不会说我们需要这种或那种能源，也不想支持一个，打击一个。相反，我认为两者都要发展，以获得最佳机会达成这些政府目标。目前，我们计划在2020年达到10000兆瓦的海上发电量，到那时陆上风能可能会超过40000兆瓦。换句话说，下一个十年陆上风能会有更快的发展，其贡献将大于海上风能。但是这不是说你可以以此反证我们就不需要在海上风能方面做努力了。我在基金会的工作就是要传播这种理念。2005年就有人问有谁愿意承担此项工作，约尔格·库比尔、约尔根·蒂勒和我本人都表明愿意接受这项工作。

基金会从阿尔法·文图斯项目中得到什么经验？

首先，基金会从项目建立的过程中就不断地学习，由于最初对项目估计不足，所以遇到了很多困难和状况，以及海上的风浪。主要是要选择适合不同气象条件的设备。阿尔法·文图斯风电场的位置选得很好，对进一步开发北海风能来说，它在浪高、水深、离岸距离及相关挑战方面是有代表性的。到2009年底，在德国的北海已有超过25个海上风电场获批。这些项目的发起人一直在关注试验风电场建设的进程。现在，试验风电场已经建立，我们还必须确保它能够成功地运行。

海上风电场的建设只是一方面，另一方面电网连接的情况如何呢？

到目前为止，阿尔法·文图斯风电场和北海的后续4个项目仅有一个电网可以连接，产能为3000兆瓦。但是穿过诺得尼岛的电缆只是计划把北海风能输上岸的四条电缆之一，因此完成铺设还需要很长时间。这样的形势使今后的开发计划变得极为困难。况且，我们要把多个区域连接起来，从长远来看，最终要建立国际性的海上电网。穿过诺得尼岛的电缆的铺设是在加速基础设施规划法案出台之前完成的，这是我们把不同项目发展商集中起来建立统一的程序，并达成合法协议的良好范例。我深信基金会作为一个协调机构，能够作出重要贡献。到

conservationists, the fishing industry and tourism. Nevertheless, it's obvious that it would have been desirable for offshore wind energy to have been able to start from the shallow areas near the coast and then move slowly into deeper waters.

What is the motivation for your work in the Offshore Wind Energy Foundation?

I have been working in the wind business since 1989 and was already very familiar with the sector on land. For me the question was, "How can we meet the climate policy objectives of the German Federal Government in the future?" Wind power is certainly a crucial component of the energy mix of the future and that needs to be utilized both onshore and offshore. I am one of those people who doesn't say we need the one or the other, or who wants to play the one against the other. Rather, I believe we need to develop both to stand the best chance of achieving these political goals. We're currently planning 10,000 MW offshore by the year 2020; by then there will probably be more than 40,000 MW on land. In other words, we will be a lot quicker in developing onshore power in the next ten years and it will thus make a greater initial contribution to energy supply than offshore wind energy. However, this doesn't mean you can use the converse argu-ment to say we don't require any work on offshore energy. My work in the Foundation is intended to propagate that idea. And when in 2005, people asked around in the wind-energy sector who would like to take on this responsibility, Jörg Kuhbier, Jörgen Thiele and myself declared ourselves willing to accept positions on the Board.

What is the offshore wind industry learning from alpha ventus?

Firstly, it has learned from the process of coming into being itself – with all the difficulties and the conditions with waves and wind on the open sea, that were initially underestimated. It's all about correctly selecting the respective equipment suitable for all weather conditions. The location of alpha ventus has certainly been well chosen; it's representative for the further expansion of offshore wind energy in the North Sea, with regard to the height of the waves, water depths and distance from the coast – and thus the challenges associated with these. In the German North Sea, over 25 offshore wind farms had been licenced by the end of 2009 and the initiators of these projects have been watching very carefully what happens in the test field. Now that the test field has been set up we have to make sure we are also successful in operating it.

Windfarms at sea are the one side of the coin. What about the other – connecting them to

目前为止，只有横跨北海泥滩国家公园的电缆铺设获得批准。可是如果计划装机容量为25000兆瓦，就要采用电缆束，否则穿过北海泥滩国家公园所需要的电缆数量会超过100条以上，这种情况是不会获得批准的。

你认为怎样才能解决这个问题？

随着2006年12月《加快新基础设施规划法案》的出台，我们就有了推进海底电网建设的基本工具。然而，我们需要制定一个海上风电总体计划，以确保所有相关的必要基础设施都能建立。毕竟，这是未来规划中必须考虑的问题。

您对海上风能的经济前景怎么看？

目前海上风电的费用是每千瓦时15欧分，这意味着海上的风电要比陆上的风电昂贵得多。二十年前，陆上风电的成本已在15分之上的水平。我认为，新的海上风能技术和相关的分析数据表明，海上风电的成本可能会大幅削减，尽管这不

the grid?

Up to now there has only been a grid connection for the alpha ventus test field and four further subsequent projects in the North Sea with a production capacity of 3,000 mega-watts. The cable through Norderney is, however, only one of a total of four clusters planned for bringing North Sea wind power ashore. Nevertheless, their implementation is still a long way off. This situation makes the planning of further development extremely difficult. Moreover, we have to think a step even further: we have to connect up the cluster areas with each other to set up, in the long-term, a transnational offshore grid. Irrespective of this, I think that with the cable solution over Norder-ney, that was implemented before the Act on Accelerated Infrastructure Planning, we have a good example of how you can bring various project developers together for a common procedure and establish legal agreements. I believe that particularly the Foundation, as moderator, can make an important contribution there. The cable through Norderney is, up to now, the only approved crossing of the Watten-meer (North Sea mudflats) National Park. If you intend to install 25,000 megawatts of generating capacity without clustering, however, you'd need a lot more than 100 cables to go through the mudflats. It'd be impossible to get that approved.

And how do you believe can the problem be solved?

With the Act on Accelerated Infrastructure Planning we have had a fundamental tool available since December 2006 to push forward the expansion of the grid at sea. However, we need a master plan for the offshore sector to ensure that all involved can rest assured that the necessary infrastructure will be set up – after all, this is essential for their further planning.

How do you see the economic perspectives of offshore wind energy?

As you know, the reimbursement for offshore wind electricity is currently 15 eurocents per kilowatt-hour, which means that wind power at sea is a lot more expensive than that on land. However,

是一夜之间能完成的。然而鉴于德国目前的机制，我认为海上风电在近十年内不会比陆上风电便宜。

您认为2030年的北海和波罗的海会是什么样，是不是像芦笋地？

这话听起来有点否定的意思。如果过几年再去北海看看，你们肯定可以看到风机。但是沿岸的居民和去那里的度假的人可能不会注意这些。我相信人们会逐渐地意识到风能所赋予北海的经济重要性。我们不要忘了，如果单就挖泥、商业捕鱼、石油和天然气开采来说，这里已经以其它方式进行了数十年的开发。

海上风能是否意味着德国海洋经济已经进入了一个新纪元？

是的，大有前途的海上风能行业已经清楚表明我们一直没像荷兰、英国、挪威和丹麦那样进行海上开发。德国在北海的专属经济区内没有石油和天然气，这就是德国没有开发海上能源业的原因。现在，海上风能是我们一个唯一的机会，我们应该加快行动，因为我们的邻国已经为海上风能开发做好了准备。我们必须要建立自己的海上产业，这也是国家的需要。为此，我们需要这个试验风电场。

您认为风能可以代替煤电和核电吗？

从长远来看，我们必须这样做。

the costs for wind power on land were above the 15-cent level almost 20 years ago. What I'm saying is, the new offshore technology and the associated learning curve mean that even greater cost reductions are possible – although such a process does not happen overnight. Nevertheless, given the framework conditions in Germany, I do not believe that offshore wind energy will be cheaper than onshore power in ten years' time.

How do you think the North and Baltic Seas will look in 2030 – something like an asparagus field?

That sounds rather negative! If you're out and about in the North Sea in a few years' time you will, of course, see the turbines. However, the inhabitants and holidaymakers on the coast won't notice them. I believe, however, that people will only slowly become aware of the economic importance that the North Sea has due to wind power. Let's not forget that it has already been exploited very intensively for decades in other ways – just think of the sand dredging, commercial fishing and the drilling for oil and gas.

Does the offshore wind energy mean a new era is starting for the German maritime economy?

The up-and-coming offshore wind energy sector has made it clear that we Germans have not been doing what the Dutch, English, Norwegians and Danes have been doing for a while at sea. The whole oil and gas industry in the North Sea is outside the German Exclusive Economic Zone, in which there are no such reserves. That's why Germany has not yet been able to develop an offshore industry. Through offshore wind energy, however, we now have the unique opportunity to build an industry of our own – if we are quick enough. Because our neighbours are in the starting blocks and would like to do the same business too. It has to be in our interest to build our own industry, basically as a task for the nation. But to do that, we need the test field.

Would you say that wind power can replace electricity produced from coal and atomic power?

In the long term, that's what we have to do.

能源公司进军海上
Power companies enter the offshore business

说实话，2005年7月海上风电基金会刚成立时，整个风能行业中有谁会料到德国首个海上风电场会由三家能源公司共同建立并运营？也许没有一个人能预料到会发生这种情况。彼时，所有人都沉浸在最初的欣喜中。德国联邦海事与水文局的批准，预示着海上风电项目将尽快得到实施，于是大家关注着各自项目的进展。将发展海上风电作为可再生能源行业、整个能源业、甚至是整个国家的共同任务——这种观念尚未形成。

随着海上能源业的先锋们进一步开展实际工作，并意识到开展海上风电项目涉及技术、物流、规划、审批及融资等多个方面，这种态度也在逐渐发生转变。许多在第一波热潮中开始海工项目的中小型项目开发商们突然遇到了严重的困难，这些困难是陆上风能开发以来所未曾出现过的。

考虑到投资额巨大以及风险难以衡量，融资问题常常成为难以逾越的障碍。许多项目停滞了，众多公司的海上梦迅速地破灭了，就和梦想产生时一样快。德国的风力发电机制造商也不愿意独自冒着财务风险去建造运营试验风电场。

该怎么做呢？在邀请德国能源业的重要决策者参加2006年4月于柏林召开的能源峰会时，德国总理默克尔一定也问过自己这个问题。海上风电是该峰会议程中一个最热门的议题。德国该采取什么样的最佳方式进入海上能源行业？这一次政府向整个行业施压，催促其采取行动。最终EWE、意昂公司和大瀑布电力公司三家能源企业向总理承诺，会联合三方力量创立海上试验场。

三足鼎立

"终于等到今天了！"德国众多海上风电企业家们感叹道。此间，由于三位CEO向德国总理做出了公开承诺，三家公司的风能部门承受了巨大的压力。但至少他们已作出了一项决定——建立博尔库姆西试验场，海上风能基金会于数月前已经获得了该地块的开发权。不过三家组织架构完全不同的公司仍需要确定合作的方式方法，诸如确定哪家公司将承担哪些任务，以便尽快地组成一个强大有效的机构。

2006年7月，能源峰会结束后仅三个月，三家能源公司中的两家共同组建了一个新公司——德国海上风电场和基础设施股份有限公司，简称DOTI。这或许是唯一一家这种类型的公司。DOTI最初由EWE股份公司和意昂的子公司意昂能源项目股份有限公司组建，后者

Let's be honest now: When the Offshore Wind Energy Foundation was formed in July 2005, who in the wind-energy business would have thought that Germany's first offshore wind farm would be jointly built and operated by no less than three power companies? Probably no-one. In that initial euphoria for offshore wind energy, as the approvals by the German Federal Marine and Hydrographic Authority (BSH) seemed to bode rapid implementation, all eyes were on the progress of each company's own projects. The idea of offshore wind energy as a joint effort on the part of the renewable energy industry, the entire energy industry as a whole – or even the state – had not yet gained a toehold.

This attitude changed gradually, as the pioneers in the offshore business got deeper into the practicalities of the matter and began to realise the sheer dimensions of the technical, logistical, planning, approval and financial issues involved. Many of the small and medium-sized project developers who had started offshore projects in the first flush of enthusiasm suddenly faced difficulties of a severity unseen since the earliest days of wind energy on land.

Financing in particular often turned out to be a seemingly insurmountable obstacle, given the large investment volumes and poorly calculable risks. Many projects stalled and many companies' offshore dreams faded away as quickly as they had arisen. The German wind-turbine manufacturers likewise were unwilling to risk the financial adventure of constructing and operating their own test field.

What was to be done? German Chancellor Angela Merkel must have asked herself that question as she invited the key decision-makers of the German energy industry to the Energy Summit in Berlin in April 2006. Offshore wind energy was among the hottest topics on the agenda. What was the best way for Germany to get into the offshore business? This time the government pressed industry to take action, and finally three power companies, EWE, E.ON and Vattenfall, promised the Chancellor that they would join forces to create a German offshore test field.

Three's company

"Finally!" said many German offshore entrepreneurs to themselves. Meanwhile, the promise the three CEOs had publicly made to the Chancellor was putting these three companies' wind-energy departments under severe pressure. At least there was one decision that had already been made – the test field would be built at the Borkum West site, the rights to which the Offshore Wind Energy Foundation had acquired a few months previously. But how the cooperative effort would actually function still needed to be worked out among the three very differently structured companies. Who would take on which

在集团内部重组后更名为意昂气候及再生能源股份有限公司。没过多久,大瀑布电力的子公司大瀑布电力欧洲新能源股份有限公司也入股DOTI,该公司从一开始便参与公司营运。在2009年春,其所持股份转让给了大瀑布欧洲风能股份有限公司。

2008年秋,EWE股份公司对DOTI进行了注资。注资完成后,其一共持有公司47.5%的资本,成为最大股东。DOTI的总部设在德国西北部的奥尔登堡市,但实际上公司从一开始就采用分散式运作模式,在奥尔登堡市和韦斯特施特德以外还设立汉堡和慕尼黑项目办公室。"从一开始我们就是个虚拟团队,分散在德国各地",DOTI的首席执行官维尔弗里德·胡贝说。胡贝在2008年秋被任命为阿尔法·文图斯的项目总监,而早在DOTI成立前,他在EWE公司就参与规划了首个海上风电场的传输网。三方合作对他而言并不算意外,因为在柏林能源峰会之前就有许多关于联合建造海上试验场的讨论。在胡贝看来DOTI只是他长期工作的延续。不同的是,DOTI为整个项目提供了坚实的基础:在电网连接、物流、试验场的建造和试运行上都有经济和技术合作。

合作的三家公司对工作进行了具体分工:EWE承担了所有与海

tasks, so that a robust, functional unit could be formed as quickly as possible?

Just three months after the Energy Summit, in July 2006 two of the three power companies founded a joint company that is probably the only one of its kind – the Deutsche Offshore-Testfeld- und Infrastruktur-GmbH & Co. KG, or DOTI for short. DOTI was initially formed by EWE AG and the E.ON subsidiary E.ON Energy Projects GmbH, which later became E.ON Climate & Renewables GmbH after internal restructuring. Shortly thereafter the Vattenfall subsidiary Vattenfall Europe New Energy GmbH joined the group, having been involved at the operational level right from the beginning. Its shares were transferred to Vattenfall Europe Windkraft GmbH in the spring of 2009.

Following an injection of capital in the autumn of 2008, EWE AG became the largest shareholder with 47.5 percent of DOTI's capital. The headquarters is officially in Oldenburg, northwest Germany, but DOTI operated decentrally right from the start, with project offices in Hamburg and Munich besides the Oldenburg and Westerstede locations. "From the very first we were a virtual team, spread throughout Germany," says Wilfried Hube, who functioned as CEO of DOTI and in the autumn of 2008 was named overall Project Director of alpha ventus. Hube was one of the people at EWE who had been working on transmission-grid planning for the first offshore wind farms even before

阿尔法·文图斯变电站的上部结构由Taklift 4浮吊实施吊装,然后从威廉港港口运至海上。
The alpha ventus transformer station's topside is taken by the hook from Taklift 4 floating crane in the port of Wilhelms-haven and moved out into the open sea.

DOTI came into being. The triple partnership did not come as a surprise for him, as even before the Berlin Energy Summit there had been much discussion behind the scenes of how to go about building a joint offshore test field. Thus, for Hube DOTI was just the continuation of something he had long since begun working on. However, DOTI now offered a solid foundation for the entire project – financial and technical cooperation for the grid connection, the logistics, and the construction and commissioning of the test field.

The work was divided up among the partner companies. EWE took on all tasks connected with undersea cables, the transformer station and control systems. E.ON Climate & Renewables concentrated on all matters concerning the wind turbines. Vattenfall was in charge of the turbine tower foundations and logistics. On top of all this, the German Federal Marine and Hydrographic Authority (BSH) needed to see a completely new Health, Safety and Environment (HSE) concept before it would grant approval. Irina Lucke of EWE was put in charge of the complex task of developing this. With the assistance of external expert Andreas Stutz, an experienced professional diver for the offshore industry, she and her team drafted an HSE manual that proved its value during the construction phase and will doubtlessly serve as a model for future offshore projects.

The first official act of DOTI after its founding was to lease the ap-

底电缆、变电站和控制系统相关的任务；意昂气候及再生能源公司的工作集中在风力发电机上；而大瀑布电力公司则负责发电机基座和物流。此外还有一项更重要的任务——为整个海上施工制定全新的健康、安全与环境（HSE）管理体系。因为只有具备完整的HSE体系，德国联邦海事与水文局（BSH）才会正式批准该项目。来自EWE公司的伊琳娜•卢克被任命为HSE体系的负责人。她聘请了安德烈亚斯•施图茨，一位海上能源领域的资深专家来协助自己。在他的帮助下，伊琳娜的团队起草了一份HSE手册。这份手册在施工阶段发挥了很大的作用，同时也将成为未来海工项目的样板。

DOTI成立后第一个正式法律行为是向海上风能基金会租借试验场的开发权。当然项目需要有一个名字。有人提议用"阿尔法12"，这个名字虽然听上去很有气势，但是总让人觉得还缺少些什么。最终意昂的经理史文•乌特莫伦和他的同事一起为整个项目起了一个好名字，他们贡献了一个希腊拉丁新词——"阿尔法•文图斯（alpha ventus）"，可以翻译为"第一阵风"。所有人一致认为这个名字很合适，于是博尔库姆西正式更名为阿尔法•文图斯。对此，DOTI新闻发言人，来自大瀑布电力公司传播部的鲁茨•维泽说，"我们希望用这个名字表达我们对这个试验场的期望，它代表共同拥有的海上风电的新开端"。

这确实是一个崭新的开始。2009年末，世界上独一无二的试验场经历三年半的时间终于完工了。整整42个月对局外人来说似乎很长，但维尔弗里德•胡贝不同意这种看法。"对建造海上风电场来说已经相当快了！"他显得非常激动，"尤其是考虑到耗费的时间和人力，包括准备招标，认真评估风力发电机、基座、专用船舶以及其它装置的投标书。"人事变动也给项目带来了不少挑战。要特别提到的是在初始阶段，各家公司为更好地发展可再生能源业务分别进行了内部重组，导致人员派遣上出现一系列的变动。尽管如此，在对项目回顾总结时，DOTI团队中几乎所有的员工都认为公司间的合作"异常出色"，都提到了"优秀的团队合作精神"。在整个项目进程中，该团队每月在汉堡项目办公室举行两次工作会议。即便是来自外部的干涉或施工工地上出现问题也不能扰乱这个日益紧密的团队。事实上三家公司对阿尔法•文图斯项目从未产生过一丝疑虑。为什么要有疑虑呢？EWE、意昂和大瀑布电力三家公司都对海上风电有很高的期望。尽管在审视他们过去、现在和未来的公司活动时可以发现这三家公司的战略基本相似，但是在阿尔法•文图斯这个先锋项目中他们拥有共同利益。

EWE公司献身于充满可能的神奇领域

EWE股份公司全称为"威悉河-埃姆斯河能源供应公司"，总部位于德国西北部的奥尔登堡市。公司从很早开始就不满足于只在当地发展了，它不断扩大供能地区，不仅在德国国内的勃兰登堡、吕根和北波美拉尼亚地区，甚至在波兰和土耳其这两个国家也表现活跃。EWE集团的业务共涉及三个领域——传统的发电、电网，还有1996年新增的电信和IT业务。现在公司为近100万客户供电，为120万客户供应天然气。

可再生能源在EWE的作用越来越大，而且公司还会持续扩大风能、生物能和太阳能发电量。公司最受欢迎的可再生能源项目很可能

proval rights for the test field from the Offshore Wind Energy Foundation. And of course the project needed a name. 'alpha 12' was mooted, but the parties involved felt that although this was promising, it lacked that certain something. E.ON-Manager Sven Utermöhlen and his colleagues found the answer – they contributed the Greco-Latin neologism 'alpha ventus' (freely translated as 'First Wind') to the pool of ideas. Everyone felt the name was appropriate, and so Borkum West was renamed 'alpha ventus' without further ado. "We wanted the name to be an outward symbol of our intention for this test field to represent a shared new beginning for offshore wind energy," says Lutz Wiese of Vattenfall Communications and DOTI Press Spokesman.

And it is indeed a new beginning – although it was to take until late 2009, another three-and-a-half years – to complete the test field, still the only one of its kind in the world. 42 months might seem a long time to some outside observers, but Wilfried Hube sees it differently: "That's really very fast for an offshore wind farm!", he enthuses, "especially given the amount of time and manpower required just to prepare the bid tenders, and then evaluate in painstaking detail the resulting bids for wind turbines, foundations, special vessels – and all the other components of this massive project." Personnel changes also brought challenges, especially during the initial phases as the partner companies restructured internally in order to focus better on renewables. This resulted in a series of changes in the staff assigned to various tasks. Nevertheless, in retrospect almost all of the employees on the DOTI team that met twice monthly in the Hamburg project office over the entire course of the project described the inter-company cooperation as "astoundingly good," and spoke of the "excellent team spirit." Even outside interference and problems on the construction site could not unsettle this increasingly tight-knit team. In fact, at no point did any of the three companies involved in DOTI express the slightest doubt that they would stay on board with the alpha ventus project. And why should they? EWE, E.ON and Vattenfall all continue to have very high expectations for offshore wind energy. This is their common interest in this pioneering project, although otherwise their company strategies could hardly be more different, as a close examination of the past, present, and upcoming activities of the three companies reveals.

EWE's commitment to the fascination of the possible

'Energieversorgung Weser-Ems' (EWE AG) has long looked beyond its home territory in northwest Germany and has greatly extended the area to which it supplies power. From its base in Oldenburg, the group is now active in Brandenburg, Rügen and North Pomerania in Germany, and as far afield as Poland and Turkey.

EWE works in three business fields. Traditionally a power-generation and grid utility, in 1996 it added telecommunications and information technology to its portfolio. Today, the company supplies electricity to around a million customers and natural gas to 1.2 million customers. Renewable energy plays a growing role for EWE and the company is steadily expanding its generation capacity in wind, biomass and solar power. Perhaps its most popular renewable energy project is the solar

2008年秋，变电站被安装至阿尔法•文图斯试验场。
The transformer station was set up in the test field in autumn 2008.

是不来梅威悉体育场外立面的太阳能电池板：其发电功率达1.2兆瓦，是世界上最大的太阳能电池板之一。公司还和两个项目伙伴在埃姆登合作运营一家总功率达20兆瓦的生物能发电厂。此外它还参与了沼气生产。

风能发电一直是EWE股份公司投资最多的业务领域，公司在风电领域积累了20多年的经验。1988年EWE在库克斯港附近建造了第一座风电场，很快又建造了其他几座风电场，大多位于德国西北部的东弗里西亚地区。公司目前最大的风电场位于维贝尔苏姆圩田区，总装机容量达79兆瓦，约三分之一已在1997年到2002年间投入运转。

array on the façade of the Bremen Weser Stadium: this can produce 1.2 megawatts and is one of the largest of its kind anywhere. In Emden the company operates a 20-megawatt biomass power plant jointly with two project partners. EWE is also involved in biogas generation.

EWE AG's greatest renewables investment so far has been in electricity generation from wind energy, and the company has over 20 years of experience in the field. The first EWE wind farm was built in 1988 near Cuxhaven and was quickly followed by other wind farms, mostly in the East Friesia region of northwest Germany. EWE's largest wind farm to date is in the Wybelsum Polder. Around a third of the installed capacity of 79 megawatts there was brought on-stream between 1997 and 2002.

向深海的危险致敬
RESPECTING THE DANGERS OF THE HIGH SEAS

迪克·延森报道 by Dierk Jensen

阿尔法·文图斯试验场的健康、安全、环境（HSE）管理体系对后续的海工项目是一笔宝贵的财富。

"你也做了一回海马？"一开始，对自升式平台上工作的装配工说的这句话，我一点都不理解。是玩笑吗？但很快我就明白了。"哦，是啊，我上过课了，在鹿特丹上的，上了三天呢。"我说。他回答："我也是。你一定也参加过Bosiet课程（海上基本安全感应和应急训练），模拟直升机坠毁在水中、消防培训、深海救助等，一整套课程。""是啊，一整套。"我想起了我们做过的众多练习中最具挑战性的一项——他们把你关在水下，关进一个被水完全淹没的小隔间里，你被困在里面只能摒住呼吸，分不清东南西北也找不到舱门可以逃至水面。

每个参与阿尔法·文图斯试验场建造阶段工作的工作人员都必须参加这项海上培训；等到阿尔法·文图斯开始运营后，所有工作人员也都必须参加此项培训。整个课程为期数日，向学员传授紧急情况下如何逃生。培训中心强调尽可能真实地模拟紧急情况，将实践知识传授给海上工作人员，便于其在突发状况下做出正确反应。因而只有那些在海上没呆多久，不知道大海有多危险的人才会称这项十分实用的培训为"海马"。

至少安德烈亚斯·施图茨是这样认为的。作为专业潜水员，他有丰富的海上潜水经验。他接受

The alpha ventus health, safety and environ-ment programme is a valuable resource for future offshore projects

"Did you also have to do the seahorse?" At first I didn't know what the fitter on the jack-up platform meant. Was it some kind of joke? But then I got it. "Oh, yes, I took the course, in Rotterdam – three days," I answered. "So did I," he said. "I bet you had to do the Bosiet course, the simulated helicopter crash underwater, fire-extinguisher training, high-seas rescue, the whole thing." "Yes," I said, "the whole thing," and thought of the most challenging of the many exercises we did – the one where they turn you around underwater in a flooded compartment while you're strapped in and holding your breath, so you don't know right from left, or which direction to go to get to the hatch and escape to the surface.

This offshore training is mandatory for everyone working in the construction phase of the alpha ventus test field, and will be requir-ed for everyone who works there when it's operational. The course takes several days and teaches participants how to stay alive in emer-gency situations. The training centres place great emphasis on simulating emergency situa-tions as realistically as possible, and on giving offshore workers the practical knowledge they need in order to be able to react appropriately in case of emergency. Only somebody who hasn't been at sea for long and doesn't know how dangerous it can be, would refer to this highly practical training as "seahorse."

At least, that's what Andreas Stutz thinks. As a professional diver with extensive offshore

experience, he was engaged by DOTI under the supervision of Irina Lucke (EWE AG) to work out the major features of the occupational health, safety and environment (HSE) scheme for alpha ventus. "Those of us in the offshore industry know the hazards of working at sea, and have the greatest respect for them. Safety offshore is our first priority," said Stutz, adding: "Safety requirements at sea have a completely different standard than on land. Nobody goes to sea unless they can prove ahead of time that they fulfil rigorously defined qualifications. If your papers aren't in order, you're staying on land, regardless of cost. No compromises." In addition to the offshore training course, everyone has to have a thorough health check, including a lung check and ECG, and must have completed a first aid course and rappel (abseiling) training. "If something can go wrong, it will, and you have to be ready for it," notes Stutz, in a reference to Murphy's famous law.

Irina Lucke, the person in charge of Approvals and HSE, calls it "great luck" that she was able to get Andreas Stutz to prepare the safety programme and to accept the post of Safety Coordinator. The biggest challenge during the alpha ventus planning phase was that Lucke, Stutz and their colleagues on this first German offshore project had no guidelines to turn to. Wherever they looked, they came up empty. "Unlike Germany, the other nations bordering the North Sea have many years' experience with oil and gas platforms and have developed guidelines that simply didn't exist in Germany."

Now alpha ventus has changed all that. The health, safety and environment programme, without which the German Federal Maritime and Hydrographic Agency would not have approved construction, provides an Operating Manual for hazard prevention that all future offshore projects can refer to and develop further as necessary. This 75-page manual covers in minute detail every individual aspect, from 'Responsibilities' to 'Personal safety equipment' to 'Rope-supported access and positioning.' Irina Lucke says of the comprehensive documentation, "For every task that is done out at sea, there must be a precisely predefined working procedure, with hazard assessment and risk analysis. Each task is described in exhaustive detail – even if it's just painting a wall. The Manual lays out what tools, what equipment, and how many people are needed for each task, as well as which hazards are involved and what measures must be taken in advance in order to minimize or eliminate these hazards", Lucke explains.

In the final analysis, the safety effort paid off. Despite a few accidents, of the kind that can always happen on an offshore construction site, the HSE concept more than proved its value. And Andreas Stutz does not tire of further publicising the need for the highest safety requirements in the offshore wind industry.

了DOTI的聘用，在来自EWE股份公司的伊琳娜·卢克的领导下，共同为阿尔法·文图斯制定了HSE管理体系的具体内容。施图茨说，在海上行业工作过的人都知道海上工作存在危险，对此都存在敬畏之心。"海上安全是最重要的"，他还强调，"海上安全和陆上安全的标准完全不同。除非能够事先证明已经完全符合资格，不然没有人可以出海。如果你的证明不齐全，你就得呆在岸上，不论这样做可能会浪费多少时间和成本。没有任何妥协。"除了要参加海上培训课程，每个人还要进行全面的健康检查，包括肺部检查和心电图，还必须完成急救课程和高空滑绳训练。施图茨引用了著名的墨菲定律，"会出错的事总会出错，而你必须提前做好准备。"

伊琳娜·卢克，审核批准和HSE管理体系的负责人，把能够招到安德烈亚斯·施图茨出任安全协调员并准备安全方案称作"非常走运"。阿尔法·文图斯筹划阶段最大的挑战就是卢克、施图茨和他们的同事找不到任何指南，可以供这个德国历史上首个海工项目借鉴，无论从哪儿找都无功而返。"和德国不一样，北海沿岸的其他国家在建造海上石油和天然气平台方面都已经积累了多年经验，纷纷制订了相关指南。这些在德国根本就没有。"

现在阿尔法·文图斯改变了一切。它的健康、安全和环境方案成为了预防危险的操作指南。有了该方案德国联邦海事与水文局才批准开工建造，而且今后各个海工项目都可以参照它，并在必要时可对其进一步修改。这份75页的指南非常详细，从"责任"到"个人安全设施"甚至"绳索支护和固定的方式"，涵盖了方方面面。伊琳娜·卢克谈及整篇文档时说，"对于每项在海上完成的任务都必须有一份事先确定的精准的工作程序以及危险评估和风险分析。每项任务都被解释得非常清楚，即使只是简单地刷一面墙。手册明确了每项任务需要使用哪些工具和设备，需要多少人员，涉及哪些危险，必须提前采取何种措施以减少或避免这些危险。"卢克解释说。

对项目进行的最终分析证实了安全上的付出得到了回报。尽管发生了一些在海上施工基地经常发生的事故，HSE管理体系还是大大证明了它的价值。安德烈亚斯·施图茨仍在继续推广海上风电行业需要的最高安全标准。

安全第一：每个在海上区域工作的人都必须接受强制性的应急训练，包括在库克斯港DEWI-OCC试验场内进行高空滑绳训练——从直升机上滑下或者从瑞能5兆瓦的风机上滑下。
Safety is first priority for anybody working in the offshore field. That's why emergency exercises are compulsory, including rapelling training from the helicopter and from a REpower 5M, located on the DEWI-OCC test field in Cuxhaven.

水中探险

2004年10月，EWE公司在埃姆登港附近埃姆斯河河口的浅水域设置了一台4.5兆瓦级的风机机组。这是在德国沿海水域的第一台风机机组——如果说它算不上真正的离岸型机组，则绝对属于近岸型机组。它让EWE有机会获取经验，并将之用于未来海工项目。一年后，在库克斯港的试验场内，EWE公司又安装了一台6兆瓦级的风力发电机，目的是在类似海上条件下测试这种风力发电机。这些宝贵经验使得EWE公司十分轻松地做出参与风电场项目的决定，并且在风电场投产后EWE就一直负责其正常的营运。公司计划在北海沿岸博尔库姆岛西北大约15公里处，即12海里领海内建立自己的海上风电场。几年后，在Riffgat风电场中将竖起24座风机，发电总量将达到阿尔法·文图斯的两倍。为了能够将风能发电中生产的大量电能暂存，需要将电力驱动汽车整合到供能系统中来。EWE股份公司正在和奥斯纳布吕克的汽车制造商Karmann合作开发研制电动汽车，其模型已在2009年汉诺威

Venturing into the water

In October 2004 EWE sited a 4.5-megawatt wind-energy converter in the shallow water of the Ems Estuary, near the port of Emden. It was the first in German coastal waters – if not quite offshore, then certainly 'inshore' – and it gave EWE the opportunity to gain experience it could apply to later offshore projects. A year later the company set up a 6-megawatt turbine in the test field in Cuxhaven, in order to test this type of turbine under offshore-like conditions. This wealth of experience made EWE's participation in the alpha ventus wind-farm project an easy decision to take, and since the farm was brought on-stream the company has been responsible for ensuring its correct operation.

The company plans to build its own offshore wind farm in the 12-nautical-mile zone, some 15 kilometres northwest of Borkum on the North Sea coast. In a few years the 24 turbines that are to be erected in the Riffgat wind farm will deliver about twice as much power as alpha ventus. In order to create intermediate storage capacity for the

展会上展出。若干年后，电力驱动汽车会成为电网的组成部分，成为移动存储中介。为了为将来的发展提供良好的科研基础，EWE公司在奥尔登堡大学成立了名为"未来能源"的研究中心，主要研究可再生能源、能源效率和能源存储。

发挥地区优势

"EWE的事业心一如既往来源于我们对充满可能的未来十分着迷。"首席执行官托马斯·诺伊贝尔说，"我们对于海洋工程技术有着极大的期待，即使在德国我们需要应对许多恶劣情况。"诺伊贝尔意识到第一步往往是最艰难的，这一点在阿尔法·文图斯施工第一阶段也得到了验证。

尽管困难重重，扩展可再生能源始终是EWE公司战略中不可或缺

electricity generated by wind power, electric cars need to be integrated into the energy-supply system. EWE AG is working with Osnabrück automaker Karmann on an electric car, a prototype of which was presented at the 2009 Hanover Fair. In a few years, electric cars will become part of the electrical grid, acting as mobile intermediate storage devices. To provide a sound scientific basis for further progress, EWE has founded a research centre by the name of 'Next Energy' at Oldenburg University. The centre is focused on renewable energy, energy efficiency and energy storage.

Making use of regional expertise

"EWE's commitment is based on our fascination for the possibilities," says CEO Thomas Neuber. "We have great expectations for offshore technology, even if for us in Germany it means that we have to cope with difficult conditions far out to sea." Neuber is aware that the first

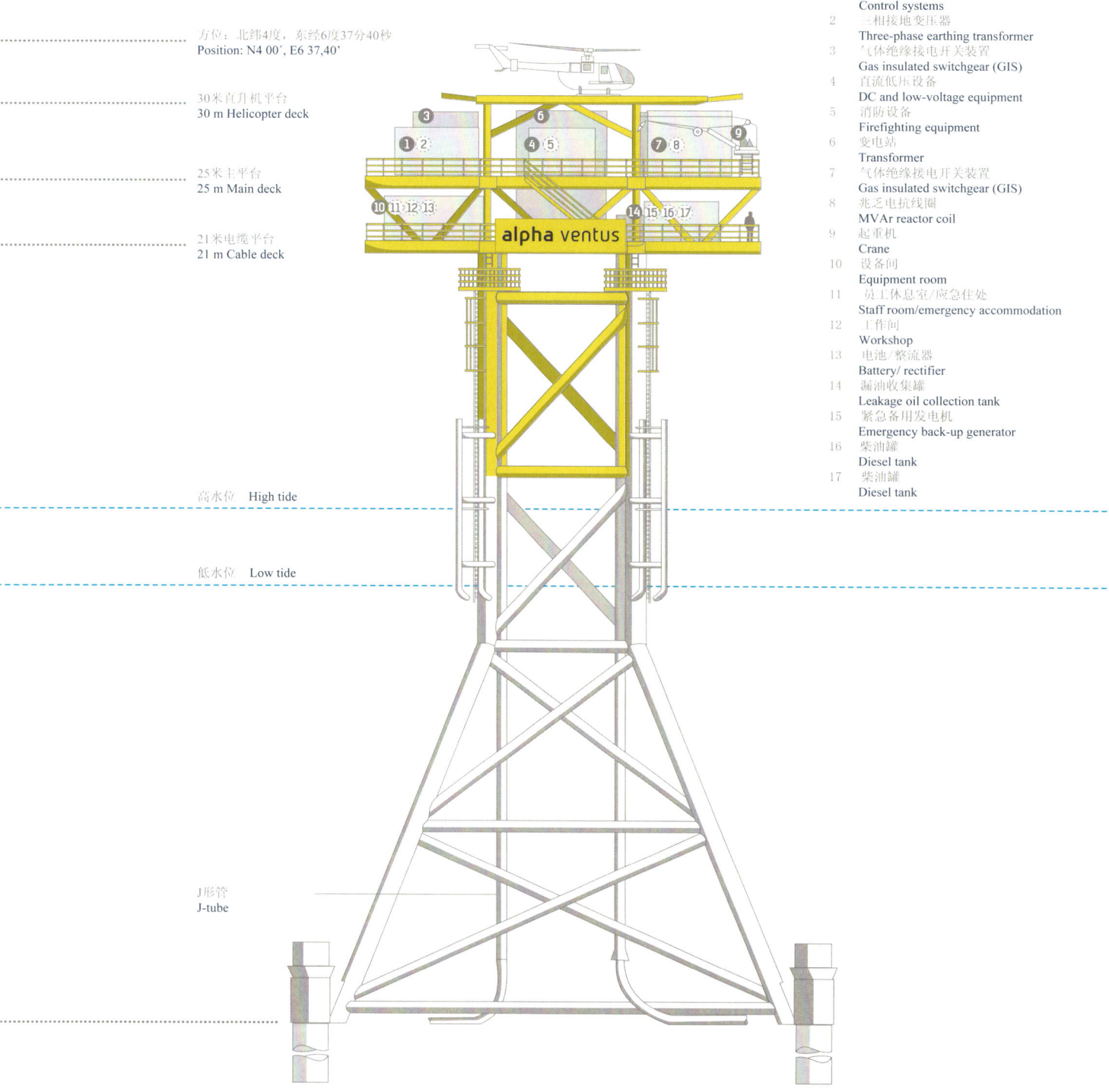

的部分。在陆上，EWE公司在埃姆斯河、威悉河和易北河间的供电区域中已经没有太多扩展空间了，因此它期待着能够利用海上的巨大潜能。

托马斯•诺伊贝尔提到，他们希望在能源生产转向可持续发展和环境保护的过程中发挥积极作用。阿尔法•文图斯项目非常重要，证明了海上风电以其发电方式为能源生产方式的转变做出了重要贡献。德国如果想实现联邦政府制定的气候保护目标，就迫切需要这方面的贡献。

此外，EWE还认为海洋工程技术在未来拥有巨大的创新和成长潜能。托马斯•诺伊贝尔说，"德国可以利用海上能源市场的巨大出口潜力来创造经济增长和就业机会。德国在风电行业总体处于领先地位，但在海洋工程技术领域还算不上领先。此外，我们生产了世界上功率最大的海上风力涡轮发电机，却没有机会在实际工程中证明它的效能。因此需要利用阿尔法•文图斯和未来海上风电场来打通出口渠道，这点非常重要。我们必须捍卫我们在风电技术上的领先地位。"

为了实现这一目标，整合现有资源将十分有意义。EWE股份公司作为发迹于此的公司，会致力于扩展和加强在德国西北部已拥有的强大竞争力。托马斯•诺伊贝尔强调，"EWE承诺将为海洋工程技术在未来获得成功而不懈努力"。

大瀑布电力公司瞄准碳中和生产

瑞典能源公司大瀑布电力也明显表现出了同样的决心。2007年4月，公司获得了距北海岛屿叙尔特岛70公里的Dan Tysk项目的开发权，这就是最好的证明。赫尔根•施托勒是该公司的施工工程师，从2007年起在DOTI参与负责阿尔法•文图斯项目的基座建造和物流工作，他也将参与Dan Tysk项目的规划和分步施工。该项目预计完工时总装机容量将达1500兆瓦，目前正处于风机和变电站招标阶段。第一个施工期定在2011年开始，计划完成400兆瓦的装机量。"我将把阿尔法•文图斯项目中获得的相关经验运用到新项目中。"施托勒提到了阿尔法•文图斯这个开创性项目的积极作用。"2009年安装基座和风机的工作同时进行期间，我们在物流上遇到了许多困难——实际上常常是焦急的发疯！"赫尔根•施托勒在描述那个关键阶段时称其是"非常困难和紧张的施工年份"。然而恰恰是那段经历使他对未来的挑战作足了准备，帮助他信心十足地展望未来。

与此同时，大瀑布电力公司计划实施"清洁电力"的战略，计划到2030年实现发电过程中二氧化碳排放量减半，到2050年电力生产达到百分之百的碳中和。很明显，风力发电将是战略实施中重要的一环。大瀑布电力公司可以利用自身丰富的经验去实现这个宏伟目标。它在30年前就开始风力发电试验，第一步是一台60千瓦的试验风力涡轮发电机，其功率与之后投入批量生产的风机相同。

在80年代初，大瀑布电力公司在瑞典哥特兰岛上建了Näsudden试验场，建造了Näsudden一号风机组，功率为2兆瓦，成为当时少有的大型试验涡轮发电机。1993年更大的Näsudden二号风机组（功率为3兆瓦）将其取而代之。Näsudden二号运作了大约15年，为世界上首台发电总量达6千万千瓦时以上的风机组，在2008年一台2.5兆瓦发

step is usually the hardest, as the first construction phase of alpha ventus showed.

But despite all the difficulties, expansion of renewable energies is a firm part of EWE's strategy. On land, however, the scope for the company to expand in its power supply area between the Ems, Weser and Elbe rivers is severely limited, and therefore EWE is looking to make use of the enormous potential at sea.

"We want to play an active role in the shift of energy production to sustainability and climate protection," notes Thomas Neuber. alpha ventus is an important demonstration that offshore wind energy can make a substantial contribution to this shift in the way energy is generated. This contribution is urgently needed if Germany is to meet the climate protection targets set by the government.

In addition, EWE sees offshore technology as having great future potential for innovation and growth. As Thomas Neuber says, "Germany has the opportunity to use the high export potential in the offshore market to create enormous growth in value creation and jobs. Our country leads in wind energy overall, but not yet in offshore technology. We offer the world's most powerful offshore turbines, but have not yet had the opportunity to demonstrate their effectiveness under real-life conditions. That is why it is so important to have an export shop window in the form of alpha ventus and future offshore wind farms. We must fight for our leadership role in wind-energy technology."

To reach this goal, it makes sense to bundle existing assets. As a company with strong roots in the region, EWE AG intends to help to make sure that the substantial expertise already present in Northwest Germany will be expanded and extended. "EWE is committed to continued effort on behalf of a successful offshore future," Thomas Neuber emphasises.

Vattenfall aims for carbon neutral generation

The same forward-looking attitude is also evident at Vattenfall. The best proof is the Dan Tysk project about 70 kilometres off the island of Sylt in the North Sea, the rights to which this Swedish energy company acquired in April 2007. Vattenfall construction engineer Hergen Stolle, responsible at DOTI since 2007 for the foundations and logistics of the alpha ventus project, will also be involved in the planning and step-by-step construction of Dan Tysk, which will have a total capacity of 1,500 megawatts when completed. The wind turbines and the transformer station are currently in the bid tender process and the first construction phase for 400 megawatts of the total is slated to begin in 2011. "I'll be able to bring very relevant experience from alpha ventus to bear on this project," notes Stolle as a positive result of the pioneering project. "In 2009, when the foundation work and the installation of the turbines were going on simultaneously, we had no shortage of logistical challenges – in fact we were often tearing our hair out!" recounts Hergen Stolle of the critical phases in what he terms a "very difficult and intense construction year." But that experience was the perfect preparation for his upcoming challenges and Stolle can look ahead to the future with confidence.

Meanwhile, Vattenfall plans to halve the CO_2 emissions of its electricity generation by 2030, through its 'Making Electricity Clean' strategy. By 2050 the company intends its electricity generation portfolio to be entirely carbon-neutral and it is clear that wind energy will play an important part in this. In moving ahead towards this ambitious goal, Vattenfall can draw on long experience with wind energy, having be-

电机将其替代。

目前大瀑布电力公司在北欧的内陆和海上安装的风力发电机的装机总量已超过900兆瓦,每年发电总计2百亿千瓦时。公司计划继续提高风力发电总量,至2030年将风力发电总量增加至总发电量的百分之十二。

2008年公司公布了"市场激励方案",旨在到2016年实现100亿千瓦时的可再生能源年发电量。其中新的水力发电厂将发电20亿千瓦时,生物能发电厂发电5亿千瓦时,风电场将生产70到80亿千瓦时的电量。这一目标要求建造装机总量为2500到3000兆瓦的风电设备。为实现该目标,大瀑布电力公司正在实施一项重要战略,包括新一代海上风机(功率达到3.5兆瓦至5兆瓦以及5兆瓦以上)和功率为2兆瓦至3兆瓦,以及3兆瓦以上的陆上风力涡轮发电机。

大瀑布电力公司数年来一直致力于海上风力发电。它在瑞典拥有三个海上风电场,Utgrunden, Yttre Stengrund和Lillgrund,在英国有一个名为Kentish Flats的风电场,拥有丹麦Homs Rev风电场百分之六十的股权,在阿尔法•文图斯项目中持股26.26%。2008年末,大瀑布电力公司获得了英国海工项目Thanet的开发权,该项目会在泰晤士河口建造100个功率为3兆瓦的风机。100个基座已于2010年1月完工,风力发电机也将于年内安装完成。如果一切都如公司战略规划者预想的一样顺利,短短数年后大瀑布电力公司的海上发电的装机总量就将达到1000兆瓦。

意昂公司投资数十亿

在瑞典公司大瀑布电力业务繁忙的时候,它的竞争对手能源供应商意昂公司也没有片刻工夫闲着。它不仅没有放松,更是把成为行业第一作为自己的目标。2007年5月意昂公司将其所有的绿色电力生产部门组合,并入了新成立的子公司意昂气候及再生能源股份有限公司。自此,总装机容量提高了5倍,风电、生物能发电和小型的水力发电厂的装机总量已达到2400兆瓦左右。公司计划在第一个四年里,即从2007年到2011年,在可再生能源领域投资80亿欧元以扩大这一部门,将其发展为集团的一个主要业务领域。集团希望可再生能源发电的总功率在2015年能达到10千兆瓦。

迅速增加可再生能源发电总量是一项壮举,只有依靠大型项目才能实现。史文•乌特莫伦,意昂气候及再生能源中欧股份有限公司的首席执行官阐述了公司战略的核心:"我们的目标是将细致工程转为工业标准化工程,从小型项目转为大规模工业化。这不仅仅是项目大小的问题,更关键的是要通过合作提升这个年轻行业的增值链,提高能效,使可再生能源更具竞争力。"

战略涵盖了太阳能和生物能发电等方面。不过在不久的将来,真正占意昂可再生能源发电总量首位的将会是风力发电。2007年8月,意昂集团通过接管某大型风电场运营商,获得了西班牙和葡萄牙的数个风电场,从而使其装机总量接近700兆瓦。

为了在欧洲以外的市场占据有力的市场地位、获得巨大的增长潜力,意昂公司在2007年10月取得了爱尔兰风电场运营商安粹风能在北美的业务,从而使整个集团的风电场装机总量又提高了210兆瓦。截至

gun experimenting 30 years ago with electricity generation from wind. The company's first step was a 60-kilowatt test turbine, which was the power class of the wind turbines then in series production.

In the early 'eighties Vattenfall set up the Näsudden test field on the Swedish island of Gotland, and built the Näsudden I wind energy converter. At 2 megawatts output, it was one of only a very few large test turbines in existence at the time. In 1993 it was replaced by the even larger Näsudden II (3 megawatts), which remained in operation for some 15 years and was the world's first wind turbine to produce a total of over 60 million kilowatt hours of electricity. In 2008 Näsudden II was replaced by a 2.5-megawatt turbine.

Vattenfall now has installed onshore and offshore wind energy capacity totalling over 900 megawatts in northern Europe, generating over two billion kilowatt hours every year. By 2030 Vattenfall plans to draw around twelve percent of its electricity generation from wind energy.

In 2008 the company publicised its 'Market Stimulation Programme' aimed at ramping up annual renewable energy generation to ten billion kilowatt hours by 2016. New hydroelectric plants will supply two billion kilowatt hours, biomass power plants 0.5 billion, and wind farms seven to eight billion kilowatt-hours. This will require the construction of new wind energy capacity totalling 2,500 to 3,000 megawatts. To reach this goal, Vattenfall is pursuing a strategy that includes the next generation of offshore wind turbines (rated at 3.5 to five mega-watts or more) and onshore wind turbines rated at two to three megawatts or more.

Vattenfall has been generating electricity at sea for some years and owns the three Swedish offshore wind farms Utgrunden, Yttre Stengrund and Lillgrund, as well as the British wind farm Kentish Flats. Vattenfall has a 60 percent share in the Danish wind farm Horns Rev, and 26.25 percent in alpha ventus. In late 2008 Vattenfall acquired the rights to the British offshore project Thanet, which will consist of 100 wind turbines rated at 3 megawatts each in the mouth of the Thames. The last of the 100 foundations was completed in January of 2010 and the turbines are also to go up in 2010. If everything goes as intended by company strategists, in just a few years Vattenfall will be producing electricity at sea with a capacity of around 1,000 megawatts.

E.ON investing billions

With all the activity of its Swedish competitor, energy supplier E.ON cannot remain idle. On the contrary, the company is aiming to claim the top spot. In May 2007 E.ON bundled all of its green power activities in the newly created subsidiary E.ON Climate & Renewables. Since then the company has increased its own generation capacity five-fold and now produces almost 2,400 megawatts from wind energy, biomass and small hydropower plants. In the first four years, i.e. from 2007 to 2011, a total investment of eight billion euros in renewable energy is planned in order to expand this sector and make it one of the E.ON Group's main business areas. By 2015 the group hopes to have reached the 10-gigawatt mark with renewable energy.

This rapid expansion of renewable electricity generation capacity is a major effort and will be possible only through very large projects. Sven Utermöhlen, CEO of E.ON Climate & Renewables Central Europe GmbH, describes the central element of the strategy: "The goal is to get from 'boutique' to industrial scale, and from small projects to industrial dimensions. This is not just a matter of project size, but also depends on improving the value-adding chain of this young industry through

2008年底，其在北美又建成了多个风电场，装机容量总计880兆瓦。

两个项目诠释了意昂公司所指的"行业规模"。2009年9月，位于美国德克萨斯州的黑豹小溪村风电场正式投入使用。它由305个风力涡轮发电机组成，总装机容量为458兆瓦。一个月后，同样位于德克萨斯州、占地400平方公里的罗斯科风电场也开始投入使用。它是目前世界上最大的风能发电场，拥有627座风力涡轮发电机，发电能力780兆瓦，可以为23万户家庭提供清洁能源。

以上风电项目的发电能力总计2200兆瓦。这些令人印象深刻的项目全都属于陆上项目。不过它们很快会因为海上风电场而失色。风在海上比在陆上上吹得更猛也更久，陆上风机发电会时断时续，而海上风能发电产生的电量可以更好地被整合进供电系统。海上风电拥有巨大的潜力，因此它将在意昂公司发挥特殊作用。

海上风电是意昂公司战略规划的重点。公司迄今为止的海工项目的总规模相当小。不过一旦泰晤士河口的伦敦阵列风电场建成后将会发电1000兆瓦，如此一来将会诞生一个新的标准。为了完成这个巨型项目，意昂公司正与丹麦能源供应商DONG以及阿布扎比零碳城市合作。第一阶段630兆瓦预计在2012年完工。目前为止，意昂公司共运营

partnerships that boost efficiency, and ultimately make renewable energies more competitive."

Naturally, solar power and biomass are part of this strategy. But for the foreseeable future, wind power will supply by far the greatest part of the electricity that E.ON gets from renewable energy sources. In August 2007 the group acquired several wind farms in Spain and Portugal through the takeover of a large wind farm operator, thereby increasing its installed capacity to reach around 700 megawatts.

In October 2007 E.ON acquired the North American business of Irish wind farm operator Airtricity, in order to open a strong market position with high growth potential outside Europe. This move gave the E.ON Group wind farms with 210 megawatts' capacity. By the end of 2008 more wind farms were completed in North America, totalling 880 megawatts.

Two projects illustrate what E.ON means by 'industrial scale'. In September 2009 the Panther Creek wind farm in Texas came on-stream. It consists of 305 wind turbines with a total output of 458 megawatts. Only a month later it was followed by the 400-square-kilometre Roscoe wind farm, likewise in Texas and currently the largest wind farm in the world. At this site, E.ON generates clean power for the equivalent of 230,000 households, with 627 wind turbines and a total capacity of 780 megawatts.

着5个海上风电场，装机容量接近300兆瓦，离实现千兆瓦的目标还有很长一段距离。

对意昂公司而言，阿尔法•文图斯项目发挥着关键作用，它是迈向更深更远海域的过程中非常重要的一步。因为在更深更远的海域，尤其在远离德国北海海岸的区域，将会遇到更极端的挑战。意昂公司凭借现有海工项目的经验，确定了20:20的活动范围，即将海区区域划定至离海岸20公里远、水深20米处。这其实是一道分界线，区分了迄今为止成功的项目和将要开始的项目。在这个范围之外建造风电场（例如阿尔法•文图斯）技术上会遇到更多挑战，对流程管理和风险管理也提出了更高要求。

意昂公司的战略明确了先在较容易的条件下建造风电场，从中汲取经验。这些风电场都位于离海岸较近且较浅的水域，主要分布在丹麦和英国。比如布莱斯海上风电场，Scroby Sands和Nysted海上风电场项目，以及2009年9月开始发电的Robin Rigg风电场和仍在建造中的Rodsand 2风电场。这些风电场中没有一个位于水深超过十米处。

意昂气候及再生能源公司的首席执行官弗兰克•马斯蒂奥克斯认为前景很乐观："公司目前运营和在建的海上风机组的装机容量已经超过了1000兆瓦。在这些项目中我们逐渐获得了所需的实践经验和专业知识，可以用于应对海上风电行业中的巨大挑战。"2007年5月，意昂公司承诺，到2030年将二氧化碳排放量减至1990年排放量的一半。如果到2050年能实现二氧化碳排放量较1990年水平减少至少50%的全球减排目标，并且到2020年或2030年实现在全球范围内确定并涵盖所有工业国家的中期减排目标，意昂公司将完成减排50%的目标提前至2020年。

到2030年，可再生能源将以36%的份额成为意昂公司能源部门内最大的分支。集团决意在未来气候保护中，在国际舞台上发挥自身影响。

规模虽小，意义重大

这些能源供应商们都为自己定下了宏伟的目标。到它们实现各自目标的那天，装机容量只有60兆瓦的阿尔法•文图斯项目很可能早就被遗忘了。但是它确实对所有发起人和参与者都意义重大，因为他们希望这个试验场可以帮助海上风电在德国和德国之外都实现突破。这种乐观不能掩盖事实，从功率上看阿尔法•文图斯似乎并不大，但是三家合作完成该项目的能源公司却承担了迄今为止风电项目开发商需要克服的最艰难的任务。之前没有人在这么极端的条件下、这样的离岸距离和水深处进行探索。尽管和未来的风电场相比该项目规模小，但是它对于可行性方面的讨论还是有很大的影响。

相比较而言，在波罗的海建风电场肯定更容易。"但是德国海上风电产业的最大机会恰恰在北海"，阿尔法•文图斯项目总负责人维尔弗里德•胡贝在施工完成之后满意地指出，"所以，将试验场安排在北海正是放对了地方"。

无论如何，在示范性的试验场内成功安装了第一批12台新一代兆瓦级的风力涡轮发电机后，胡贝比以往更相信从阿尔法•文图斯中"将

These impressive wind power projects, which have a combined capacity of 2,200 megawatts, are all onshore. However, they will soon be eclipsed by offshore wind farms. For E.ON, the enormous potential of offshore wind energy gives it a special role: the wind blows stronger and steadier at sea than on land, allowing an energy utility to integrate offshore electricity into its transmission system better than the less consistent power generated by onshore wind turbines.

Offshore wind energy is a strategic priority for E.ON. Its offshore projects up until now have been relatively small, but the London Array wind farm planned for the mouth of the Thames will then produce one gigawatt (1,000 megawatts) and in doing so will set a new standard. To handle this gigantic project, E.ON is working together with the Danish energy supplier DONG and the Masdar Initiative (Abu Dhabi). The first construction phase (630 megawatts) is planned for completion in 2012. Currently E.ON operates five offshore wind farms with just under 300 megawatts capacity, so there is still a long way to go to reach the first gigawatt at sea.

The alpha ventus project plays a key role for E.ON in this effort. It is a major step towards the deeper water and greater distances from shore that present such extreme challenges, especially off the German North Sea coast. From its experience with existing offshore projects E.ON has defined a 20:20 radius of action, marking the zone up to 20 kilometres from shore and 20 metres water depth that is the approximate dividing line between the projects that have been successful thus far, and the projects that will now be started. Building wind farms outside this radius (such as alpha ventus) is technically more challenging and places higher demands on process and risk management.

E.ON's strategy is to first gain experience with the construction of wind farms under less demanding conditions. These farms are in shallower water nearer the coast, primarily in Denmark and Great Britain. Examples are the Blyth, Scroby Sands und Nysted projects, the Robin Rigg wind farm that generated its first electric power in September 2009, and the Rødsand 2 wind farm currently under construction. In none of these farms is the water deeper than ten metres.

Frank Mastiaux, CEO of E.ON Climate & Renewables, has a positive outlook: "E.ON already has over 1,000 megawatts of offshore wind power in operation or under construction. With these projects we have gradually gained the practical experience and expertise we need to meet the great challenges of the offshore business." In May 2007 E.ON committed itself to halving its specific CO_2 emissions from the 1990 level by 2030. If it is possible to achieve a global reduction goal of at least 50 percent by 2050 from the 1990 level, accompanied by medium-term reduction goals for 2020 and 2030 at the international level and including all industrialised countries, E.ON will move its 50 percent reduction in specific emissions goal to 2020.

In 2030, renewable energy will then have a 36 percent share and will be the largest single position within E.ON's energy portfolio. These commitments emphasize that the company is determined to play a leading international role in future climate protection.

Small size – large importance

These energy suppliers have set themselves ambitious goals. When they reach them, alpha ventus with its mere 60 megawatts of output will probably be long forgotten. But that is actually in the interests of all involved, because they want this test field to help offshore wind energy achieve a breakthrough, in Germany and elsewhere. This optimistic

获得对今后项目十分重要的经验"。这些经验特别与变电站的规划（包括应急用电理念）相关，从整体上看又与电网连接相关。胡贝还说，"我们还获得了有关基座以及在深海安装基座方面的宝贵知识。"作为能源工程师，他认为对海洋工程技术最大的挑战无疑是"将基座置于水中，并将其安全地固定在海底。即使风速很低，北海上激起的浪高也会让目前使用的特种船舶无法工作。"但是胡贝知道这一切很快就会改变，因为新一代更大型的船只很快就会离开造船厂。胡贝已经开始忙于规划博尔库姆Riffgat海上风电场了，他在阿尔法•文图斯中取得的经验将会派上用处。然而，在相当长的时间内这绝对不会是天天都发生的事。它可能会发生在2029年。到那个时候阿尔法•文图斯达到了设计的使用年限，运营商们可能需要开始考虑对海上现有设施进行再利用。

outlook should not conceal the fact that as modest as alpha ventus may seem in terms of wattage, the three energy companies building it have taken upon themselves what may be the toughest assignment ever attempted by any wind energy project developers. No one has ever before ventured out into this combination of extreme conditions, distance from shore and water depth. Although the project may be small-scale when compared with the dimensions of future farms, it is making a very big impact on the feasibility debate.

A site in the Baltic would certainly have been easier. "But the biggest German offshore potential just happens to be in the North Sea," pointed out overall project leader Wilfried Hube with satisfaction after construction was completed. "So, by being in the North Sea, this test field is right where it needs to be."

In any case, after the successful installation of the first dozen new-generation, multi-megawatt turbines at this pioneering site, Hube is more convinced than ever that with alpha ventus "we'll gain experience that will be absolutely critical for the success of future projects." This experience relates to the planning of the transformer station in particular (including the emergency power concept) and to the grid connection as a whole. "We've also gained invaluable knowledge about foundations and how to construct them on the high seas," said Hube. As a power engineer, he considers far and away the greatest challenge within the entire adventure of offshore technology to be "getting foundations into the water and anchoring them securely to the sea-floor. Even relatively low wind speeds kick up wave heights in the North Sea that make it impossible to work with the specialised ships currently available." But that will change soon, as Hube knows, because a new generation of larger ships will soon leave the shipyards. Hube himself is already busy with the planning for the Borkum Riffgat offshore wind farm, where all of the experience gained at alpha ventus will be put to good use. However, it won't be a routine process for a long time yet. That might start to happen in 2029, when the turbines at alpha ventus have reached the end of their planned lifetime and the operators may begin to think about repowering at sea.

WeserWind股份有限公司的员工在威廉港的不伦瑞克码头安装变电站的管道架结构。
WeserWind GmbH employees assemble the transformer station's jacket structure at Braunschweigkai in Wilhelmshaven.

变电站的变压器模块(上部结构)已准备完毕,可以运至海上。
The transformer module (topside) of the transformer station is made ready to go to sea.

从上方观察，一切是如此简单：Odin自升式平台正在阿尔法·文图斯变电站旁工作。DOTI的技术师乘坐直升飞机或双体船"Windforce I"到达那里。
No big deal when you see it from above. The Odin jack-up barge is working at the alpha ventus transformer station. Technicians from DOTI reach the building by helicopter or by the catamaran "Windforce I".

研究和测量技术
Research and metrology

海上风电是一项新技术。虽然若干年前在丹麦、瑞典和英国沿海已经建造了一批风电场，但是这些试验性项目全部都属于近岸项目，位于较浅水域，使用较小的风力涡轮发电机，而且它们都没有安装使用过装机容量为5兆瓦以上的风机。这是新一代的多兆瓦级风机组，它们往往被安装在远离海岸线的深水海域，需要面对恶劣天气条件下波涛汹涌的大海，还要接受极端温度变化的考验。那么，这类风机怎样才能经受住时间的考验？材料和机器设备又必须承受多大压力？

对于上述问题，迄今为止只有部分模糊的猜测以及一些保守预期，可以说整个海上风电行业此时此刻才刚刚起步，还有许许多多东西需要学习。类似问题还涉及海上风电场和作为生物栖息地的大海两者之间的关系——海上巨型机组会对鸟类、海洋动物以及生活在海床中和海床上的植物群和动物群产生什么影响？在阿尔法•文图斯施工阶段，工程师、装配工、物流专家和项目经理都获得了丰富的经验。这些专业知识无疑会有助于形成新点子和新方法，有利于今后安装海上风机，而且也将应用于风机运营阶段。估计运营时间至少是20年。

德国作为世界主要风能利用国家之一，它的首个海上风电场不仅是经济和能源政策上重要的范例，更是今后相当长一段时间内深入研究的课题。各个研究所的科研人员都急切期待着在接下来的几年内对一些关键问题进行科学验证，找到答案。例如：天气情况究竟如何？基座、塔架、机舱和叶轮如何应对长期的风浪？在陆上得到认可的风力涡轮发电机技术能否在海上也能获得成功？极端天气情况多长时间会出现一次？风力和天气对工作人员抵达阿尔法•文图斯产生什么影响？海上风电场的扩张和运营是否会妨碍鼠海豚——一种生活在北海、长约1.8米、属于小型齿鲸的哺乳动物？风机会不会扰乱鸟类生活？风力和潮汐情况是否将发生变化？海底沉淀物处于什么情况？海浪有没有可能会冲走基座？

在技术和生态问题之外，运营海上风电场还涉及到了许多经济问题。哪种材料性能最好？怎样可以缩短停工期？如何能迅速组织运输，将人员和材料运至风电场？未来的施工物流会是怎样的？如何节约成本？以及海上风电设备生产的电能如何能以最经济的方式传输并接入联合电网？

广泛的科研计划

为了在试验场对这些复杂问题开展有序研究，德国联邦环境部

Wind energy at sea is a new technology. The wind farms off the Danish, Swedish and British coasts are just a few years old. But all these groundbreaking projects are nearshore in relatively shallow waters and they have used comparatively small turbines. On the other hand, virtually no experience has been gained with the new generation of multi-megawatt wind turbines with a capacity of five megawatts and more. These wind-energy converters are located far off the coasts in deep waters, subjected to rough seas in harsh climates and exposed to extreme fluctuations in temperature. So how will they stand the test of time? What stresses will materials and machines have to cope with under these conditions?

To date, only vague guesses or cautious expectations have been made at best. The offshore wind-energy industry is still at the very beginning of a long learning curve. The same applies to issues concerning the relationship between offshore wind farms and the sea as a natural habitat. What impact will these new giant structures in the sea have on bird life, the wildlife that inhabits the sea and the flora and fauna living in and on the seabed? During the construction phase of alpha ventus, the engineers, fitters, logistics experts and project managers gained a huge range of experience. The expertise acquired will definitely shape new ideas and methods which again will be of huge benefit when constructing offshore turbines in the future. This also applies to the operational phase, which is scheduled to last for at least 20 years.

The first German offshore wind farm is not just an important model in business and energy policy terms for one of the world's premier wind energy nations, but will also be the subject of intensive research over a long period of time. Researchers from many institutes are waiting impatiently in the wings to provide scientifically verified answers to the several key questions over the next few years. What really are the weather conditions? How will the foundations, towers, nacelles and rotorblades react to wind and waves in the long term? Will the wind-turbine technology, proven onshore, also prove itself at sea? How often do extreme weather conditions actually occur? How do wind and weather affect access for service personnel? Will the porpoise, a marine mammal that grows to around 1.80 metres in the North Sea and belongs to the family of small-toothed whales, be adversely affected by the expansion and operation of the offshore wind farms? Will the turbines bother birds? Will wind and tidal stream conditions change? How will sediments behave? Could the force of the sea possibly wash away the foundations?

In addition to technical and ecological aspects, operating wind farms at sea also throws up a number of business-related questions. Which material will perform best? How can downtimes be minimised? How can the transportation of personnel and material to the offshore wind farms

（BMU）将所有相关研究项目组合成了一个"研究阿尔法•文图斯"的计划，简称RAVE。德国政府在五年时间内共投资5000万欧元，支持RAVE中跨学科项目的工作。期间，生物学家、地理学家、地质学家、鸟类学家、材料研究员、洋流专家、物理学家、海洋学家、经济学家、机械工程师以及电气工程师一起开展测量工作，采集并分析数据。而在这个计划之前，从来没有人对风电场进行过如此细致的研究。在安装风机组之前，各种测量设备被一一装在风机上。总计安装了约1200个传感器，能日夜不停地发送数据。因此，所有的一切都能被有效监测。大部分的对比数据（包括风力、海浪和洋流数据，声学测量数据以及在风机上测得的负荷数据、工作性能和其它运转数据），都被直接提供给RAVE计划委派的科研人员。

德国联邦环境部（BMU）委派了尤里希研究中心（PtJ）负责整个研究计划的行政管理工作，RAVE计划的协调工作由位于卡塞尔市的弗劳恩霍夫风能及能源系统技术研究所（IWES）主管，此外德国联邦海事与水文局承担了提供并组织生态研究的工作。尤里希研究中心负责RAVE计划和FINO 1研究平台的约阿希姆•库切尔博士特别指出，"德国联邦环境部的目标从一开始便是为未来海上风电场积累更多经验，而不仅仅是在试验场上安装风机。"

15个研究项目

截止至2010年二月，共有15个RAVE项目正在进行中（www.raveoffshore.de）：

1. 基座项目调查风浪和风机运转对基座的影响。

2. GIGAWIND阿尔法•文图斯项目旨在采用整体确定尺寸理念改进支撑结构，目的是将这种结构发展为经济可行的、可批量生产的产品。

3.-6. 在北海开始大规模建设海上风电场之前，从规划、建造和运营阿尔法•文图斯试验场中得到的经验和教训将被拿来用于发展技术。瑞能叶轮项目主要研究叶轮。瑞能组件项目研究整个系统中的交互。阿海珐Multibrid的5兆瓦改进项目研究在苛刻的海上条件下如何在改进风机组件上取得创新。海上风机（OWEA）项目对海上风电机组设计和运营中关键技术的可靠性进行验证。

7. 激光雷达（LIDAR）项目将调查在海上风机上使用现代化的风电场测量技术的情况（LIDAR：激光探测和测距）。同时，项目也尝试提升运营管理。

8. 来自德国卡塞尔市的弗劳恩霍夫风能及能源系统技术研究所（IWES）的研究人员凭借着多年监管风电场的经验，收集风机组的重要运营数据（诸如发电量、停工期、可用性等等），以便接下来进行进一步评估。他们工作的基础便是RAVE计划中的风力测量和评估项目（海上WMEP项目）。该项目旨在覆盖所有未来将被安装至北海和波罗的海的风机。

9. 电网整合项目制定、实施和展示将海上风电发电量整合入德国国家输电网的战略。目标是确保未来电力供应，确保和常规发电一样

be organised quickly? What will installation logistics look like in the future? How can costs be saved? And finally: how can the electricity generated at sea be transported and fed into the interconnection grid most economically?

A wide-ranging research initiative

In order to research these complex matters in the test field in a structured way, the German Federal Ministry for the Environment (BMU) has combined all related research projects in a programme called 'Research at alpha ventus', or RAVE for short. The German government is funding RAVE's primarily inter-disciplinary work over a five-year period to the tune of 50 million euros. During this period, biologists, geographers, geologists, ornithologists, material researchers, ocean current engineers, physicists, oceanographers, economists, as well as mechanical and electrical engineers will carry out measurements, collect and analyse data. Never before has such detailed research been carried out on a wind farm. Extensive measuring devices were fitted to selected turbines before they were installed. As a result, around 1,200 sensors are in operation delivering data around the clock. Nothing goes unobserved. The majority of data collated (for example wind, wave and ocean current data, acoustic measurements, as well as the load data, performance characteristics and other operational data measured on the wind turbines themselves) are delivered to accredited researchers as part of the RAVE initiative.

The BMU has appointed the Projektträger Jülich (PtJ) as Administrative Project Sponsor to supervise the research activities. The RAVE programme is being co-ordinated by the Fraunhofer Institute for Wind Energy and Systems Studies (IWES) in Kassel, whereas the German Federal Maritime and Hydrographic Agency (BSH) is in charge of providing and organising ecological research. "Right from the outset, it was the BMU's intention not to use this test field only to set up wind farms, but to obtain as many results as possible for future offshore wind farms", emphasises Dr. Joachim Kutscher, the Jülich manager responsible for RAVE and the research platform FINO 1.

Fifteen research projects

As of February 2010, work on a total of 15 RAVE projects (www.rave-offshore.de) is in progress:

1. The Foundations project examines the effects of wind, waves and turbine operation on the foundations.
2. The aim of GIGAWIND alpha ventus is to improve the support structures using holistic dimensioning concepts. The project aims to develop these structures into an economically viable mass product.
3.- 6. Before large-scale installation of offshore wind farms in the North Sea begins, experience gained and lessons learnt from planning, setting up and operation of the alpha ventus test field are to be applied in developing the technology. The REpower Blades project will look at the rotor blades. REpower Components will investigate interactions in the overall system and the AREVA Multibrid M5000 Improvement project will conduct research on how selected components of the wind turbine can be improved. The OWEA project will verify key aspects required for the reliable design and operation of offshore wind-energy converters.

上图：三脚式桩基是诸如防腐蚀测试等多个研究项目的研究对象。
下图：基座成功固定后，潜水员们正在检查测量设备运行是否正常。

Top: The tripod is object of various research pro-jects such as corrosion protection testing.
Bottom: After successful anchoring of the foundation, divers check to make sure if the measurement equipment is in good working condition.

研究和测量技术 Research and metrology 95

具备高质量和高可靠性的海上风电在其中占有较大比例。

10. 生态项目开展生态研究，旨在了解建造和运营海上风电场对海洋环境的影响（包括海底生物诸如海螺、蠕虫和蟹类，鱼类，栖息的鸟类和候鸟，海洋哺乳动物）。

11. 地质学项目测量重要的海洋和地质数据，以便了解和评估风机周围和整个风电场内的沉积动力学。对支撑结构的冲刷（冲蚀）是沉积动力学最明显的表现。该项研究将为设计海工结构提供可靠依据。

12. 运行噪声项目测量风机在水下发出的噪声。项目关注所有会影响海洋生物尤其是海洋哺乳动物生活的噪声。

13. 降噪项目（"水下噪声"）研究如何在施工阶段降低噪声。在打桩过程中从橡皮管中冒出的覆盖整个支撑结构的气泡帷幕已经接受了测试。

14. 声纳应答机项目旨在避免军用潜艇撞上风机基座。安装在风机组上的声纳应答器能帮助防止潜艇在危险情况下撞击风机。

15. 此外，来自德国哈勒-维滕贝格大学的一个工作组正在研究全社会对海上风电场的接受程度。研究团队为政策制定者拟定了一些扩大海上风电应用的建议，尽可能减少争议，提高海上风电应用的接受度。

除了15个已获批准的项目，还有一个项目正在规划中。该研究项目简称为UFO，全称为"周边情况对海上风机组的影响"。项目申请单位为fk-wind，即不来梅哈芬应用技术大学风电研究所。

FINO 1研究平台

相比RAVE计划必须在阿尔法•文图斯开始运作后才能真正起步，位于北海和波罗的海的FINO 1研究平台早在2003年便在如今海上试验场所在区域的附近成功设立。自那时起，平台上的仪器就开始不断提供大量有价值的数据。其中最重要的是从八个不同的高度进行风速和风向测量得出的数据。此外，安装的设备还收集和记录气象、海洋和生态方面的参数。

FINO 1研究平台是德国可再生能源法范围内建立的第一个测量设施，之后波罗的海和北海地区又建立了多个研究平台，全部由德国联邦环境部资助。FINO 1研究平台是观察阿尔法•文图斯的重要前哨，因为研究平台上安装了一个网络摄像头，可以持续地显示阿尔法•文图斯的实时变化。这项服务十分受欢迎，尤其是在施工关键阶段。

安装FINO 1研究平台的工作委派给了汉堡的F+Z建筑有限责任公司和不来梅港的拖轮、海运和海上救助有限公司组成的工作组。德国劳氏船级社负责协调施工、建造和运营工作。平台甲板建在类似于管道架基座的钢结构上，支撑着六台瑞能风机组。研究平台的管道架更"向外伸出"，它由钢管材料组成，与海床接触的基座面积为26x26米，而位于平台甲板下方的顶部面积则为7.5x7.5米。20米高的平台上竖立着80米高的测量架。

2003年6月，ENAK浮吊将导管架桩基从不来梅港运出，运至工

7. The LIDAR project (Light Detection and Ranging) will investigate the use of modern wind field measurement techniques on offshore turbines. At the same time, it will try to discover any improvements that are possible in operational management.

8. With their years of experience in wind-plant monitoring, Fraunhofer IWES researchers in Kassel, Germany, collect essential operational data (such as energy yields, downtimes, availability etc.) of wind energy converters for subsequent evaluation. As part of the RAVE initiative, the Wind Measurement and Evaluation Programme (Offshore WMEP) provides the cornerstone for their work. The aim of the Offshore WMEP is to cover all wind turbines which are to be set up in the North Sea and the Baltic Sea over the next few years.

9. The Grid Integration project develops, implements and demonstrates strategies for integrating offshore wind energy into the German grid. Its goal is to reduce the backup and balan-cing reserve capacities by using new forecasting tools, without having a negative impact on the safety and availability of the interconnection grid.

10. to obtain information on the impact of construction and operation on the marine environment (benthos, i.e. marine snails, worms and crabs, fish, resting and migrant birds, marine mammals).

11. Part of the Geology project is to measure key oceanographic and geological data in order to collect and evaluate sediment dynamics in the immediate vicinity of the turbines and across the whole wind farm. Sediment dynamics can become parti-cularly noticeable as washing-outs (scour) on the support structures. The goal of the research is to provide a reliable basis for the design of offshore structures.

12. Underwater noise emissions from the turbines are measured in the Operational Noise project. The project looks into all noises that affect marine life, marine mammals in particular.

13. The Noise Reduction project ('Hydrosound') examines how noise can be reduced during the construction phase. Bubble curtains have been tested which emerge from hoses and cover the structure during ramming work.

14. The Sonar Transponder project focuses on avoiding collisions of military submarines with turbine foundations. Sonar transponders, fitted to wind energy converters, should help prevent any collisions of submarines with turbines in dangerous situations.

15. Furthermore, a work group from the German Halle-Wittenberg University is looking into the acceptance of offshore wind farms by society at large. The research team will draft recommendations for political decision makers to help expand offshore wind power use so that as few disputes as possible are caused and the acceptance of wind energy usage is enhanced.

In addition to the 15 already approved projects, another one is in the pipeline. It is a research project called UFO, in short, "Impact of ambient conditions on offshore wind energy converters". The project has been applied by fk-wind, the Institute for Wind Energy at Bremerhaven University of Applied Sciences.

FINO 1 Research platform

While RAVE will only really get going once alpha ventus goes online, FINO 1, the research platform in the North Sea and Baltic Sea was al-

FINO 1研究平台的基座结构上已长满了贝类和海葵。植物群和动物群对海上风机组会作出什么反应呢？
The FINO 1 research platform's foundation structure has become covered with a
growth of mussels and sea anemones. How do flora and fauna respond to offshore
wind energy converters?

ready set up at the rim of today's offshore test field in 2003. The instruments on the platform have been providing a host of valuable data since that time. Top priority is measuring wind speed and wind direction at eight different heights. The installed devices collect and record the entire meteorological and oceanographic conditions as well as ecological parameters.

FINO 1 was the first measuring facility in the German EEZ, followed later on by further platforms in the Baltic Sea and North Sea, all funded by the German Federal Ministry for the Environment (BMU). At any rate, FINO 1 was an important outpost for observing alpha ventus, as a webcam constantly showed the changing status quo. This service was very popular, especially during the critical construction phase.

A consortium of F + Z Baugesellschaft mbH, Hamburg, and the Bugsier Reederei- und Bergungsgesellschaft mbH & Co, Bremerhaven, was commissioned with installing FINO 1. Germanischer Lloyd (GL) coordinated construction, setting up and commissioning. The platform deck is based on a steel construction similar to the jacket foundations that support the six REpower wind-energy converters. However, the FINO 1 jacket structure protrudes further. It consists of steel-tube profiles with a 26 x 26-metre base on the sea floor and a head width of 7.5 x 7.5 metres beneath the platform deck. A measuring mast 80 metres in

地。接下来，4根桩柱穿过桩套筒，由打桩机打至海底30米深处。

仅在紧急情况下允许在平台过夜

FINO 1研究平台为无人操作平台，平台上的仪器在德国劳氏船级社的照管下完全自动运转。只有当部件需要修理或更换时才有人前往平台。根据不同天气条件共有三种不同方式可以达到FINO 1研究平台。风平浪静时，研究人员可以坐船前往。在这种非常有利的天气情况下，他们可以从船上爬上两个扶梯中的任意一个，沿着管道架的桩腿爬到平台上。不过这要求船只必须能够固定在钢结构旁，因而只有小型轮船和小艇可以做到。

研究人员也可以选择第二种方式：轮船停靠在距导管架数米远的地方，遥控起重机从平台上放下升降梯，将研究人员运送到平台上。但是这种方法很少使用，因为即使是微风或者微小的涌浪，从船上转移人员也有危险。

第三种方式，同时也是最贵的方式就是乘坐直升机前往FINO 1研究平台，它适用于任何天气条件。从不来梅港出发，飞行时间只要40分钟，而乘船则需要耗费7至8小时。因为只有紧急情况下才允许留在FINO 1平台上过夜，所以在平台上实际工作的时间非常短暂。因此，绝大多数情况下使用乘坐直升机的方式。

强风巨浪

连续六年在FINO 1平台进行测量后，气象学家现在可以非常精准地确定阿尔法·文图斯所在区域的年平均风速——10.06米每秒，因而可以预计风电场将会达到预期的高发电量。然而，风速时常有很大波动，在海上亦是如此，因此统计风速等级的时间分布数据十分重要。分析表明在一年中的8000小时里风速至少为4米每秒（3级风）。风机的叶轮正是被设置成以该风速运转。因为一年总计有8760小时，所以在高技术可用性下，阿尔法·文图斯风电场的叶轮基本上不会停止转动。

还有更多的喜讯：风速在2000多个小时内可达每秒12至13米（6级风）。在该风速下风机达到额定最大发电功率。测量数据显示12台5兆瓦风机每台每年可发电2250万千瓦时，等于以额定功率运转4500小时（即4500个年全负荷小时数），比陆上风机年发电总量的两倍还多。

以上结果令人振奋，但是算不上不出人意料，因为北海素来以风速高著称。此外，海浪高度的测量结果也令人惊叹。2006年11月1日和2007年11月9日，两场大风暴席卷北海，激起巨浪，从平台的毁坏程度可以明显感觉到当时海浪有多高，击打FINO 1研究平台的力量有多大。2006年和2007年，高达15米的海浪造成了周边工作平台的损坏：因为从来没有人能预料到海浪能将这些沉重的钢质栏杆折弯。

最高的浪达到了16.5米左右。结果，工作平台被浸在1.5米深的水中，浪尖离主工作平台仅3.5米。值得注意的是如此大规模的风暴和涨潮在两年内接连发生。尽管遇到了风暴，德国劳氏船级社工业服务

height is located on the 20-metre high platform.

In June 2003, the ENAK floating crane moved the jacket out from Bremerhaven and positioned it on site. Subsequently, the four piles were threaded through the pile sleeves and rammed thirty metres deep into the seabed.

Overnight stays only in emergencies

The instruments on the platform are looked after by Germanischer Lloyd (GL) and operate fully automatically. FINO 1 is unmanned and only visited if anything needs to be repaired or replaced. Depending on weather conditions, the platform can be approached in three different ways. When there is a lull in the wind and the sea is dead calm, a ship brings the researchers to FINO 1. In these very favourable weather conditions, they can reach one of the two ladders from the ship that lead from the legs of the jacket foundation up to the platform. The condition is, however, that the vehicle can moor alongside the steel construction – which is only possible for small ships or dinghies.

There is also a second alternative: the ship moors at several metres' distance from the jacket, while the remote-controlled crane lets down a personnel lift cage from the platform to convey visitors to the top. These forms of access are rarely possible, however. Even if there is just light wind and a slight swell, transfer from the ship can be dangerous.

The third and most expensive option, but possible in any weather, is to fly by helicopter to FINO 1. From Bremerhaven the flight takes just 40 minutes, while the passage by ship takes seven to eight hours. Overnight stays on FINO 1 are only possible in emergencies. Consequently, there is very little time to actually work on the platform. Therefore, the helicopter is used to reach the platform in the majority of cases.

Strong winds, extreme waves

After six years of taking measurements at FINO 1, meteorologists are now able to identify the annual mean wind speed at the alpha ventus site with fairly high accuracy: it's 10.06 metres per second on average, and the wind farm is expected to generate the high yields hoped for. However, wind speeds fluctuate heavily, even at sea. Which is why the wind-speed distribution over time into wind-speed classes is so essential. The analysis showed that for 8,000 hours per year, wind speeds of at least four metres per second (Beaufort Force 3) can be expected. The wind turbine's rotor blades are set in motion at this wind speed. By comparison, there are 8,760 hours in a year. Subject to high levels of technical availability, the rotor blades at the alpha ventus wind farm will probably hardly ever stop turning.

There is also more good news to report: for more than 2,000 hours, 12 to 13 metres per second (Force 6) were measured. At this wind speed the turbines reach their rated capacity. The data indicates probable production of 22.5 million kilowatt hours per year by each of the twelve 5-megawatt turbines. This is equivalent to 4,500 hours at rated capacity (i.e. 4,500 full load hours), more than double than what these turbines would produce at good onshore sites.

These results are pleasing, but not surprising because the North Sea is known for its high wind velocities. On the other hand, the measurement of wave heights produced astonishing results. On November 1, 2006 and on November 9, 2007, two heavy storms raged across the North Sea whipping up the waves to extreme heights. The damage

部的副总裁克里斯蒂安•纳什，FINO 1认证的负责人，对此无保留意见，他认为"平台的设计完全合理"。面对仅一些辅助设备遭到损坏的事实，他说这是为了应对罕见风暴可能造成的损坏而特别设计的，并且还能降低项目的总成本。该研究平台的主层结构是超过海平面20米。

采用激光束研究风速

FINO 1研究平台除了使用传统的风力测量方法，目前正在使用激光束测量风力，这也是RAVE计划中的一部分。测量对象是发射出激光束后大气微尘和悬浮物质反向散射的回波。这种技术被称为激光探测和测距（LIDAR），探测范围可达上百米，是一种遥感技术。

这项测量技术不需要安装测量架，测量仪器可以放置于风机旁：可以垂直向上发射激光束，在不同高度测量风速。测量结果很有趣，距地面高度越大风速越大，这一现象在叶片扫过的横截面积即在距地面50至150米的区域尤为明显。叶轮在旋转中风速会有很大变化，对叶片材质会产生压力。虽然这种情况在海上没有像在陆上上那么明显，但是了解叶轮扫过的横截面积内的垂直风速仍然相当重要。

to the FINO 1 research platform hints at just how high the highest waves were and the force at which they hit the platform. In 2006 and 2007, waves towering up to 15 metres caused damage to the peripheral work platform: nobody had expected it was possible for these to bend the heavy steel railings.

The highest waves reached some 16.5 metres in height. Consequently, the work platform was submerged by about 1.5 metres of water and the wave crests towered up to 3.5 metres beneath the main work platform. It is remarkable that storm and swell incidents of such magnitude could happen within two successive years. In spite of such critical incidents, Christian Nath, Vice President of Germanischer Lloyd Industrial Services, who was responsible for the FINO 1 certification, had no reservations and commented: "The platform's design is adequate." Only auxiliary extensions were damaged and he went on to say that these had been purposely designed to cope with damage in certain rare storms and as a result had led to a more cost-effective total cost of ownership. The main level of the research platform protrudes 20 metres over the sea.

Laser beams investigate the wind flow

In addition to the traditional wind measurements carried out on FINO 1, laser beams are now also being used as part of RAVE. Backscatter-

在相当长的一段时期内，无人值守的FINO 1研究平台是阿尔法·文图斯唯一的观察前哨。FINO 1研究平台设立于2003年，一直在提供重要的天气数据，专家会定期对其进行检查。德国联邦环境部的乌多·帕什达格正在访问研究平台（左下图）。
The unmanned FINO 1 research platform has been alpha ventus's lonely outpost
for a long period. Set up in 2003, it provides vital weather data and
is regularly checked by experts. Udo Paschedag
(left bottom), member of the BMU, is visiting the platform.

研究和测量技术 Research and metrology

在RAVE计划的激光雷达项目中,一台激光雷达测量仪器自2009年6月起被安放在了FINO 1研究平台上,用于验证该技术是否适用于海上测量,具体测量工作由德国风能研究所进行。同时激光束也可用于横向测量,目前斯图加特大学的一个风能工作小组(SWE)正在研究这方面的课题。吹过风电场的风并不是持续不断的,经常会出现大风和湍流天气情况。因此对风机的设计者而言,尽可能多地掌握气流以及尾流方面的知识是非常必要的。

斯图加特大学风能工作小组(SWE)最初选择了一台位于不莱梅港附近的陆上的Multibrid 5兆瓦风机,将一台激光雷达测量仪器安装在其机舱上。从中获得所有的研究发现和测量技术将在2010年被应用在阿尔法·文图斯海上风电试验场中(RAVE计划中的海上风机项目)。为了取得风速数据并且能够提前预防强风,测量将从机舱向前进行。研究人员希望能更快弥补强风对叶轮转速的影响,以便减小叶轮、传动系统和塔架所受的压力和负载。

此外在测量功率曲线时还会对流入风场的风力进行横向测量。风速测量和由此得出的整个叶片面积上的分配值提供了陆上及海上发电功率与风力间的比率。为了瞄准表面的多个测量点,特别研发了一种扫描仪,可以根据需要将激光束集中。测量还会从机舱向后进行,以便获取尾流数据。叶轮在运转中当然会影响风速,在风机后部会形成尾部湍流,所以必须保持风机间最小间距,防止对风电场内的其他风机产生过多压力。由于使用激光雷达技术远程遥感,数字式尾迹模型将会得到改进,并被应用于今后的风电场规划之中。

气泡帷幕降低噪声

在风电场施工阶段干扰海洋生物生活最大的噪声来自于基座桩柱的打桩过程。Multibrid风机组伫立在六个三脚式桩基上,每个三脚式桩基都由三个桩柱固定在海底。瑞能风机的导管架基座甚至需要四个桩柱。因此,总共要固定42个桩柱。每个桩柱需要锤击大约14000次才能使其沉入30至40米的海底。打夯产生的噪声在水中比在空气中传播得更快、更远,因而在20公里以外也能听到噪声。这种噪声对海豚的干扰尤其大。根据离噪声源的距离,噪声可能会妨碍海豚之间的交流,或者在它们捕食时损害其回波定位导航系统。此外噪声可能会使动物的听力受到暂时性损伤或永久性损伤,并且影响动物数量:当频繁地进行打夯工作时,海洋哺乳动物将会在一段时间内或者长久地远离它们的栖息地。

为了密切观察海豚的行为,海洋生物学家在打夯工作开始前、打夯期间和打夯工作结束后分别从飞机和船只上对这些生活在北海南部的哺乳动物进行了统计,并使用水下麦克风对它们进行了录音。由于海豚的听力非常敏锐,因此在嘈杂的锤击工作开始前采取了许多工作将它们从基地附近赶走。在距离噪声源20公里远的地方进行水下分贝测量也证实了噪声确实会传到很远的地方。

为了降低打夯产生的噪声进行了多次气泡帷幕试验。汉诺威大学静力学和动力学研究所(ISD)对每次试验都进行了监督。试验原理很简单:从围绕着噪声源的细导管中升腾起小气泡,形成帷幕;小气泡

ing of the bundled laser light by the ever-present dust particles and aerosols is measured. The technique is called Light Detecting and Ranging (LIDAR) and has a range of several hundreds of metres. In other words, this is a remote sensing technique.

A measuring mast is not required, but the measuring device can be placed next to a wind turbine: it directs the laser beam vertically upwards to measure the wind speed at several heights. The results are interesting because the wind picks up speed with increasing height above ground. This is particularly obvious in the area swept by the rotor, or between about 50 and 150 metres above ground. The rotor encounters very different wind speeds during a rotation, resulting in material stresses. While this is not as pronounced at sea as on land, knowing the vertical wind speed profile within the area swept by the rotor is still important.

During the RAVE LIDAR project, a LIDAR measuring device has been placed on the FINO 1 research platform since June 2009 to verify whether the technique is also suitable for measurements at sea. Measurements have been conducted by the German Wind Energy Institute DEWI. Laser beams can also measure horizontally. This direction of measurement is what a wind-energy Working Group at Stuttgart University (SWE) is working on. The wind flowing through a wind farm is not constant, but often gusty with occasional turbulence. For designers of wind turbines, it is therefore essential to gain as much insight into the oncoming wind flow as well as the wake flow as possible.

The SWE initially installed a LIDAR measuring device on the nacelle of a Multibrid M5000 located onshore near Bremerhaven. In 2010, the findings and measuring techniques gained are to be put into practice at the alpha ventus offshore wind test field (RAVE project Offshore Wind Energy Converter – OWEA). Measurements are made from the front of the nacelle in order to capture the incident wind and to be able to detect gusts in advance. Researchers hope to compensate for the impact of gusts on the rotor speed more quickly in order to reduce the loads on the rotor blades, drive train and tower.

Horizontal measurements of the inflow wind field are also to be applied when measuring the power curve. Measuring wind speeds and the resulting distribution across the entire rotor area provides information about the ratio of the power produced per wind inflow – both onshore and offshore. A scanner has been specifically developed to focus the laser beam as required to target several measuring points across the surface area. Measuring is also performed from the nacelle towards the rear to capture the wake flow. The rotor does of course affect the wind flow it is moving in. Wake turbulence forms beneath a wind turbine, so that minimum distances must be kept in order to avoid placing too much load on other wind turbines in the wind farm. Thanks to remote sensing using LIDAR, numerical wake models will be improved and used for future wind-farm planning.

Bubble curtain to cut noise

The loudest noise to disturb marine life is created when ramming in the foundation piles. Each of the six tripods on which the Multibrid wind turbines are mounted is anchored to the seabed by three piles. REpower turbine jacket foundations even need four piles each. Ramming had to be done a total of 42 times. A pile needed to be hit some 14,000 times just to sink it 30 to 40 metres into the seabed. Noise caused by ramming is transmitted faster and over much longer distances through

海洋生态保护是一个重要问题。鸟类学家知道在将要建造海上风电场的区域生活着哪些鸟类以及会有多少鸟类定期迁徙。
Bird protection at sea is a key issue. Ornithologists find out which bird populations and which
migrant birds can be encountered at potential offshore wind farm locations.

帷幕（LBC）将降低噪声传播。在应用该原理的过程中，四根导管将Multibrid风机AV09的三脚式桩基基础围起来，围成一个圈。这些导管被焊接在基座的各个角上，像笼子一样围绕住桩套筒。

2009年5月气泡帷幕首次正式使用，在桩柱穿过桩套筒时，气泡帷幕便开始升起。同时在离噪声源大约500米处研究人员使用水中测音器对产生的噪声进行测量，以验证帷幕的减噪能力。试验表明气泡帷幕的减噪作用很大程度上受到洋流强度和方向的影响。在打夯过程中，在水中升起的气泡帷幕会顺着洋流的方向被冲散。因此，一边是气泡帷幕没有实际效果，而另一边则是减噪达12分贝（db）以上。研究人员计划不久之后进行更多气泡帷幕方面的试验，帷幕将离噪声源更远。目前这一理念已经在FINO 3研究平台施工中得到成功运用。

对海洋环境的影响

运营商必须在试验场内开展生态研究，所有研究必须在德国联邦海事与水文局监管下进行。在阿尔法•文图斯项目中调查海上风电场对海洋环境的影响时，第一次应用了调查研究标准。它在未来会强制推行，正式名称为StUK3。此外，德国联邦海事与水文局还协调组织了另一个生态研究项目，名为StUKplus，主要研究一些相关的特殊课题。根据研究结果将会对StUK3进行适切性和有效性方面的检查与评估。

开展生态研究的目的是进一步了解风电场的建设和运营对海洋环境的影响，使海上风电的发展尽可能不危害环境。生物学家采用前后对比的方式来确定风电场对海底生物（包括海螺、蠕虫、蟹类等）、鱼类、栖息的鸟类和候鸟以及海洋哺乳动物的影响。"在建造阶段发生了一些暂时性的破坏。"来自环境数据管理系统公司的格奥尔格•内尔斯博士给出了这样的评论，在阿尔法•文图斯施工过程中他一直对海豚的行为进行观测。"海豚会明显地避开阿尔法•文图斯的基地，保持15到20公里左右的距离。"尽管如此，内尔斯仍然期望海豚可以"在阿尔法•文图斯运营期内像以前一样生活在自己的栖息地内"。此外，在阿尔法•文图斯试验场还必须开展长期研究，以观察动物们对建造在其栖息地内的风电场的反应。

候鸟项目的内容包括使用新摄像机、热成像摄影机和雷达记录鸟类撞击转轮叶片的事故，以避免类似情况的发生。上述设备都是第一次应用在海上。

水下照片显示在很短时间内，相邻的FINO 1研究平台的基座就变成了人工礁，长满了贝类、海葵甚至牡蛎。相同情况极有可能会发生在阿尔法•文图斯的12台风力涡轮发电机的基座上。结果是几年后，到了夏天装置的总重量将达到6吨。可食用蟹和绒蟹将在装置旁的细砂海床上定居；这两种蟹通常只出现在暗礁或沉船残骸附近。

鱼类、栖息的鸟类和海洋哺乳动物的栖息地也会有所改变。在运营过程中，风电场的灯光和噪声会产生干扰；而另一方面，它又为渔业提供了保护区，因为某些种类的鱼甚至海豚可能喜欢靠近风电场的海域。这个问题也将会成为未来几年内的一个研究课题。

water than through the air. Therefore, the noise can be heard even at distances of more than 20 kilometres. This noise particularly disturbs porpoises. Depending on the distance from the source, the noise impairs communication between the animals, or their navigation system called echolocation while hunting. The risk that the animals suffer reversible or irreversible damage to their hearing cannot be ruled out either. In terms of population, there is reason to fear that these marine mammals will abandon their habitats in the medium or long term when ramming work is performed more frequently.

In order to keep a close watch on the porpoises' behaviour, marine biologists on planes and ships counted the mammals in the southern part of the North Sea during and after ramming and recorded them with underwater microphones. Because porpoises have such sensitive hearing, steps were taken to scare the animals away before loud hammering started. Measuring underwater sound at distances of up to 20 kilometres has confirmed that the noise travels great distances.

Tests using a bubble curtain were conducted to reduce the noise produced during ramming. The Institut für Statik und Dynamik (ISD) at the University of Hanover oversaw these tests. The principle is straightforward: they made small air bubbles rise from thin tubes surrounding the noise source to form a curtain. This purpose of this Little Bubble Curtain (LBC) is to reduce the noise spreading. To put the principle to the test, they surrounded the tripod base of Multibrid turbine AV09 with four tubes forming a ring. These tubes enclose the pile sleeve and are welded to the base point like a cage.

When first implemented in May 2009, the bubble curtain started to rise while the ram pile was driven through the pile sleeve. The noise emitted was measured at a distance of about 500 metres using hydrophones to verify the curtain's ability to cut noise. It emerged that reducing the noise caused by the bubble curtain heavily depended on the strength and direction of the ocean current. During the ramming process, the bubble curtain rising in the water body was driven away with the direction of the current. So on one side the bubble curtain had virtually no effect, while on the other, noise reduction of twelve decibels (dB) and more was measured. More tests based on a bubble curtain concept are soon planned. The concept means it is possible to maintain a greater distance from the noise source and has already been successfully used while installing the FINO 3 research platform.

Impact on the marine environment

Ecological research has to be done in the test field by the operator and monitored by the German Federal Maritime and Hydrographic Agency (BSH). The standard investigation concept on the effects of offshore wind farms on the marine environment was applied for the first time at alpha ventus. The concept will be compulsory in future and is known officially as StUK3. The BSH also coordinated a project on secondary ecological research (called StUKplus) in which specific associated research issues are looked at. Based on the results, StUK3 is to be checked and thus evaluated for its level of adequacy and effectiveness.

The goal of this ecological research is to increase knowledge on the impact of wind-farm construction and operation on the marine environment and to make the expansion of offshore wind energy as environmentally friendly as possible. Biologists use before-and-after comparisons to identify the effect of the wind farm on benthos (snails, worms and crabs), fish, resting and migratory birds, as well as marine

研究成果将造福整个欧洲

尤里希研究中心的库切尔博士说，"阿尔法·文图斯绝对不会是最后一个海上风电研究项目"。他期待着在未来数年内技术得到进一步发展，可以增加风电设施安装的安全性、降低成本并帮助提高风电场的运营管理和提升生态环境的友好性。"所以科学研究并不会仅仅局限于阿尔法·文图斯。"RAVE计划将成为整个欧洲今后开展的项目的科技典范。"阿尔法·文图斯的科学发现将被应用于任何有相似自然条件的地方。在英国东海岸以及西班牙大陆架上也会遇到与德国海湾相类似的水深和风浪条件。"德国劳氏船级社的克里斯蒂安·纳什补充道。

因此，FINO 1研究平台和RAVE计划的研究成果会对整个欧洲的海上规划有所帮助，将有助于确保欧洲迫切需要的气候环境保护型电力绝大部分来自于海上风电。

mammals. "Temporary disruptions occurred during the construction phase", comments Dr. Georg Nehls of Bioconsult SH, who observed the behaviour of the porpoises when alpha ventus was being set up. "The porpoises clearly avoided the site, keeping a distance of 15 to 20 kilometres". Nevertheless, Nehls expects the porpoises to "use the marine environment during the operational phase of alpha ventus, just as they did before". However, long-term research is still required to observe the precise reactions of the animals to the wind farm in their natural habitats.

As part of the migratory bird projects, new video and thermal imaging cameras as well as radars are used to record any collisions with the rotor blades, or any attempts made by the birds to avoid them. This equipment is being used for the first time on the high seas.

Underwater photos show that the foundation structure of the neighbouring FINO 1 research platform developed an artificial reef of mussels, sea anemones and even oysters within just a short space of time. The same will also probably happen to the 12 foundations of the wind turbines. As a result, in just a very few years, the weight of the installations will increase by up to six tonnes in the summer months. Edible crabs and velvet crabs will settle on the fine sandy seabed near the installations; these crabs are usually otherwise only found on reefs or wrecks.

The habitat will also change for fish, resting birds and marine mammals. During operation, the wind farm will create a disturbance due to light and noise emissions. On the other hand it will offer protected areas from commercial fishing operations. Therefore, some species of fish and possibly even porpoises might prefer to come to the area near the wind farm. This issue will also be the subject of research over the next few years.

Research results to benefit all of Europe

"alpha ventus will definitely not be the last word in offshore wind energy research", comments Dr. Kutscher from project sponsor Jülich. Over the next few years he expects further technical developments to increase the safety of wind-energy installations, cut costs and help enhance operational management and the eco-friendliness of the wind farms. "Therefore, scientific studies will not just be limited to alpha ventus". Nevertheless, RAVE will become a scientific role model for upcoming projects in the whole of Europe. "The scientific findings at alpha ventus can be applied to wherever we find similar natural parameters. Water depths, wind and wave conditions, such as those we experience out in the German Bight, can also be encountered on the east coast of Britain and the Spanish continental shelf", adds Christian Nath of Germanischer Lloyd.

Therefore, the findings gained from FINO 1 and the RAVE initiative will benefit offshore planning right across Europe. The results will help to ensure that a major proportion of the climate- and environmentally-friendly electricity that Europe so urgently needs is produced offshore.

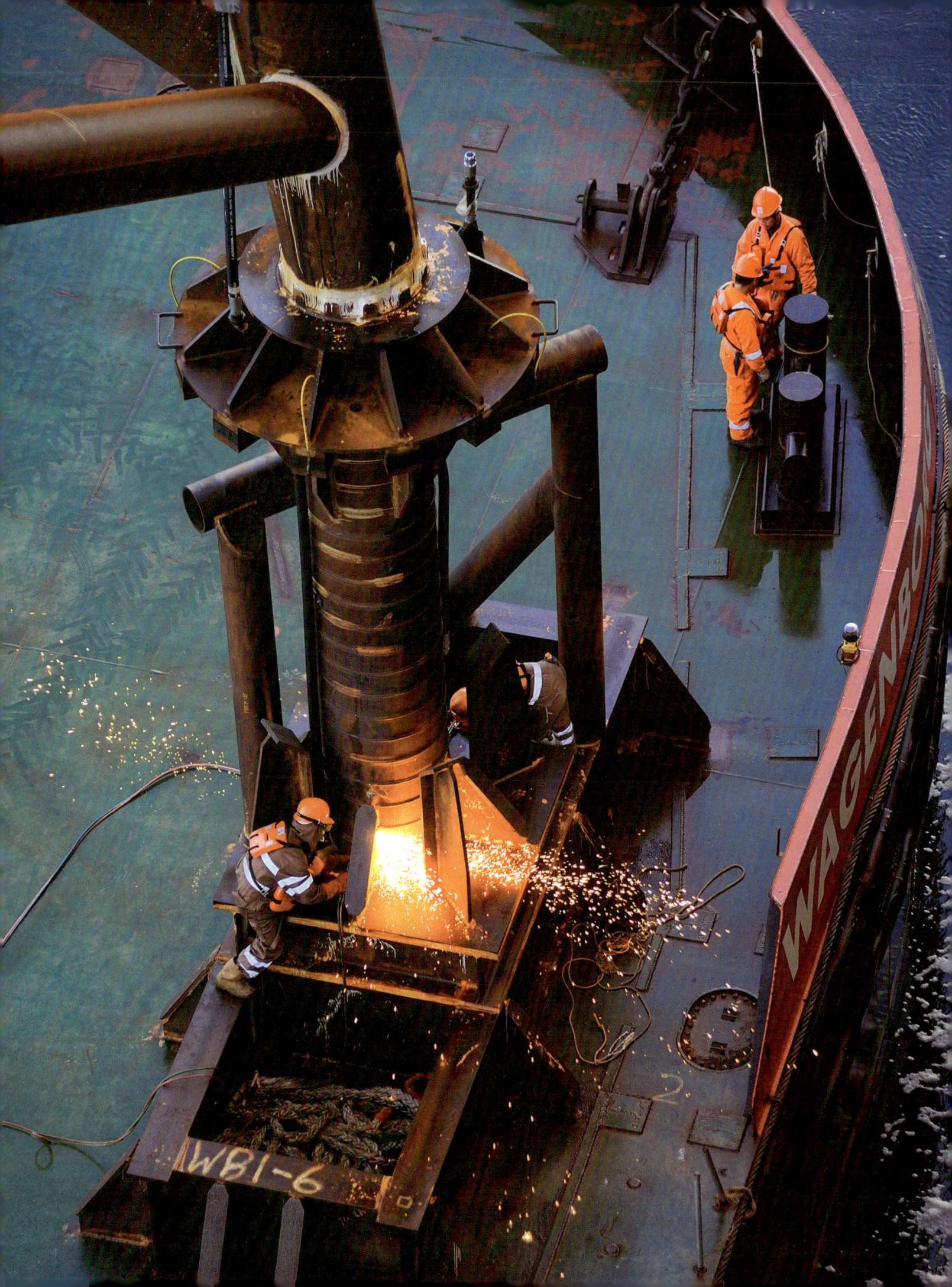

岸上工作为海洋工程技术服务
Work on land for technology at sea

所有的海工项目均从岸上开始。海上风电场的制造商们在各自工厂里建造了机舱、塔身和电动风叶,制造地非常理想,就在码头边上。钢结构件制造商通常位于海港附近,他们将钢结构组件装配成基座结构。其它企业负责复杂的物流运输工作,将单个组件运送到港口,使用各种专用船舶,再从港口运输至海洋工程现场。最后,专业建筑公司将巨型钢结构在海上搭建起来。当然,这些工作都要衔接得"恰到好处",不能耽误。

这个复杂的建造过程所需的基础设施还从来没有在德国近海建造过。如果还要面对并战胜海上风电场新时代的挑战,必须先扩建德国北部港口。同样重要的是未来海事物流链的开发,须配备新型船舶,可以装载5兆瓦及以上的大型海上发电机及其基座。未来几年还要在港口建立大量物流设施,并发展造船业,以确保这个增值的建造过程和德国北部地区工程的顺利进行。海洋工程组件的制造和运输需要其专用的工业和物流基础,而这些基础还处于初建时期。如果要使雄心勃勃的海工计划在未来几年付诸实现,德国必须加强所需的基础建设投资。

海洋工程的团队合作网络

位于威悉河畔的德国港口城市不来梅是一个优秀的先例,展示了海洋工程和物流基础设施扩建后的样子。近几年来,不来梅已经发展成德国北部海岸最大的海上风能支持基地。在此之前,她经历了有计划的长期投资过程,进行了富有远见的城市开发,为不来梅港口创造了4000个新就业岗位,主要集中在货物处理、集装箱和公路运输货物终端等行业。风能业也为港口的动态经济增长作出了重要贡献。这一扩建在很大程度上是由不来梅港投资促进和城市发展有限公司(BIS)推动并进行协调。追溯到2000年,第一个海上风电场开发项目获得最初的批准之前,BIS已经看出了时代的迹象,当时的港口设施和传统物流设施已明显无法满足海上风能组件频繁的制造和运输需求。

为了将不来梅港早早定位于大有前途的海上风能业务,BIS对港口的市场潜力进行了调研。其初期优势在于现有的工业不动产和专家力量,其中包括一批非常优秀的资深海事工作者。2001年11月,当地政府邀请风能业及其供应商召开了一个经济发展会议。其反响极其热烈,共有200名与会者出席会议,是预期人数的四倍。这些与会者不仅来自当地政府所在地区,而是来自整个德国。如此积极的响应促使BIS

All offshore projects start onshore. Manufacturers of offshore wind energy converters build nacelles, towers and rotor blades in their factories, which are ideally located dockside. Steel fabricators, usually near the harbour, assemble steel components into foundation structures. Other companies handle the complex logistics involved in getting the individual components to port and from there to the offshore site, using a variety of specialised vessels. Finally, specialist construction firms set up the steel giants out on the open sea. Naturally, all this should happen 'just in time' and without delays.

This complex production process requires an infrastructure that formerly did not exist on the German coasts. Further extension of the northern German ports must be a priority, if the challenges of the new offshore wind energy era are to be met and mastered. No less important is the further development of a maritime logistics chain, with new vessels that can handle the huge dimensions of offshore turbines of five or more megawatts capacity, plus their foundations. In the next years there will need to be a logistics offensive in harbours and the shipbuilding industry in order to keep the value-creation process and its jobs in the north German region. The manufacture and transportation of offshore components requires its own industrial and logistical basis, which is still in its infancy. If Germany's ambitious offshore plans are truly to come to fruition in the coming years, the country will have to boost its investment in the infrastructure needed to make it happen.

A network for the offshore industry

The German port city of Bremerhaven on the River Weser gives a good example of how expansion of the offshore industry and logistical infrastructure might look. In recent years the city has developed into the largest offshore wind-energy support base on the German North Sea coast. This was preceded by a long and systematic investment process and accompanied by forward-looking urban development which created 4,000 new jobs in Bremerhaven, primarily in cargo handling and at the container and road-freight terminal. The wind-energy sector is also making a significant contribution to the port's dynamic economic growth. This expansion was driven and coordinated in large part by the Bremerhaven Economic Development Company Ltd. (Bremerhavener Gesellschaft für Investitionsförderung und Stadtentwicklung mbH, BIS). Back in 2000, even before initial approval was granted for development of the first offshore wind farm, the BIS read the signs of the times. It was obvious even at that early date that the existing port facilities and conventional logistics were not up to the manufacture and transportation of offshore wind energy components on a regular basis. In order to position Bremerhaven early on for the promising offshore

成立了不来梅港/不来梅风能协会（wab），旨在最大程度地开发地区潜能。仅仅几年时间，wab协会就在威悉地区创建了综合的风能专家团队网络，集结了风能企业和当地海事业以及科研院所。这是一个成功先例，至今协会旗下已有220家企业和研究机构。

不来梅港作为一个港口城市的特性大大增强了该地区的吸引力，不来梅港长期以来以渔业、造船业和海事经济为优势，并拥有充足的可用空间。不来梅还拥有大量教育和培训机构，能在短期内为新岗位培养优秀的工作人员。BIS经济和技术促进部主任尼尔斯•施诺伦贝格记录过："2008年末，有约4000万欧元投资于作为商业地区的不来梅港。其中，2500万欧元投资于当时所需的任何基建项目；1500万欧元直接用于风能。"不来梅花费的这些资金是一项明智的投资，风能行业获得了当地政府和德国联邦政府的支持，至2008年底已经在不来梅港投资了2.5亿欧元。

多家制造商和供应商在不来梅港建立了设施，其中有阿海珐Multibrid、瑞能系统和PowerBlades，这三家公司均参与了阿尔法•文图斯的建造。仅这三家就创造了1000个新岗位。此外，威悉风能公司即将在不来梅港的渔业码头"渔港"开设一家工厂，用于制造变电站使用的海上风能发电机和平台的基座。该地区还进驻了两家研究机构，Fraunhofer风能和能源系统技术研究所（IWES）以及一个叶轮测试场，和Deutsche WindGuard有限公司，这家公司建造了一个风洞。最后同样重要的是，几年来大量小型供应企业和服务供应商入驻该地区，在不来梅港-不来梅地区的海洋工程发展初期创造了具有吸引力的就业机会。许多事情已经实现，但在海洋工程支持基地全面完工之前还有很多事情要做。海上风电场的物流设施和预装工程需要大量额外空间来中转存放各种组件，如基座结构、塔身分段、机舱和叶轮。当时的港口只能通过船闸到达，如果不来梅港要成为海上风电场的建造基地，就必须有一个无障碍的入海口，否则阿尔法•文图斯项目启动后，势必迫使项目负责人通过荷兰的埃姆斯港来处理所有物流工作。这样将意味着，在不来梅"渔港"码头附近的生产工厂制造的风机机舱必须先通过双船闸送入威悉河，然后进入北海，最后送到威悉河西岸的埃姆斯港。这种费时费力的调动是一种完全不经济的方法，因为届时每年将有100台甚至200台风能风机要从不来梅港运送到北海。海洋工程企业都要求组件能从港口直接进入威悉河，即无需通过船闸。这意味着需要一个新港口。

然而，不来梅港不是唯一一个希望从海上风电场项目中获益的港口，德国其它沿海城镇和港口也看到了这一新兴行业带来的机遇。其中，埃姆登港、库克斯港和施塔德港都已改建了基础设施，并成功吸引了海上风能企业进驻。例如，库克斯港竭尽全力，使库克斯港钢结构件公司（CSC）和旭普林建筑工程公司在当地制造的基座能快速运出。为此，库克斯港建造了新的堤坝，改进了进入易北河的通道，并大量扩建港口，使基座能以最直接的方式运送到码头。

埃姆登港也投入了不少努力，逐步成为了又一个重要的海洋工程生产中心。位于埃姆登的Bard集团生产机舱和叶轮，而负责蒂森北海工程的萨尔福工业股份公司（SIAG）于2009年9月并购了一家塔架制造商，并将其落户在这个城市。SIAG船厂不再造船，而是转向生产风

wind energy business, the BIS investigated the market potential of the port. In its favour from the beginning were existing industrial real-estate and expertise, including a good supply of skilled maritime workers. In November 2001 the local government invited the wind-energy industry and its suppliers to an economic development conference. The response was overwhelming – 200 visitors came, about four times more than expected. They came not just from the region, but from all over Germany. This lively interest encouraged the BIS to found the Wind Energy Agency Bremerhaven/Bremen e.V. (wab) to maximise the potential of the area. In just a few years, the wab was able to create a comprehensive wind energy expertise network in the Weser region, bringing wind-energy companies together with local maritime industry and scientific institutions. This was a success and today over 220 companies and institutes belong to the association.

The attractiveness of the area was enhanced by the character of Bremerhaven as a port city, which had previously always lived from fishing, shipbuilding and the maritime economy, and had ample available space. The city also had the education and training facilities to qualify workers for new jobs in a short time. "By late 2008 about 40 million euros had been invested in Bremerhaven as a business location. Of this, 25 million euros went to infrastructure projects that were necessary in any case. 15 million were earmarked directly for wind energy," notes Nils Schnorrenberger, Director of the BIS Department for Economic and Technology Promotion. The money the city spent was a wise investment, as the wind energy industry, with state and German federal support, had invested about 250 million euros in Bremerhaven by the end of 2008.

Several manufacturers and suppliers have opened facilities in Bremerhaven – AREVA Multibrid, REpower Systems and PowerBlades, all of which were involved in the construction of alpha ventus. These three companies alone created over 1,000 new jobs. In addition, the WeserWind company will soon open a plant in the 'Fischereihafen', Bremerhaven's fishing harbour, for the manufacture of foundations for offshore wind turbines and platforms for transformer stations. The city is also receiving two research institutes, the Fraunhofer Institute for Wind Energy and Energy System Technology (IWES), with a rotor-blade test facility, and Deutsche WindGuard GmbH, which has built a wind tunnel. Last but not least, over the past few years numerous small suppliers and service providers have settled in the area, creating attractive job opportunities in the incipient offshore boom in the Bremerhaven-Bremen region. Much has happened – but much still remains to be done before the conversion to an offshore support base is complete. The logistics and pre-assembly of offshore wind farms will require much additional space for the intermediate storage of components such as foundation structures, tower segments, nacelles and rotor blades. The harbour, currently reachable only through locks, needs unhindered access to the sea if Bremerhaven is to become a base for the construction of offshore wind farms. The lack of this free access to the sea when construction started on alpha ventus forced the project leaders to use Eemshaven in Holland for all the logistics. This meant that the nacelles for the turbines, which were manufactured in two dockside production facilities in Bremerhaven's Fischereihafen, first had to be shipped through the double lock to the River Weser, then to the North Sea and finally to Eemshaven on the west side of the River Ems. This very time-consuming manoeuvre will become completely uneconomical when 100 or even 200 wind turbines per year soon begin leaving Bremerhaven for the North Sea. The offshore companies require com-

瑞能的5兆瓦机舱正在不来梅港的拉柏多重载码头进行装载。该机舱的生产场就在码头旁边。
At the heavy-load quayside in Bremerhaven's Labrador-harbour the Repower 5M nacelles are loaded. The produc-tion hall is right next to the quayside.

岸上工作为海洋工程技术服务　Work on land for technology at sea　　109

力发电机的塔架和基座。同时，施塔德港在短短几年间进行了大规模的生产结构改革，位于易北河南岸的Bützfleth港口的Bützfleth工业区也是如此。那里以前是原子能和铝的生产基地，如今从其它燃料中产生替代能源，生产生物燃料，PN Rotor股份有限公司为阿海珐Multibrid 5兆瓦制造叶轮。

由其它国家生产的三脚式桩基和风机支架

尽管各地政府、志愿者和政治家们都不遗余力地努力，但德国的生产能力仍然无法满足阿尔法•文图斯的建造工程。乐观地来看，这个问题可以解释为，其它港口城市，如罗斯托克、斯特拉尔松、吕贝克、基尔、弗伦斯堡和布伦斯比特尔，能在海洋工程领域继续书写新的篇章。但在当时，阿尔法•文图斯的项目负责人不得不寻求德国以外的制造商，因为不来梅港的WeserWind当时还在建造中，还不能生产基座结构。所以，挪威的阿克克瓦纳船厂负责制造三脚式桩基，苏格兰的Burntisland船厂负责风机支架的制造。因此，这些基座结构穿越北海，千里迢迢地回到工程现场。最终由位于五个国家的五大生产基地共同为阿尔法•文图斯风电场服务。而根据德国五个沿海地区的政府所言，未来绝大部分的组件制造将集中于德国境内。对于北海和波罗的海沿岸的各国而言，在未来很长一段时期内，风能开发将会成为一项重要的任务。

海上建造使用的专用船舶

在海上建造风电场必须快速施工，在气候无常的北海上更是如此。春季和秋季的风暴季节在4月中旬到9月中旬之间留出了一个空隙，只有这段时间内的风速和浪高较低，才能允许施工。当然，即使在夏季正当中，也会突然掀起剧烈的海风，迫使施工中止。无干扰的连续施工期往往只有几天的时间。

为了最大程度地利用好这些时间，所有基座、塔身、机舱和叶轮必须从港口以最快的速度、最直接的方式运送到海上施工现场。港口必须靠近施工现场，距离越近，组件就能越快地送达。比如，从埃姆斯港出发，拖船只需要12至14小时就能将自升式平台拖运到阿尔法•文图斯风电场。埃姆斯港需要足够的空间来装配叶轮和轮毂，这两个组件是由瑞能和阿海珐Multibrid在岸上工厂为阿尔法•文图斯制造的，以节约海上施工的宝贵时间。然而，搭建12座风机仍然花费了约7个月的时间，从2009年4月中旬一直持续到11月中旬。这段时间内需要利用足够多的天气好的日子，风缓浪低，才能使施工顺利进行。未来的风电场施工将要在相同时间内搭建10倍于本次工程的风机，不仅需要更多

不来梅港，5兆瓦的机舱正在装载到Mega-Motti推进自升式平台上。
The nacelle of the M5000 are loaded onboard the Mega-Motti pusher barge in Bremerhaven.

ponents to get from the harbour to the Weser directly, i.e. without going through locks. A new harbour is needed.

But Bremerhaven is not the only port hoping to benefit from offshore wind energy. Other German coastal towns and ports also see opportunities in this new industry. Emden, Cuxhaven and Stade have made infrastructure improvements that have succeeded in attracting offshore wind energy companies early on. For example, Cuxhaven went to great lengths so that the foundations built there by the companies Cuxhaven Steel Construction (CSC) and Züblin could be shipped out as fast as possible. The city built a new dyke crossing to improve access to the River Elbe, and considerably enlarged the harbour so that the foundations could be shipped to the dock by the most direct route possible. Emden went to no less effort, and has step by step become another important production centre of the offshore industry. The Bard Group has located there to fabricate nacelles and rotor blades, and a tower manufacturer has also taken up residence, through the September 2009 acquisition by Schaaf Industrie AG (SIAG) of the Thyssen North Sea Works. Now the former shipyard no longer builds ships, but instead makes towers and foundations for offshore wind-energy converters. Stade, meanwhile, has undergone a breathtaking structural change in just a few years, with the Bützfleth industrial zone at the harbour of the same name on the south bank of the Elbe. Where formerly atomic energy and aluminium were produced, today alternative energy is generated from other fuels, bioethanol is produced and PN Rotor GmbH manufactures rotor blades for the AREVA Multibrid M5000.

Tripods and jackets from other countries

Although municipalities, pioneers and politicians have gone to great lengths, the construction of alpha ventus has showed that production capacity is still lacking in Germany. Viewed positively, this unmet need can also be interpreted to mean that other port cities such as Rostock, Stralsund, Lübeck, Kiel, Flensburg and Brunsbüttel have the opportunity to write their own new chapters in the offshore story. But initially, the alpha ventus leaders had to look outside Germany for manufacturers, because WeserWind in Bremerhaven was still under construction and therefore not yet able to fabricate the foundation structures. Instead, the Aker Kværner shipyard in Verdal, Norway, built the tripods, and the Burntisland shipyard in Scotland fabricated the jackets. This meant that the foundations travelled great distances across the North Sea and then back out to the construction site. In the end, five production sites in five countries were involved in building the alpha ventus wind farm, although in future component construction will be concentrated to a much greater degree in Germany – at least according to politicians in Germany's five coastal states. Of course, over the long term, exploitation of North Sea and Baltic wind energy will be a task for all coastal countries.

Special ships for construction at sea

To build a wind farm out at sea you have to work quickly. This is especially true under the rough weather conditions in the North Sea. The spring and autumn storm seasons leave a window of good weather from mid-April to mid-September. This is the only time wind speeds

上图：由AMBAU公司制造的5兆瓦塔身分段在不来梅装载上船。
Above: The M5000 tower sections fabricated by AMBAU GmbH are loaded onboard in Bremen.

下图：阿尔法·文图斯的变电站基础结构正在威廉港进行建造。
Work proceeds on the transformer station's foundation structure for alpha ventus in Wilhelmshaven.

施塔德的易北港口，5兆瓦的风叶正在装上 Mega-Motti推进自升式平台。
The blades of the M5000 are loaded onboard the Mega-Motti pusher barge in the Elbe port of Stade.

运输船和工程船，还需要更长的风暴季节空隙。唯一的解决方法是使用更多能在恶劣海况下工作的专用船舶。对阿尔法•文图斯施工过程的评估具有重要意义，评估结果有助于创造更合适的设备和船舶，为未来的挑战做好准备。

到目前为止，用于海上风电场施工的船舶数量依然相对较少。原因之一是阿尔法•文图斯建造计划中的浮吊和自升式平台的数量限制，该数量是正常情况下海上油气作业所需的合同签订的使用量。如果海上风电业不仅是一个填补空隙的角色，而是要加快风电场建设的步伐，就需要尽快拥有专用的大型船舶，针对该行业的需求和规模而专门进行设计。造船厂已经积极回应了该需求，第一艘专用船舶正在建造中，将于2010年启用。

海上能源千里迢迢从海洋输送至大陆

海上风能转换装置（WEC）已进入公众视线，人们可以远远地看到它们矗立在海上，大幅度地旋转着。当风机制造商们因其出色的工程技术而赢得赞誉时，人们往往容易忘记一点，风机必须由电缆连接，才能将电能传输至岸上，比起这一点，风机制造商们也只能隐藏

and wave heights are low enough for construction. Of course, even in high summer the wind can freshen sharply and force a cessation of work. The periods during which construction work can proceed without interference are often a matter of just a few days.

To make the best use of the short time available, all of the foundations, towers, nacelles and rotor blades need to get from harbour to offshore site as quickly and directly as possible. The port should be close to the site – the shorter the distance, the faster components can get there. For example, from Eemshaven, tugs needed only about 12 to 14 hours to tow the jack-up platforms to the alpha ventus test field. The harbour needs enough space to permit the assembly of rotor blades and hubs, which the manufacturers REpower und AREVA Multibrid did on land for alpha ventus in order to save precious time at sea. Nevertheless, setting up the twelve turbines took from mid-April to mid-November 2009, or around seven months. This was the time needed to accumulate enough good-weather periods of low wind and moderate wave height during which work could proceed. Future wind farms, involving the construction of ten times as many turbines in the same amount of time, will require not only many more transport and assembly vessels, but also longer time windows. The only way to achieve this is with larger, specialised vessels that can work in rougher weather. Assessment of the work processes for alpha ventus is of great importance because it

穿过浅滩和岛屿的电缆
A CABLE THROUGH MUDFLATS AND ISLAND

海底电缆穿越北海的诺得尼岛。
The subsea cable crosses the North Sea island of Norderney.

在路德维希•萨尔维留斯先生的办公室里堆得高高的活页笔记本，书脊上整齐地贴着标签"Eon Grid Offshore"、"Plambeck Godewind"或"Nature conservation part"。作为诺得尼岛行政区的市长，萨尔维留斯先生不得不连续多年处理这个复杂的海上风能项目，这是岛上居民经常热议的争议性话题。这些输送阿尔法•文图斯海上风电场电力的电缆从岛的正中间穿过，将来很快就会有东Frie-sian海岸的更多风电场加入。

这一切是从1999年开始的，那时有一个来自莱尔附近的Prokon北方公司的英戈•德布尔，来到诺得尼岛上，讲述了他的公司计划在距离临近的博库姆岛45公里的海上建造几台风力发电机。他坚定地说："它们是史无前例的。"市长先生对第一次见面的情景依然记忆犹新："我马上就清楚地意识到，我们作为一个海岛行政区，必须非常小心，不能眼睁睁地看着这些事情在我们周围发生，而我们突然沦为了旁观者。"有一大堆未知的问题，使得规划中将要铺设在这个度假岛屿上的电缆成为了炙手可热的话题："最初对此的讨论常常是一片混乱"。但是萨尔维留斯先生对此的印象却是"激动人心的时期"，整个岛区成了新的技术研讨区，人们甚至在讨论是否能利用电缆发散出的热能。

岛上居民是持怀疑态度的，许多人都认为海上风能会损害岛上的旅游业。而如今，风能这个

起他们的美誉光环。人们无法看到电缆,因为它们静静地躺在海底或者埋在海底。海底电缆是海上风能运行的一大瓶颈。没有它们,就无法将电力传输到岸上。但是,电缆的规划和铺设所需要的努力大大超过了人们的想象。仅次于海上风能转换装置和基座结构,电力输送是这项海洋工程的第三大投资要素。

最终要归功于德国议会(联邦议院)于2006年10月通过的一项法案,阿尔法·文图斯才得以按时完成并网发电。该法案因其不够优雅的名称——《加快基础设施规划法案》——而遭受了些非议。政治家们不遗余力地拟订、表述该法案,使其能加快落实重要的基建项目,如联邦高速公路、铁路、水运河道和机场。直到联邦议院的最终版,才在该法案中加入了一段对海上风能至关重要的章节。在这一章节中规定电网运营商必须负责海上风电场至其所在区域内的电网连接点的连网。这意味着电网运营商被法律绑定,负责安装"海底线路"。

这项法案一举改变了整个局面。规划人员不用再像以前一样,为每个海上风能项目安排电力线路接至电网连接点。基于该法案,就能使几个海上风电场的电能通过一条电缆集中传输,这一优化后的输电路径规划不仅降低了成本,而且大大减少了对自然和环境的影响。

will assist in creating the right equipment and vessels to be prepared for future challenges.

Up until now the number of vessels available for offshore wind energy work has been relatively low. One of the factors in planning the construction of alpha ventus was the limited availability of floating cranes and jack-up barge platforms, which are normally contracted for offshore oil and gas work. If the offshore wind industry doesn't want to just be a gap-filler, and wants to ramp up the pace of wind-farm construction, it will need its own large ships as soon as possible, specially designed for the needs and dimensions of the industry. Shipbuilders have already responded to the demand; the first specialised vessels are under construction and will be available in 2010.

Offshore power on a long haul from sea to mainland

Offshore wind-energy converters (WECs) are in the public eye. They can be seen from afar as they rotate spectacularly above the sea. While turbine manufacturers win admiration for their engineering skills, it is easily forgotten that manufacturers can only garner the glory because their turbines are connected by cables that bring the power to shore. Escaping the notice of the observer because they lie hidden on the seabed or are even buried in it. Subsea cables are the bottleneck of off-

In Ludwig Salverius' office the ring binders are piled high. Their spines are neatly labelled 'Eon Grid Offshore', 'Plambeck Godewind' or 'Nature conservation part'. As Mayor of the island community of Norderney, Salverius has had to deal with the complicated subject of offshore wind power for years, a controversial topic often hotly discussed by the islanders. The cables carrying wind power from the alpha ventus test field run right through the middle of his island, soon to be joined by others from more wind farms on the East Friesian coast.

It all began in 1999, when a certain Ingo de Buhr from the company Prokon Nord in nearby Leer came to the island and spoke of his company' intention to set up a few wind turbi-nes some 45 kilometres off the neighbouring island of Borkum. "You won't even see them", he promised. These first encounters are still fresh in Mayor Salverius' memory: "It immediately became clear to me that we, as an island community, had to be very careful that we didn't all of a sudden become mere spectators watching all this going on around us." With numerous questions left unanswered, the planned laying of the cable over this holiday island was a particularly touchy subject: "The initial discussions with those involved were frequently chaotic". Nevertheless Salverius remembers this as an "exciting period", when the community was breaking new technolo-gical ground. It was even discussed whether the heat emitted from the cables could be used.

The island's inhabitants were sceptical, as many of them believed that offshore wind energy would have a negative impact on tourism on the island.

话题已经具有了积极的内涵。从这个岛上获得的经验有助于抚平岛上居民最初的担忧,他们开始接受:可持续发展的旅游业和"清洁能源"似乎可以结合得非常好。

虽然如此,在做出关键决定之前还是花了相当长的时间。萨尔维留斯先生是这样描述那场最终达成各方接受之协议的马拉松式大讨论:"这儿的生活空间不大,没有什么能在这里隐藏很久,岛上发生的任何事情都没法保密。所以我们不断地讨论直到得到可行的最佳方案,使铺设的电缆穿过浅滩和我们的岛。"每个人都希望得到一个既影响小又安全的电缆铺设方案,这就意味着电缆只能从地下穿过。

所有参与方最终达成协议。萨尔维留斯愉快地眺望着大海,双足稳稳陷在诺得尼岛的沙丘中,他说:"我们最终接受了海上风力发电。路线就从这里通过。"他一边说着,一边用张开的手臂在这一带画了一条弧线。但这只是想象中的路线,据电网营运商Transpower透露,该电缆最高可输送3000兆瓦的电力。由于电缆深埋在地下3米的深处,任何人或动物都不会感觉到其散发的热量。

Nowadays, however, the subject of wind power has fundamentally positive connotations. The experience gained on the island contributed to calming the islanders' initial fears, as they began to accept that sustainable tourism and 'clean energy' seemed to fit together very well.

Nevertheless, a lot of time passed until the key decisions could be taken. "There's not a lot of space to live on here – nothing stays hidden for long, and whatever happens on this island you can't keep plans like these under wraps. That's why we didn't stop fighting until we got the best-possible solution for laying the cable through the mudflats and our island", is how Salverius describes the discussion mara-thon needed to reach an agreement acceptable to all sides. Everyone wanted a low-impact, cautious laying of the cable – meaning it defi-nitely had to go underground.

All involved were able to finally reach an agreement. Happily looking out to sea with his feet planted firmly in the sand of the Norderney dunes, Salverius states: "We've come to accept wind power at sea. That's where the route goes", he says, tracing an arc across the terrain with his outstretched arm. But this is an imaginary line, as the cable – which according to grid operator transpower can carry a maxi-mum of 3,000 megawatts – is three metres underground. So deep that no person or animal would ever notice any heat from the cable.

高潮和低潮之间：电缆铺设工作在诺得尼岛的朝海一侧进行。
Between high and low tide: cable-laying work proceeds on Norderney's seaward side.

为了尽可能减少对生态系统的影响，穿过"下萨克森州北海浅滩海国家公园"的海底电缆铺设工程必须遵守严格的自然保护条件。

To minimise the impact on the ecosystem, subsea cable laying through the "Lower Saxony Wadden Sea National Park" was subject to strict nature conservation conditions.

作为相关系统的运营商，transpower stromübertragungs股份有限公司（其前身为意昂Netz）做了详细的研究。该公司为此成立了一家子公司，transpower offshore股份有限公司，由其母公司委托任务，规划和铺设从海上风电场到岸上电网连接点的连接电缆。第一个项目就是将阿尔法•文图斯风电场接入电网。这个连接工作可不是短短几周就能完成的。约70公里长的60兆瓦电缆从阿尔法•文图斯海上风电场旁边的变电站出发，向东南方穿过旅游胜地诺得尼岛，经过下萨克森州北海浅滩海国家公园，最终到达Hagermarsch变电站。在那里，海上风能产生的电力并入110千伏的电网。这个过程中有三大建造部分：穿越诺得尼岛、铺设浅滩海的海底电缆，以及连接到阿尔法•文图斯海上风电场变电站的海底电缆。

穿越诺得尼岛

这个巨大工程首先从穿越诺得尼岛的海滨度假小岛开始。在非常早的阶段，规划人员就考虑了如何尽可能将这项工程对大自然的影响降低到最小，尽管需要建造起多个电网线路。最终的解决方案是采用空心管道，铺设在现有的道路下。在这个1.5公里长的结构中，包含了至少35根的空心管道，其目的也是为未来的项目做好准备。根据国家

shore wind-power operations. No electric power would ever reach the shore without them. However, the effort required for planning and laying the cables far exceeds what some might think. Next to WECs and foundation structures, power transmission is the third-largest investment factor in the offshore business.

Ultimately, it was thanks to a law passed by the German Parliament (Bundestag) in October 2006 that grid connection of the alpha ventus test field could be completed in time. The law has achieved some notoriety because of its unwieldy name – the Infrastructure Planning Acceleration Law. Politicians went to great lengths in framing and formulating this law to enable implementation of major projects such as federal highways, railway lines, waterways and airports faster than had previously been possible. It was not until the final reading in the Bundestag that a section was incorporated into the law which was of key significance for offshore wind energy. In this section, grid operators were obliged to provide for the connection of wind farms to the grid in their balancing zone. This meant that transmission system operators were bound by law to install the 'outlets in the sea.'

This law turned the tables in one fell swoop. No more did the planners have to arrange for their own line to the grid connection point for each offshore project, as had previously been common practice. All of a sudden, on this legal basis it became possible to connect several offshore wind farms to the grid, bundled via one cable. The optimised

route planning is not only supposed to cut costs but also considerably mitigate the impact on nature and the environment.

As the responsible system operator, transpower stromübertragungs GmbH (formerly E.ON Netz) is under close scrutiny. The company established a subsidiary for this task, transpower offshore GmbH, which was commissioned by its parent company to take on the planning and laying of connection lines at sea to the grid node-point on land. The first project was to connect the alpha ventus test field to the grid. This connection could not be made in just a few weeks. With a transmission capacity of 60 megawatts, the approximately 70-kilometre-long cable starts at the transformer station next to the alpha ventus offshore wind farm. It then runs southeast to the resort island of Norderney, crosses the island, and then passes through the Lower Saxony Wadden Sea National Park, to finally terminate at the Hagermarsch transformer station where the wind power produced at sea is fed into the 110-kilovolt grid. Three construction sections had to be managed: crossing the island of Norderney, laying the submarine cables in the Wadden Sea and continuing at sea to the transformer station at the alpha ventus test field.

Crossing Norderney

The extensive works started with the crossing of the coastal resort island of Norderney. At a very early stage, planners considered how the impact on nature could be reduced to a minimum, in spite of the multiple grid connections that were to be built. The solution was hollow ducts which were laid beneath an existing road. No fewer than 35 hollow ducts were integrated into this 1.5-kilometre-long structure, in order to be prepared for future projects as well. According to state regional planning procedure, a total of around 3,000 megawatts can be connected via Norderney. The first work started in early 2007 and the companies involved completed construction of the hollow ducting in early 2008.

In addition, in the summer of 2007 transpower carried out four horizontal subterranean drillings under the dunes and dykes of Norderney and near Hilgenriedersiel on the mainland. This procedure, commonly called horizontal direct drilling (HDD procedure), consists of three steps. First a pilot drilling is performed with a measuring probe in the drill head, which finds its way through the ground at depths of more than 20 metres. Then a further drilling follows using a bigger drill head: this leaves a borehole in which, in the third step, workers lay the cable ducts and then insert the cables. Transport vessels brought materials and equipment from the port of Norddeich through the shipping lane to Baltrum. The first cable entry for the line to alpha ventus was laid in May 2008. At the same time, in April 2008, transpower started building the feed-in point on land, the new Hagermarsch transformer station, to which a 4.5-kilometre buried cable was laid from Hilgenriedersiel.

地区规划程序，最高可通过诺得尼岛连接总计约3000兆瓦的电力。第一项工程于2007年年初启动，参与项目的各家企业在2008年年初完成了空心管道的施工。

此外，在2007年夏季，Transpower在诺得尼岛的沙丘和堤坝下以及大陆上靠近Hilgenriedersiel的区域执行了四次地下水平钻掘。这种技术通常被称为"水平定向钻掘"（HDD）工艺，由三个步骤组成。首先执行试钻，钻头上配备有测量探头，能够在地下超过20米的深度下寻找通路。然后，使用较大的钻头进行进一步钻掘：这样能够留下钻孔，在之后的第三步中，工作人员将在其中铺设电缆管道，然后插入电缆。运输船通过通往Itrum的航道，从诺德代希运来材料和设备。阿尔法·文图斯海上风电场于2008年5月铺设了首个电缆入口。与此同时，在2008年4月，Transpower开始建造陆地馈送点——Hagermarsch变电站，并且铺设了从Hilgenriedersiel到此长达4.5公里的直埋电缆。

铺设穿越潮坪和海底的电缆

陆地上的电缆长度较短，显然是整个输电工程中最为轻松的部分。在海床上铺设穿越潮坪和海底的电缆，通往变电站，则更为复杂。由于电缆的直径为18厘米，每米重量接近53公斤，自然不难明白为什么必须采用特殊的设备。除此之外，不同类型的海床需要不同的电缆铺设方法。在海中，使用两条船只，用10米深的线路铺设和直埋电缆。但即使在开工之前，糟糕的天气也造成了工程延误。只有在经过5天的耐心等待后，海面又再次恢复了平静，足以让电缆铺设船上的"阿曼队"工作人员将5公里长的电缆绕上"安装者号"船只。然后"安装者号"朝着诺得尼岛进发，而"阿曼队"则朝着风力发电场铺设电缆。电缆通过垂直喷射器或犁机射入海床。而在远海地区，安装人员们将电缆连接到变电站上。

由于存在特殊限制，下萨克森州北海浅滩海国家公园地区的电缆铺设需要特别小心。事实上，通常这个国家公园内不允许进行任何施工。负责的政府部门允许在极其有限的路线内铺设电缆，而且必须对所计划的工作提交详细描述和具体程序后，方可施工。为了遵守北海地区每个工程阶段的严格限制，Transpower派遣了来自德国莱尔的Ecoplan景观规划公司，在施工过程中提供环境保护咨询。Ecoplan公司记录了施工流程，为项目领导层和工程公司提供有关各类环保问题的咨询，并且作为Transpower和政府部门之间的中间人。Ecoplan公司还监控了生物群落生境、鸟类、土壤和水保护等各种指标。

事实证明，穿过北海的潮坪地带铺设电缆十分困难，因为工作人员必须尽可能减少重型机械的移动，而维修和技术问题却需要多次运输。此外，所采用的铺设工艺也并未像预想得那样奏效。由于电缆在高潮时期铺设，其结果只有在下一个低潮时才可看到。在很大程度上以这一经验为基础，下一年实施的另一个电缆铺设项目则选择了另一种技术：振动犁机。"时间缩短了一半，而且占用的空间也小得多，因此，也大大减少了对国家公园的环境影响。"项目总主管马蒂亚斯·门辛如是说。

门辛的经验是：游客对这项工程十分好奇。"通常人们都对正在

Laying cable across tidal flats and under the sea

The short length of cable on land was certainly the easiest section to build of the entire power transmission line. Laying undersea cable across the tidal flats and on the sea floor to the transformer station was much more involved. With a cable measuring 18 centimetres in diameter and weighing almost 53 kilograms per metre, it's easy to see why special equipment would be necessary. In addition, different types of seabed require different cable-laying methods. At sea, the cable was laid and buried from the 10-metre depth line with two ships. But before they could even get started, bad weather forced a delay. Only after five days' patient waiting did the sea again become calm enough for the crew of the cable-laying ship 'Team Oman' to wind five kilometres of cable onto the ship 'Installer'. Then 'Installer' set out towards the island of Norderney, while 'Team Oman' laid the cable towards the wind farm. The cable was injected into the seabed with a vertical injector or plow. Far out to sea, the installers connected the cable to the transformer station.

Cable laying in the Lower Saxony Wadden Sea National Park required special care due to the special restrictions in force there. In fact, normally no construction of any kind is allowed in the Park. The responsible authorities granted permission to lay cable within a very tightly defined route, and then only after a detailed description of the planned work and its exact procedure had been submitted. In order to comply with the restrictions at every phase of the work in the Wadden Sea, transpower tasked landscape planning company Ecoplan from Leer, Germany, with environmental protection consulting to accompany construction. Ecoplan documented the construction processes, advised the project leaders and construction companies on all questions surrounding environmental protection and acted as a go-between for transpower and the authorities. Ecoplan also monitored all measures for biotope, bird, soil and water protection.

Cable laying across the tidal flats of the Wadden Sea proved difficult, since the crew had to keep heavy machinery movement to a minimum, while repairs and technical problems necessitated more traffic than planned. In addition, the laying technique used did not work as well as projected. Since the cables were laid at high tide, the results were visible only at the next low tide. Based in large part on this experience, for another grid connection project the following year an alternative technology was chosen, the vibration plow. "It takes only about half the time and uses much less space, so it has considerably less environmental impact on the National Park," says overall project leader Matthias Mensing.

Mensing's experience is that tourists are quite curious about the work. "Generally people are interested in what's going on, and ask astonishingly detailed questions," he reports. "And when you explain what you're doing, most people express their approval, combined with the hope that it all works properly when finished."

But it's not just a matter of the right technology. The time window is particularly narrow in the National Park. The weather doesn't have quite the same influence as on the high seas, but dyke and bird protection are priorities. Dyke protection legislation prohibits any work before the 15th of April and after the 31st of August of any given year. This time period is overlapped by the protected breeding season for birds, which lasts until the 15th of July. That leaves the period between the 15th of July and the 31st of August for work in the Park. In exceptional cases an extension can be granted, but only until the 30th of Sep-

执行的工作很感兴趣，而且会提出极其详细的问题。"他说："而当向他们详细解释目前的工作后，大多数人都表示了支持，同时还希望所有工程在竣工时能够顺利运行。"

但问题并不仅仅在于选择正确的技术。国家公园的施工期限非常紧张。天气的影响不如外海严重，但堤坝和鸟类保护却成为首要任务。堤坝保护立法严禁在每年的4月15日之前和8月31日之后进行任何施工。然而，这个时间段正好与鸟类的保护繁殖季节重合，后者直到7月15日结束。因此，只有7月15日至8月31日之间的时间可以在公园内施工。在例外情况下，可以批准略微延长，但也只能延长到9月30日。在这个期限以外，在潮坪区域执行任何陆上作业都是非法的。换而言之，在国家公园内铺设电缆，只有一个半月的时间，最多也只有2个半月。

外海的变电站

在风力发电机所产生的电力输送到岸上之前，将通过风力发电场，通过发电场内部的电缆连接到变电站，然后在那里从30千伏变压到110千伏。

Bilfinger Berger集团、Hochtief工程集团和WeserWind有限公司都是负责为这个海上变电平台进行施工和安装的公司。这三家公司为这个项目组建起联盟。从2008年3月至9月，位于德国威廉港的Braun-schweigkai公司预先装配了基础结构和最上层结构的导管架式桩基，包括直升机坪、主甲板和电缆甲板在内。变压器本身在2008年8月初从阿海珐工程技术有限公司送达，安装在最上层结构的主甲板上。

早在2008年9月中旬，Taklift 4水上浮吊就构建起了导管架式桩基，稍后，变电站将安装在上面，并定位到安装现场。整个导管架式桩基为45米高，重达650吨。和其它导管架式桩基（FINO 1和6个瑞能5兆瓦风机）一样，上宽下窄的直桩套筒分别焊接在四个脚上，插入长度为35米的桩子，打入海床。

浮吊将上层变压器模块放置到导管架式桩基上后，变电站在9月下旬准备投入运行。此时，尚未安装风机。因此，直到2009年年初，海底电缆方才连接到这个平台。最后，2009年5月，经过长达24个月的项目深化期以及对所有部件的彻底检验后，这个平台开始投入使用。

海上变电站必须经过严格保护，避免受到含有盐分的腐蚀性空气的侵蚀。"整个变电站安装在类似集装箱的结构中。"伊莉娜•卢克说，接受DOTI的委托，他负责变电站的施工与安装："或者可以说是采用气候控制系统的海上集装箱。当工作人员进入集装箱时会带入含有盐分的潮湿空气。但是，气候控制装置可以确保进行快速气体排放，将含盐的潮湿空气排出集装箱。"特殊的四层涂层系统保护着集装箱和变压器的外壁。石油和天然气行业的事实已经证明，这个系统能够十分有效地对抗天气影响。

变电站停止运作将是最糟糕的情况，因为这样会造成通往大陆的电流中断。因此，采用了一切可能措施，预防这种情况发生。"我们通过摄像头和远程控制工程技术监控整个变电站。"伊莉娜•卢克自信地说着："此外，我们还将每月定期出海1到2次，检查所有组件。"

简而言之，未来前景似乎颇为光明。

tember. Outside this period it is illegal to do any land-based work in the tidal flat zone. In other words, only one-and-a-half months, or at the very most two-and-a-half, are available for cable-laying work in the National Park.

Transformer on the high seas

Before the electric power produced by wind turbines can flow to the shore it is bundled via intra-farm cabling to the transformer station at the wind farm, and there transformed from 30 to 110 kilovolts.
Bilfinger Berger AG, Hochtief Construction AG and WeserWind GmbH were the companies in charge of construction and installation for this offshore transformer platform. The trio formed a consortium for this project. The jackets for the foundation structure and the topside super-structure including the helicopter, main and cable decks were pre-assembled at Braunschweigkai in Wilhelmshaven, Germany, from March to September 2008. The transformer itself was delivered from AREVA Energietechnik GmbH in early August 2008 and installed on the topside's main deck.
As early as mid-September 2008, the Taklift 4 floating crane moved out the jacket foundation, onto which the transformer station was later mounted, and positioned it at its installation site. The jacket is 45 metres high and weighs 650 tonnes. As is the case with other jacket structures (FINO 1 and the six REpower 5Ms), a vertical pile sleeve that widens upwards was welded to each of the four legs, into which a pile 35 metres in length was inserted and rammed into the seabed.
The transformer station was ready for service in late September, after the floating crane had placed the topside transformer module onto the jacket. At that point in time, no wind-energy converters had yet been set up. It was therefore not until early 2009 that the submarine cable was connected to the platform. At last, in May 2009, the platform went online after a project development period of 24 months and thorough inspection of all components.
The transformer station at sea must be protected from the corrosive salt air. "The entire transformer station was installed in a container-type structure", reports Irina Lucke, who was in charge of construction and installation of the transformer station commissioned by DOTI. "In other words, climate-controlled offshore containers." Humid salt air cannot be prevented from entering the container when a person comes in. But the air conditioning ensures an active air exchange that removes the salty air relatively quickly from the container. A special four-layer coating system protects both the container's and the transformer's outer walls. This system has already proved to be very weather-resistant in the oil and gas industry.
A breakdown of the transformer station would be the worst-case scenario, because it would bring the electric power flowing to the mainland to a halt. Therefore all possible measures are taken to prevent this from happening. "We monitor the entire transformer station via camera and telecontrol engineering", Irina Lucke conveys confidently, "and in addition, we will routinely be out at sea once or twice a month to check everything."
In short, prospects for the future look bright.

右图：只要看一看位于梅西尔的巴提斯兰德施工现场，就能发现导管架式桩基的真实尺寸。稍后将打入海底的基桩仿佛一支巨大的箭。

Photo on the right: A look at Burntisland's production site in Methil reveals the jacket's true dimension. The base which will be rammed into the seabed later on resembles a huge arrow.

右图：5兆瓦风机导管架式桩基通过Thialf特种船只的重型起重机定位。
Right: The 5M jacket foundation structure is positioned by the heavy-lift crane of the Thialf special vessel.

一艘拖船将挪威Verdal制造的三脚式桩基拖向威廉港。
A tug tows the tripods manufactured in Verdal, Norway, to Wilhelmshaven.

左上：来自阿海珐Multibrid公司的罗伯特·
努克利希和帕得里克·伯恩哈特。
Top left: Robert Nuglisch and Patrick
Bernhardt from AREVA Multibrid.

Taklift 4水上浮吊将三脚式桩基运往施工现场。基础结构在预定位置下沉。然后Menck液压锤将基桩打入海床。
The Taklift 4 floating crane ships the tripod to the construction site. The foundation structure is lowered at the planned position. Then the Menck hydraulic hammer rams the piles into the seabed.

大图：迈克尔·克林格和亚历山大·克勒姆特站
在三脚式桩基下。
小图：在将基桩引入三脚式桩基时，需要高科
技和辛勤努力。
Big photo: Michael Klingele and Alexander
Klemt standing beneath the tripod.
Small photo: Hi-tech and hard work are required
when introducing the piles
into the tripod.

在秋季风暴期间迎来激动人心的收尾工作
Exciting finish between autumn storms

负责人迪尔克·罗兰从写字桌后跳起来，透过小窗向远处张望，然后打开窗户。新鲜空气顿时涌入他位于"Buzzard"号自升式平台上的闷热办公舱内。此时的北海波浪翻滚，他仔细地观察着左舷的Multratug拖轮正在做些什么。"我还是没有接收到任何卫星信号"，比利时GeoSea公司的员工罗兰喃喃自语道，"所以，我们至今仍是在没有GPS的情况下慢慢接近"Goliath"。他那单调的语气明显泄露了他是来自德国鲁尔地区。他慢慢地将眼镜推向高高的额头上。"电子技术非常不错，眼睛同样如此。"

为使锚索保持拉紧状态，Multratug的船长使引擎一直保持在全速运转的状态，因此Multratug号的烟囱一直冒着浓浓的黑烟。而"Sea Bravo"号拖轮则在右舷做着相同的工作。通过无线电的完美协调，两艘拖轮把"Buzzard"拉往正确的方向。这看上去像是孩童的游戏，但这里的拉力却是非常之大：分别有5000和3500马力作用在缆索上以操纵"Buzzard"号及其贵重的货物——一台瑞能5兆瓦风机前行，距离其巨型姐妹自升式平台"Goliath"大约100m的距离——"Goliath"原意为圣经中被牧羊人大卫杀死的巨人，使用这个名字，可见该自升式平台的巨大。毕竟有2000吨东西要转移到Goliath上去。自升式平台已经在前一天紧靠导管架式桩基提升到了北海海平面50米以上。

把"Buzzard"拖到准确的位置需要耐心以及专业的方法。帕斯卡·泽特韦也是GeoSea公司的职员，他作为"Goliath"负责人，与罗兰承担着相似的职责。泽特韦索而下并登上"Buzzard"，希望能与罗兰及另外5名船员完成精确定位。现在离"Goliath"的距离只有大约100m，于是两艘拖船分别抛下锚，"Buzzard"从此刻起将自己掌握命运。使罗兰感到高兴的是，卫星接收器再一次接受到信号，这意味着所有导航设备都可用于最后的定位。在风机架之前，所有事都必须精确地按计划进行。船员们借助指向绞盘的摄像机密切地关注着锚索的状态。就算是两艘自升式平台并拢前的最后几米，甚至几厘米，这对船员来说也不是简单的任务。"Buzzard"船长是比利时人约翰·凡·登·贝格，他与他的团队不仅拥有强壮的体魄，而且心思敏锐。他专注地站在控制台前，他轻轻推动四根操纵杆，以精确到厘米的程度牵引、停止并控制着四根锚索。

2009年10月的最后一夜，四周一片漆黑，此时"Buzzard"正将其长长的桩腿降到阿尔法·文图斯试验场海底的准确位置。然后自升式平台开始慢慢升起。晚上10点，比Buzzard高20米的"Goliath"放下

Superintendent Dirk Rolland jumps up from behind his desk, looks out of the small window and then opens it. Fresh sea air floods into his overheated cabin-office on the jack-up barge 'Buzzard'. The Superintendent watches carefully to see what the tug 'Multratug' is doing on the port side in the billowing North Sea. "I still haven't got any satellite reception", mumbles Rolland, employee of the Belgian company GeoSea. "That's why we've had to approach the 'Goliath' up to now without any GPS." His singsong voice is an immediate giveaway: he's a Ruhr Valley man. He slowly slides his glasses over his high forehead. "Electronics are good – eyes too, though."

Meanwhile the funnel of the 'Multratug' is belching dark smoke as her skipper keeps her engines on full ahead to keep the anchoring cable tight. The tug 'Sea Bravo' is doing the same job on the starboard side. Coordinating perfectly by radio, both tugs are pulling the 'Buzzard' in the right direction. What looks like child's play is, in fact, pure force: 5,000 und 3,500 HP respectively are pulling on the cables to manoeuvre the 'Buzzard' with her valuable freight, a REpower 5M wind turbine, up to about 100 metres from her enormous sister jack-up barge 'Goliath' – whose name says it all. After all, there are 2,000 tonnes that need moving over to the Goliath. The jack-up platform had already lifted itself the day before 50 metres above the waves of the North Sea, directly next to the jacket foundation.

Getting the 'Buzzard' in the right position requires patience. And professionalism. Pascal Soeteway is also a GeoSea employee and, as Working Manager, is Rolland's counterpart on the 'Goliath'. Soeteway has abseiled down and with a subsequent tug transfer has boarded the 'Buzzard' in order to achieve a precision landing together with Rolland and his five-man crew. Now that the distance to the 'Goliath' is only about 100 metres the tugs drop anchor, leaving the 'Buzzard' in sole control of its destiny. To Rolland's delight his satellite dish is once again receiving signals from space, meaning he has all navigation instruments available for the final positioning. Everything has to go exactly to plan before the wind turbines can be set up. Using cameras pointed at the winches, the crew keeps a clear eye on the anchoring cables. Particularly the last few metres, even centimetres, of bringing the two jack-up barges together are no easy task for the men responsible on the bridge. Aboard the 'Buzzard', Belgian skipper Johan van den Berghe and his men not only have strong backs but also great sensitivity. Deep in concentration in front of his console, he gently nudges its four joysticks to pull, stop and control the total of four anchoring cables to the centimetre.

It's been pitch-black for a while now as the 'Buzzard', on this last evening of October 2009, lowers her long legs in exactly the right

舷梯。此时，风力开始加强，天下起毛毛细雨，借着探照灯的光亮，依稀可见烟波浩渺的北海海面。帕斯卡·泽特韦非常高兴，因为过程进行得相当顺利。他身穿一件红色防风衣，手里拿着对讲机，独自一人在甲板上站了好久。他看了看黑色的天空，又过了一会儿，他年轻的脸上终于露出了一丝微笑。"在过去几个星期内，所有事情就进行的非常顺利。我们很幸运，物流方面安排的很好，船员非常优秀，连天气也非常配合，"这位三十出头的年轻人在"Buzzard"号狭小、欠舒适的餐厅内微笑着叙述过去一周的成功。毕竟，他们破纪录地在风电试验场内架起了第四台瑞能风机：从装载到"Buzzard"号的返回仅用了4天时间。然而出色的表现背后总有辛勤的付出。满面胡须、面露倦色的帕斯卡·泽特韦简单地向大家道了声晚安，大口喝掉杯中的咖啡，然后慢慢地走上通往"Goliath"的舷梯。

有些工作已经完成，而另一些工作却刚刚开始。晚上10点刚过一会儿，来自瑞能公司的装配小组和来自柏林Seilpartner公司的攀爬专家从"Goliath"号来到"Buzzard"号的甲板上。虽然风力加强了许多，但是小组成员们还是打算立刻开始第一个塔架部分的安装工作。"现在风力是10米/秒，我们能够处理，"Seilpartner公司一名配备整套攀爬工具的职员这样说到。如果天气允许的话，工作将24小时展开。凌晨两点，第一个塔架部件已经由"Goliath"号上的起重机吊起，然后慢慢降下至导管架式桩基，然后由装配小组用螺栓固定。大约在早上5点时，第五台发电机第一步装配工作已经完成。

前一夜午夜12点整，"Buzzard"从荷兰埃姆斯港起航。船上装载着用于阿尔法·文图斯试验场的第五台5兆瓦风机，这次起航的时间比原计划早很多。中午十分，大家还觉得必须在清晨之后才能起航，但与天气预报相反，风机轮毂可以在午夜前一段很短却足够的时间间隙内运上船。于是"Buzzard"号解开缆绳。在"Multratug"的牵引下，它驶离港口，经过埃姆斯河，最后来到北海。船上装载的货物被牢固的固定着，其中包括两个塔架部件、风机机舱和轮毂，叶片朝三个方向伸出栏杆。

关于"时间间隙"这个概念，这无疑是德国海上风电产业的"年度词汇"。在建造60兆瓦阿尔法·文图斯海上风电场的背景下，这个词很有可能是使用频率最高的词。风力和浪级是定义时间间隙的参数，可用于整个物流和建造环节。"即使航运物流再完善，近海供应船和自升式平台再大，人类还是无法控制天气。"迪尔克·罗兰看着他那关于北海相关海域潮汐表的小册子这样说到；这本小册子记录了所有涨潮和低潮，这对每项海上作业都至关重要。"而且我们也不可以改变天气和潮汐"，他意味深长地补充到。

11月的第一场暴风雨来临了。周日晚上，风击打着甲板，在船楼的各个角落呼呼作响，天上的雨几乎是横向倾下。天空一整天都是灰蒙蒙的，试验场内已经竖起的风机外廓依稀可见。在船上进行任何动作都是在和风进行作战。船员们穿着防雨装备，弯腰做着必须完成的工作。虽然不是寒冷刺骨，因为北海仍在释放它夏季储存的热量，但这种天气还是令人感觉不快。这个季节，海上的温度通常要比陆地高。即使不考虑温度，大风也在呼啸着吹向两艘非常靠近的自升式平台。"我刚刚用风速计测量过，风力为8级。"土木工程师托马斯·施

place onto the sea floor of the alpha ventus test field. Then the jack-up platform starts slowly pushing itself up. At ten o'clock in the evening the gangway is slid out from the 'Goliath', which is 20 metres higher. In the meantime the wind has picked up strength and an all-pervasive drizzle sets in, with the lurching North Sea moon-grey in the spotlights. Pascal Soeteway is pleased: the operation went very well. In a red cagoule, walkie-talkie in hand he stands there for a few moments on the deck completely alone. He briefly looks up into the darkness of the night. After a while he finally allows himself a little smile, his youthful face relaxes. "In the past few weeks everything has gone superbly. We've been lucky, they got the logistics right, the crew were fantastic and the weather even played along – simply great", beams the thirty-something a bit later in the small, not-so-cosy canteen of the 'Buzzard', recounting the successes of the past week. After all, it has now been possible to set up the fourth REpower turbine in the test field in record time: just four days from loading to the return of the empty 'Buzzard'! An outstanding performance – which, however, has taken its toll. Unshaven and with tired eyes Pascal Soeteway says a brief "Good night" and takes his last swig of coffee before slowly climbing up the gangway to the 'Goliath'.

For some work has been completed, for others it is just about to start. Shortly after ten in the evening the assembly team arrives from REpower and the climbing specialists from Berlin-based firm Seilpartner come down onto the deck of the 'Buzzard' from the 'Goliath'. Although the wind has picked up noticeably, the team intends to start fitting the first tower section immediately. "It's ten metres a second, we'll manage", says one of the Seilpartner employees in his full climbing gear. Wherever possible, work is carried out around the clock – weather permitting. And the first tower segment really is lifted at two o'clock in the morning by the crane operator on the 'Goliath', lowered into its foundation jacket and bolted down tightly by the installation team. At about five in the morning the first step in the assembly of the fifth turbine has been completed.

One night earlier, at exactly midnight, the 'Buzzard' had put to sea from the Dutch port of Eemshaven. Loaded with the fifth 5M turbine destined for the alpha ventus test field, it started off a lot earlier than had been originally planned. At about midday it seemed that it would not be possible to set off until early morning, but contrary to the weather forecasts the rotor hub was able to be lifted on board in a small, but sufficient time-window before midnight. The 'Buzzard' then cast off. Pulled by the 'Multratug' it floated first out of the port, then onto the River Ems estuary and finally onto the open North Sea. Its cargo was carefully secured: two tower sections, the nacelle and the rotor hub, with the rotor blades protruding on three sides over the railings.

On the subject of 'time windows', this is certainly the term of the year for the German offshore wind-power industry. There have probably been no other words used more frequently in the context of the construction of the 60-megawatt offshore wind farm alpha ventus. Wind and waves are the parameters that define the much-quoted time window for the complete logistics and construction. "As good as maritime logistics may be, and as large as the offshore ships and jack-up barges are, we humans still can't turn off the weather", says Dirk Rolland looking into his small booklet of tide tables for this area of the North Sea; this contains all the high and low tides all so critical to every offshore operation. "And it's good that we can't change the weather and tides", he adds, philosophically.

The first November storm has come. Early on Sunday evening the wind is beating over the deck, whistling around the corners of the superstructure and the rain is almost horizontal. The whole day long it has been grey and foggy, with only the dim outlines of the other turbines already erected in the test field visible. Every step on board is a small battle against the wind. Bent over and in their rain gear the crew members are only doing the work that absolutely has to be done. Truly unpleasant, even if it is not yet that bitingly cold, as the North Sea is still giving off the heat that it has gathered over the summer. During this season it's usually warmer at sea than on land. But irrespective of the temperature, the wind is blowing powerfully through and over the two jack-up barges sitting close to each other. "Wind-force Eight. I measured it just now with an anemometer" says Civil Engineer Thomas Schramm. He works for the Hamburg-based engineering company IMS that has been commissioned by DOTI to coordinate all the work on board the 'Goliath'. To make sure that it is done properly there is a works meeting every day, at which Schramm, the Superintendent Engineer from REpower, the captains of the barges and Works Manager Pascal Soeteway from GeoSea all coordinate their operations. Although the construction of wind turbines is new to 48-year-old Schramm he is, after all, the expert in all things offshore. In the past he has planned and built various flood barriers. He also

准备出海。牢固的鞋子、保暖的衣物、具有防护性的外衣以及头盔，这些都是基本装备。这毕竟不是一次轻松愉快的乘船旅行。
Getting ready to go to sea. Firm footwear, warm clothing, protective outerwear and helmets are essential. It is not a pleasure boat trip.

2009年秋，拂晓下的埃姆斯港。
Eemshaven at daybreak in autumn 2009.

拉姆说到，他是汉堡IMS工程公司的一名员工，该公司受DOTI委托，负责协调"Goliath"号上的所有工作。为了确保每项工作的有序进行，每天都要召开一个工作会议，施拉姆、瑞能公司的负责工程师、自升式平台的船长以及GeoSea公司的工程经理帕斯卡·泽特韦都会在会上协调各项操作。对于48岁的施拉姆来说，虽然他并不了解风机的结构，但他却对海上的一切了如指掌。他曾设计并建造了各种拦洪坝，他也在法属圭亚那海岸参与了阿利亚纳失事火箭的救援工作。

蒲福风力等级这样精确地描述海上8级风力："中高浪级，破峰白沫成条。空气中有明显的飞沫。"这种天气显然不适合安装5兆瓦风机，所以他们停止了工作，机械装备工居住舱内开足了暖气。

施拉姆坐在"Goliath"多层桥楼上的一间船舱内，氖灯照亮了整间舱室。其中两面墙上贴满了起重机、风机和自升式平台的结构图。他坐在桌子处便可以看到施工现场所发生的一切。右边是"Buzzard"，左边是突出海面20米的管道架，管道架上的第一个部件已经在昨天完成安装。他的正前方，也就是"Goliath"的甲板中间，竖立着一台比利时Sarens公司的Liebherr LR 1800起重机。"我对海上作业的评价一直很高，"施拉姆坐在电脑前并强调，"无论吊起的重量是一吨或

worked on the salvage of the Ariane launch rockets off the coast of French Guyana

What Force Eight means on the open seas is described by the Beaufort Scale very precisely: "Moderately high waves with breaking crests forming spindrift. Well-marked streaks of foam are blown along wind direction. Considerable airborne spray." Certainly no weather for assembling a 5-megawatt turbine. So they stop work and the radiators in the mechanical fitters' cabins are turned on full.

Schramm is sitting in a cabin on the multi-storey bridge of the 'Goliath', lit with bright neon light. Two of the walls have been completely wallpapered with numerous construction plans of cranes, the turbine and the jack-up barge. From his desk here he can see everything that is happening on the construction field. To the right the 'Buzzard', to the left the jacket protruding 20 metres out of the sea with the first tower segment that was fitted to it the day before. Right in front of his nose – in the middle of the deck of the 'Goliath' – there is the powerful Liebherr crane LR 1800 run by Belgian company Sarens. "I have always held offshore work in high esteem", emphasizes Schramm from behind his computer. "It doesn't matter whether you have a tonne or several on the hook. You can only work out here with the weather." Always the weather. Even Schramm mentions the words "time window" more than once. He points to the five-day weather forecast from the British MET

出海前,瑞能公司的员工在Buzzard号上固定5兆瓦叶轮。
Repower staff attach the 5M's rotor star on the Buzzard before going to sea.

几吨,你都必须与天气一同工作。"还是天气。甚至施拉姆也不止一次地提到了"时间间隙"这个词。他指着英国国家气象局发布的未来5天天气预报,这份天气预报他已经打印过多份:预报上有许多分成行和列的数字。中间是施拉姆用一支记号笔画的一条线。他把星期三晚上之后的所有风力等级都做了标记。根据这项天气预报,风力将从那时起开始减弱,并将保持在10米/秒以下直到星期五。"这就是我们的时间间隙,从现在看来,我们能一下子完成塔架第二个部件和叶轮的安装工作。"施拉姆自信地解释到。若想吊起叶轮,连续12小时内的风速最高只能为8米/秒。

如果气象学家预报准确,那么从星期天到星期三这三天,施工现场必须停工。这将是一个艰难的任务,因为停工对两艘自升式平台上的船员以及瑞能公司的机械装配工来说都是一项挑战,不仅是身体上的,更是心理上的。"没有别的事情可做,你必须准备好面对这样的情形。"这就是施拉姆所知道的。这里与外部世界几乎没有任何联系,无法联系到朋友、家人,也没有手机信号,网络也是时断时续——即使网络通了,速度也非常慢。有些人不断看电影来打发无聊,有些人选择看书,其他人则轮流玩电脑游戏。在这样的等待期

在秋日的暴风雨中迎来激动人心的收尾工作 Exciting finish between autumn storms

一艘拖轮将Buzzard自升式平台拖到安装地点。
A tug tows the Buzzard jack-up barge to the installation site.

内,膳食便成了重中之重。来自德国莱茵地区的Guido在"Goliath"上烹饪美味,"Buzzard"号主厨是秘鲁人拉莱·萨拉特,也尽力烹制美食,还在星期日晚上做了一道沙爹烤肉配甜花生酱。这段时间内吸烟的人要比平时多,门前垃圾桶内堆积的烟蒂便证明了这一点。

对于值夜班的船员唐纳德·凡·托雷来说,每天夜里在"Buzzard"桥楼上巡逻时并不会看到什么特别的事情。但这位经验丰富的比利时海员已经习惯了这些,因为他已经在海上度过了无数个夜晚。当渔夫已经有30年的他常常驾驶一艘拖网渔船出到北海以及大西洋,捕捞鳕鱼、安康鱼、海鲈鱼、鳎鱼、鲑鱼和绿鳕。然而,过去几年中鱼类资源急剧减少,他每次出海的收入越来越少,最终他放弃了这份工作,最近受聘于GeoSea公司。"捕鱼配额的减少肯定有原因,"凡·托雷站在桥楼上微微叹息。由于参与了阿尔法·文图斯试验场项目,54岁的凡·托雷第一次有机会近距离接触海上风电产业。"我以前都是远远看到风机,我并不了解这些机器,也不知道它们的工作原理,"他说到,"然而,我知道在海上安装这些风机意味着什么。"凡·托雷认为海上风电场范围内可能会禁止捕鱼,从而成为鱼群的庇护所,"但现在讲这些为时过早。"

Office, which he prints out more than once: there are loads of numbers, split into numerous lines and columns. In the middle a small line that Schramm has drawn with a marker pen. He has highlighted all the wind strength values from Wednesday evening onwards. According to the forecast the wind will drop then and remain under 10 metres per second until Friday. "That's our window in time. As it looks at the moment we will be able to install the second section of the tower and the rotor in one go", explains Schramm confidently. In order to lift the rotor the wind should only have a speed of maximum eight metres per second in 12 consecutive hours.

Should the meteorologists' predictions turn out to be true there will be 3 days of standstill on the construction site from Sunday until Wednesday. Not an easy exercise. Because waiting represents a real challenge for the crews of the two jack-up barges and the team of mechanical fitters from REpower. Not so much in a physical sense, but all the more in a psychological one. "There's nothing to do instead, you have to be made for such a situation", is what Schramm knows. There is hardly any contact to the outside world, with friends and family, as there is no mobile phone communication out there at sea, and the Internet does not always work – and if it does it is extremely slow. Some get through the boredom by continually watching films, others get down to their reading, others in turn play on the computer. During such a waiting pe-

凌晨5点成功完成安装后，装配工安迪•施罗德在Goliath号自升式平台的餐厅内休息。
Fitter Andy Schröder has a break in the Goliath jack-up barge canteen after successful assembly at 5 o'clock in the morning.

riod the supplies are the be-all-and-end-all for the atmosphere. While Guido, who comes from the Rhineland, conjures up culinary delights on the 'Goliath', the Peruvian chef on the 'Buzzard', Lara Zarate, also does his best and for the Sunday evening meal serves sate kebabs with sweet peanut sauce. During the waiting period you can rest assured that there will be more cigarettes smoked than normal, as demonstrated by the piles of butts in the ashcans in front of the doors.

There won't be much exciting to see for crewmember Donald van Torre during his night watch on the bridge of the 'Buzzard'. But that's what the experienced Belgian seaman is used to, as he's spent countless nights at sea. He spent 30 years as a fisherman and sailed the North Sea on a trawler, right out into the Atlantic to catch cod, monkfish, sea bass, sole, redfish and pollack. However, fish stocks have fallen dramatically in the past few years. As the wages became more and more miserly he finally gave up his job and was recently hired by Geo Sea BV. "The fishing quotas have been reduced for a reason", says van Torre on the bridge with a small sigh. The deployment in the construction field of alpha ventus is the first time the 54-year-old has had close contact with the offshore wind power industry. "I used to see turbines like this from a distance, I knew nothing about them, nothing about how it all worked at all", he admits. "However, now I know what it means to install these turbines at sea." Van Torres sees the possibility

在AV 3安装之前，用于浇铸导管架式桩基的软管被拆除。
Shortly prior to starting the AV 3 installation, the hoses with which the jacket foundation was moulded, are dismantled.

of the offshore wind farms becoming fishing-free havens for schools of fish to retreat to, "however, it is still too early to be able to say anything definite about that yet."

Contrary to all predictions the wind does abate in the night before Monday – which changes all plans from the day before. Early in the morning the 'Multratug' approaches the 'Goliath'. On board there are twelve well-slept mechanical fitters from REpower and the company SSC Montage to take over from their colleagues who have already been working for 14 days. Amongst the newcomers there is Finn Kleinwort from REpower, who is to take over the job of Superintendent Engineer from Jens Fricke for the next two weeks. The atmosphere is good, as the weather conditions mean that all of a sudden a promising time window has opened up. All those responsible on the bridge of the 'Goliath' agree and decide to start assembling the second section of the tower and nacelle as early as midday.

The sun's rays break through the clouds, as the Sarens crane operator lifts the second tower section, manoeuvring it between bridge and crane safely over the deck of the 'Goliath' and places it onto the first section as if it were routine work. Everything seems to be going smoothly; some are even secretly expecting the 'Buzzard' to be able to set off for Eemshaven in thirty-six hours to pick up the last 5M from land and bring it into the construction field.

天气预报并不准确，风力在星期一前一晚才开始减退，从而打乱了前一天的所有计划。"Multratug"在清晨慢慢接近"Goliath"，12名来自瑞能公司和SSC装配公司的、休息充分的机械装配工将替代已经工作了14天的同事。瑞能公司的芬恩•克莱因沃特也是新来的工作人员之一，他将在接下来的两周内接替总负责工程师延斯•弗里克的工作。船上的工作气氛很不错，因为天气情况的转好，突然之间有了一个良好的时间间隙。所有"Goliath"相关负责人一致同意并决定从正午起开始装配塔架的第二个部件以及风机机舱。

阳光穿过云层，Sarens公司的起重机操作员吊起第二个塔架部件、使其安全地穿过"Goliath"的甲板，然后将其吊放在第一个部件上。所有一切都进行的非常顺利，看上去更像是常规作业；有些人甚至暗自预计"Buzzard"会在36小时内返回埃姆斯港，然后将最后的5兆瓦风机运往施工现场。

就在此时，事情突然出现了意外的转折。听到一名机械装配工的叫喊声，起重机操作员立刻发现起重机的一根钢制起重绳出现损坏：上方的多股钢绳出现卷曲。工程经理帕斯卡•泽特韦立刻接到通知，然后将这个坏消息直接传达给施拉姆、弗里克、克莱因沃特和自升式平台的船长。情况相当糟糕，为了避免出现任何风险，装配工作立刻暂停。泽特韦焦虑地看着其他人。亚历山德斯•卡拉库洛夫斯受德国劳氏船级社的委托担任海洋授权检查员一职，他一丝不苟地监督着瑞能5兆瓦风机的装载、运输和建造工作；他靠近损坏点、检查并用相机拍下出现损坏的地方。所有相关人员都很清楚这一点，即关于是否继续工作的任何决定都必须保证船上所有一切的安全。如果起重绳在起吊过程中断裂，那么将会出现无法预计的、也可能是灾难性的后果。

Sarens起重机公司的比利时总部首先接到消息。针对钢绳的破损问题，他们必须决定是否能够承担继续吊起重型机舱的责任。施拉姆对待这个事件的态度非常严肃："虽然从外观上看来损坏并不十分严重，但所有的材料都有很长记忆性。"与此同时，DOTI公司位于德国奥尔登堡的总部也接到消息。一番激烈的讨论之后，终于做出决定：为了保证安全，将塔架的部件吊回"Buzzard"上。芬恩•克莱因沃特清楚地知道，如果起重机吊索不修好，那么他的团队将无法进一步开展工作。接着，所有人都通过电子邮件和电话了解了现在的决定，没人提出异议。这个决定也得到了来自德国巴登的起重机操作员法尔科•泽纳的支持。"如果我们吊起风机机舱时起重绳断了，你觉得会出现什么情况？它将直接砸向甲板，而我们所有人都将淹死，"他解释到。那么起重绳到底出现了什么情况？泽纳轻轻地摇着头："从纯逻辑的角度看来，一头大象是无法穿过钥匙孔的……但这种情况也不是不可能发生。"

船上展开了各种活动。负责人们在桥楼通道内讨论着各种可行的方案，大家都有些烦闷。"停下来，大家歇一歇。"这一解决方案警告性地挂在施拉姆办公室前的通道上：暂停手上的工作，然后冷静、理性地处理下一步。50多名工作人员、一台庞大的起重机、一台兆瓦级风机和两艘大型自升式平台都静静地停留在北海海面，随时准备开始下一步工作。而现在，几根只有几毫米粗的钢丝却摧毁了人们迅速结束阿尔法•文图斯试验场最后两台风机安装工作的希望。但抱怨是无

Then suddenly everything takes an unexpected turn. One of the mechanical fitters calls out and the crane operator notices that one of his steel hauling cables is damaged: there are a few strands twisting out on the upper edge. Works Manager Pascal Soeteway is informed immediately, who then passes on the bad news straight away to Schramm, Fricke, Kleinwort and the barge skipper. It's an extremely difficult situation. So as to avoid any risk whatsoever, the assembly work is immediately halted. Soeteway looks worriedly at the others. Aleksandrs Karakulovs, who has been commissioned by Germanischer Lloyd as Marine Warranty Surveyor, has been meticulously monitoring the loading, transport and set-up of the REpower 5M; he moves closer to inspect and take photographs of the damage. It is clear to all involved that any decision made on whether to continue work must ensure, in particular, the safety of all on board. Should such a cable break during lifting work it would have unpredictable and probably catastrophic consequences. First the Belgian head office of the crane company Sarens is informed of the problem. With regard to the torn cable strands they are to decide whether they can accept responsibility for continuing work with the heavy nacelle. Schramm is taking this incident very seriously: "From the outside, the damage doesn't look particularly bad. However, all materials have a long memory." At the same time the head office of DOTI in Oldenburg is informed. After animated discussion a decision is finally taken: to keep things safe the tower section is to be lifted back onto the 'Buzzard'. At this point in time Finn Kleinwort knows that there is "nothing more to do" for his team until the crane cable is repaired. Following e-mails and telephone calls via satellite, everyone else agrees. The decision has the full support of the crane operator from Baden, Falko Söhner. "What do you think would happen if we winched up the nacelle and then that cable broke? It would crash right through the deck and we'd all drown together", he explains. So what exactly has happened to the cable, then? Söhner gently shakes his head: "From a purely logical point of view you can't get an elephant through a keyhole either ... but somehow this sort of thing seems to happen anyway."

There is a flurry of activity. Those responsible are discussing all possible scenarios, somewhat annoyed, in the corridors of the bridge. The solution: "Stop. Take five." is hanging as a clear warning in the corridor in front of Schramms' office door: suspend current work, and then coolly and thoughtfully tackle the next step. More than fifty men, one whopping crane, a multi-megawatt turbine and two huge barges are standing there in the North Sea ready to do their job. And now a few millimetre-thick strands of cable have dashed any hopes of a quick end to the construction of the last two turbines in the alpha ventus test field. But moaning won't help. The safety of the crew takes precedence – no matter what it costs. The priority is finding a well-considered, constructive way out of a tricky situation.

On the evening of this cursed Monday all decision-makers get together. They discuss in great detail the two options that are available: either the cable is shortened on site or the 'Goliath' has to go back to Eems-haven to get the repairs to the crane carried out there. The former would be a first and therefore, in insurance terms, questionable; however, it would be less time-consuming and thus probably also less expensive. It is late that evening when a final decision is reached: the 'Goliath' has to go back to port. They were so close to the finishing line – and now all of a sudden the goal vanishes into the distance. Everyone's patience is tested again on Tuesday, as a storm is brewing from the west. Waves are building to reach up to three meters in height. Jacking up the barge is

用的。无论付出什么代价,必须将船员的安全放在首位。大家都在寻找一个考虑周全的、具有建设性的方法来解决现在的困境。

所有决策者在这个黑色星期一的晚上集聚在一起,讨论两个备选方案的细节:一是现场剪短起吊绳,二是"Goliath"回到埃姆斯港并在那里维修起重机。前者是一项创新之举,但在保险章程方面将被置疑;然而,这一方案耗时较少且成本较低。当晚的晚些时候,大家终于做出了最后决定:"Goliath"必须回到港口。眼看着工程就将结束——而现在这一目标却遥遥无期。每个人的耐心在星期二再次受到考验——一场暴风雨在西面开始形成。3米高的浪逐渐形成,将自升式平台顶起是绝对不可能的,因为这种做法十分危险。"Goliath"在波涛汹涌的海面摇动,时而传来金属碰撞的声音。于此同时,船员们正在测试船上的所有装备、容器和其它设备,并检查所有物品是否都已系牢。晚上6点左右传来警报:所有人顶着强风跑到甲板上参加一项演练,练习穿着救生衣。

暴风雨在第二天清晨便停住了,天气开始转晴:明媚的阳光照在深蓝的海上,能清晰地看到地平线。不仅如此,连海浪也十分配合:海浪将自升式平台推离导管架式桩基,意味着"Buzzard"又可以在安全距离之外重新定位。在"Goliath"回来之前,"Buzzard"

out of the question, as this would be much too dangerous. The choppy sea rocks the 'Goliath', causing occasional metallic bangs. In the meantime the crew is testing all the gear, containers and other equipment on board, and checking that everything is fastened in a seaworthy manner. At around 6 in the evening an alarm goes off: everyone rushes in the heavy gusts of wind to take part in an exercise on deck, in which they practice getting into the survival suits.

The storm has dropped the next morning. The weather has cleared up: the sun is shining, there is a clear view to the horizon and the sea is a deep blue. What's more, the tide is playing along too. The rising high tide pushes the jack-up barge away from the jacket, meaning that the 'Buzzard' can be repositioned at a safe distance. It will have a lonely existence there until the return of the 'Goliath'. Squeaks are heard as the latter lifts her steel stilts until the jack-up platform is floating on the calm North Sea. After the hauling cable has been fastened the 'Multratug' pulls the assembly platform slowly away from the farm. And it's already long past midnight before it makes fast at the quay in back in Eemshaven.

The 1,300-metre long replacement cable is already there, waiting ready for the crane. Under time pressure the workers on shore get ready to make the replacement. The task is completed within a day, the crane is now ready for use again and the 'Goliath' can be tugged back to her place of deployment in the alpha ventus test field.

轻质坚固

简单来说,导管架就是一个水下的格子形基架,只有其上部的框架型钢结构露在海平面以上。钢制平台设于导管架的顶部,并由此延伸出一段管状部分,用于5兆瓦风机的塔架的安装。在海底,长方形导管架的每个角上都连带有打入海底的钢桩,并用特殊的灰泥进行灌浆固定。导管架的稳固程度受两个因素的影响,一是支承表面,二是钢桩深度。

瑞能系统公司选择的桩基结构在石油及天然气钻井架领域已有多年应用。阿尔法•文图斯风电场六台5兆瓦风机的导管架均由挪威OWEC Tower工程局设计,并由Burntisland公司在苏格兰制造。

"导管架的几何结构刚度大,也就是说这种结构特别能抵抗波浪压力,"专家马克•塞德尔这样解释,作为这一支工程小组的一员,他主要负责设计、计算并证明汉堡瑞能公司海上风机的支承结构。

格子形导管架结构让波浪压力迅速通过,这一点对非专业人士而言也非常容易理解。特别是在风急浪高的情况下,特别能显现出这一结构的优点。阿尔法•文图斯风电场所在海域的浪高可以达到17米,让这种巨浪通过支架无疑比直接拦截它们更好。

导管架的重量相对较轻。用于阿尔法•文图斯试验场的支承结构大约重500吨,总高度为55米(含所有延伸部分在内)。用于将导管架固定在海底的四根钢桩重约200吨。

导管架被涂成亮黄色,60厘米直径的管道构成其框架,90厘米直径的桩腿。这些管道直径都符合工业标准,所以管道生产商可以进行批量生产。为了进一步优化生产流程,瑞能公司和WeserWind公司合作研发了其特有的导管架,这种导管架使用特殊的铸钢节点进行组装。在这一设计中,焊接节点并不直接位于管道相接的地方,而是位于距相接点一段距离的位置,从而允许使用自动环缝焊接。毫无疑问,导管架也是一门科学。

LIGHT YET STRONG

A jacket is, simply put, a subsea lattice tower. Only its upper end with its trusslike structure rises above sea level. A steel platform is located on top. From this extends a short tubular section on which the 5M tower is mounted. On the seabed, at the bottom, the rectangular jacket is attached at each corner to steel piles driven into the seabed and firmly grouted using special mortar. The stability of the jacket's footing is based on the footprint and pile-drive depth.

This foundation structure favoured by REpower Systems AG has already been used to install rigs in the oil and gas sector for many years. The six 5M turbines in the alpha ventus test field are mounted on jackets manufactured in Scotland by the Burntisland company and designed by the Norwegian OWEC Tower engi-neering bureau.

"The jacket geometry translates into high rigidity, which means that the structure is especially resistant to wave pressure," explains expert Marc Seidel. As part of a small engineering team, he designs, calculates and certifies the support structures for the offshore wind turbi-nes of Hamburg-based manufacturer REpower.

The trusswork-like jacket structure lets wave pressure pass through readily, as is immediately evident even to non-specialists. This feature is an advantage especially in gales with towering waves. At the alpha ventus site, rogue waves can reach incredible heights of up to 17 metres. Letting waves of such magnitude pass through is certainly better than trying to resist them directly.

The jacket is relatively lightweight. The support structure for the version used in the test field weighs 500 tonnes and has an overall height of 55 metres, including all extensions. The four steel piles anchoring the latticework structure to the seabed add another 200 tonnes.

The jacket is painted bright yellow and consists of 60 cm-diameter pipes at the bra-cings, and 90 cm-diameter pipes at the legs. These pipe diameters are industrial standard, and pipeline manufacturers can mass-produce them easily. In order to further smooth the production process, REpower and WeserWind GmbH have worked together to develop their own jacket variant, which is assembled using special cast steel nodes. In this design, the welded joints are located not directly at the node sections where the pipes meet, but instead at some distance from them. This permits the use of straightforward automatic circumferential seam welding. It's clear that jackets are a science unto themselves!

在秋日的暴风雨中迎来激动人心的收尾工作 Exciting finish between autumn storms

只能孤零零地待在那边。"Goliath"咯吱咯吱地升起它的钢支柱,直到自升式平台浮在平静的北海海面上。固定好牵引绳之后,"Multratug"拉起组装平台慢慢驶离风电场。当它被固定在埃姆斯港的码头上时,已经过午夜很久了。

长1300米的替代起吊绳已经就位。在时间紧迫的情况下,岸上的工人们早早地做好了更换起吊绳的准备。任务在1天之内就完成了,起重机又能再次投入使用,"Goliath"也可以被拖回原地从而服务于阿尔法•文图斯试验场项目。

一切工作步入正轨,所有必要的任务都顺利完成了——仅在两天之后,也就是星期天晚上,轮毂已经牢牢固定在机舱上。"Buzzard"向埃姆斯港出发并将最后一台风机运抵风电场的同时,各个公司的员工、各部门领导、船员的妻子、女友和无数风电爱好者都在通过网络摄像头观看着FINO 1上的安装工作,紧张地等待着最后时刻的到来。海员和装配工程师能否战胜时间?大西洋上反复的低压槽之间会不会出现另一个时间间隙?事实上,所有人都希望到现场一看究竟,而每天通过网络摄像头观看现场情况也成了每日例行公事。2009年11月16日清晨,激动人心的时刻终于来临:上午7:13分,最后一根螺栓被固定

It's time for fortune to favour the bold. All necessary tasks are now completed like clockwork – and after just two days, late on Sunday evening the rotor hub stands fixed firmly to the nacelle. While the 'Buzzard' now goes to fetch the last turbine from Eemshaven, employees, politicians, wives, girlfriends and numerous wind power enthusiasts watching via the webcam installed on the FINO 1, tensely await the final act. Will the seamen and fitting engineers win their race against time? Will there be another time-window between repeated Atlantic low-pressure troughs? In fact, everyone wants to see for themselves live what is happening at sea and it has become a daily ritual to have a look at the scene from the webcam. And finally, early morning on the 16th November, 2009, it's time: the last bolt is tightened on the REpower 5M at exactly 7.13 a.m. "An Even Dozen", is the title of the press release from the DOTI consortium of operators that same day. At this moment of success all the sweat, frustration and costs recede into the background: the first German offshore wind farm is up and running. "We have climbed a very steep learning curve", beams Oliver Funk, Managing Director at DOTI. And most importantly, everyone involved in the project has come home safely. There was no accident victim during the construction phase, no disaster, no irreparable damage. alpha ventus has also become a role model for the nascent offshore industry, not least thanks to the strict safety precautions implemented.

在瑞能5兆瓦风机上。"An Even Dozen"是当天DOTI新闻发布稿的标题。在这个胜利的时刻，所有的汗水、挫折和代价都不再重要：德国第一个风电场已经建成并开始运转。"我们的学习曲线很陡，"DOTI总经理Oliver Funk微笑着说到。最为重要的是，参与工程的每名成员都安全回家了。在建造阶段，没有出现一个任何事故受害者，没有灾难、没有出现无法弥补的损失，阿尔法·文图斯已经成为了新生海洋工业的榜样，这些尤其要归功于所履行的严格安全预防措施。

信息量巨大的工程阶段结束后，极具吸引力的风电场运行阶段开始了，在这个阶段中研究工作将成为重心。生态学家、工程师、技术人员、物理学家、海洋学家都希望能获得重要的新发现。说到这里，人们似乎忘记了这个先驱风电场将为50000多个家庭提供可再生能源。然而，由于距离和地球曲率的问题，陆上的电力用户将无法看到风机旋转的叶片。能源在海上产生，比起世界上其它地方，短暂与永恒在这里离得最近。

The richly informative construction period has been completed. Now the operation phase starts, one that is just as fascinating, in which research will be the focal point. Ecologists, engineers, technicians, physicists and oceanographers are all hoping for important new findings. In this respect, it has almost been forgotten that this offshore pioneering farm will provide renewable energy to more than 50,000 households. However, due to the distance and the curvature of the Earth, those electricity consumers on land won't see the rotating blades of the turbines. The power is being generated out there on the open sea, where transience and eternity come closer together than anywhere else in the world.

5兆瓦风机机舱被安装在塔架的顶部。螺栓将把机舱与塔架固定在一起。
The M5 nacelle is mounted on top of the tower. The bolts are ready to attach the nacelle to the tower.

又是夜班时间了。瑞能公司的装配小组和柏林Seilpartner公司的攀爬专家利用短暂的时间间隙,在黑暗中竖起5兆瓦风机。

下方小照片:来自Seilpartner风电有限公司的Sven Winkler在施工现场。

Night shifts time and again. The REpower fitter team and "Seilpartner" climber-experts from Berlin use the short time-windows and erect the 5M in the darkness. Small photo below: Sven Winkler from Seilpartner Windkraft GmbH on the construction site.

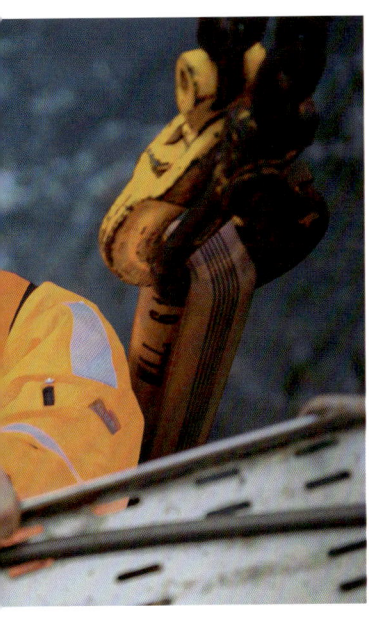

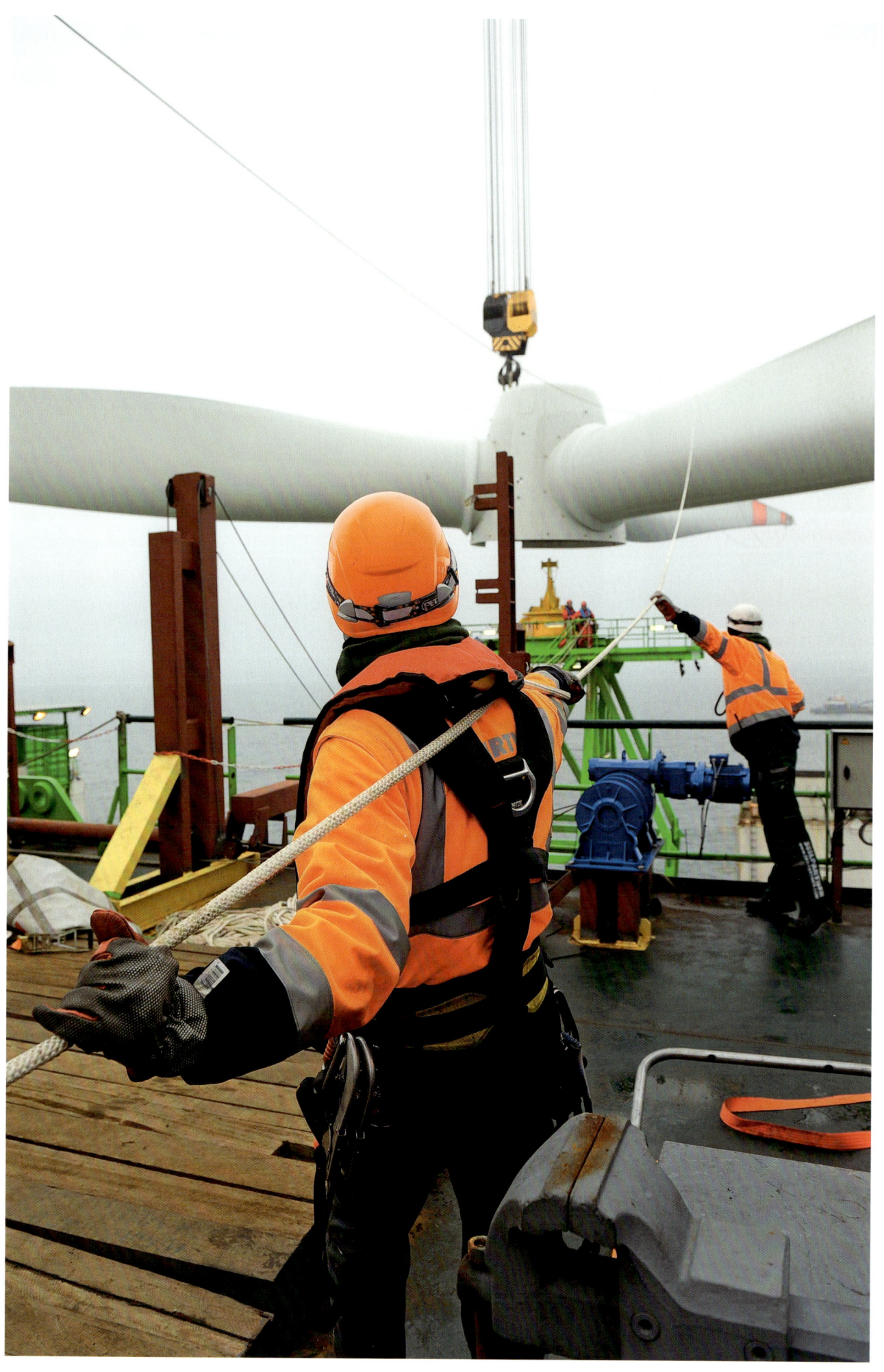

在海上风电场的整个安装过程中,吊起叶轮是最为复杂的一项操作。装配小组将叶轮带到准确的位置,然后起重机可以在不损坏叶轮的情况下将其吊高。这项操作只能在低风速时进行。
Hoisting the rotor star is the most complex operation during the offshore wind-energy converter's installation. The rotors are brought into the right position by the fitter crew so that the crane can hoist the rotor up high without any damage. This can only be done when there is low wind speeds.

主要的推动力 Key impetus

马蒂亚斯·舒伯特——瑞能系统股份公司首席技术官
MATTHIAS SCHUBERT, CHIEF TECHNOLOGY OFFICER, REPOWER SYSTEMS AG

马蒂亚斯·舒伯特
Matthias Schubert

在2001年4月以来,马蒂亚斯·舒伯特一直是瑞能系统股份公司的首席技术官(CTO)。他曾在波恩、柏林和安阿伯(美国密歇根州)学习,并获得流体动力学硕士、航空航天工程学硕士(MSE)。毕业之后,他主要担任独立应用型风能系统研究员一职。自1991年起,他就开始涉足风能产业,并担任过许多职位。他曾是伦茨堡pro & pro能源系统公司的总经理,在2001与瑞能公司合并之前,该公司自主研发了全套风能系统,该系统还成为了授权产品。

舒伯特先生,什么时候开始产生研发5兆瓦风机的想法的?

关于5兆瓦风机的问题,有一点非常有趣,早在1999年我们就开始研究大型风机到底会是什么样,当时还是伦茨堡pro & pro能源系统公司的时代,之后公司与瑞能系统公司合并。那时最大的量产风机是由我们研发的1.5兆瓦风机(MD 70),竖立在Kaiser-Wilhelm-Koog。最早的将风机建造在德国沿海地区的想法也在那时产生,很明显,海上将会出现许多风电项目。这也是我们思考海上风电产品雏形的起点——海上风机将会是什么样,应该是什么样。我们很清楚一点,那就是海上风机无论如何都要大,这样才能相对降低昂贵基础、海底电缆的成本;我们希望风机架设在离海岸线35千米以外、深30米以上的海域,并能获得经济上的收益。于是我们自发组织了德国北部海洋产业联合集团,成员包括pro & pro公司、Jacobs公司和诺德克斯公司。我们在这一集团内部组建了一个小组,专门研究5兆瓦风机的可行性研究工作。令人惊讶的是,当时的初步技术概念竟与现在5兆瓦风机的基本参数相差无几。

您是如何获得那些参数的?

那时,我们去拜访供应商并询问他们能够建造的产品尺寸。什么产品才具有经济和技术意义?这就是我们获得这些参数的方法——与此同时,我们还获得了深层次技术想法的框架。最后,我们主要考虑的问题是:齿轮箱能传递的转矩为多少,叶片长度为多少时才可行。

Matthias Schubert is Chief Technology Officer (CTO) of REpower Systems AG since April 2001. He studied in Bonn, Berlin and Ann Arbor (Michigan, USA) and finished his studies as a Graduated Engineer in the field of fluid dynamics and as Master of Science in Engineering (MSE) for Aerospace Engineering. After his studies, he worked amongst other jobs as an expert for the Ministry of Research in the field of wind-power systems for grid independent applications. He has been working in the wind industry in different positions since 1991. As Managing Director he led the engineering company pro + pro Energiesysteme in Rendsburg, that developed and licensed complete wind-power systems until its merger with REpower 2001.

Mr. Schubert, how long ago was it that the first ideas emerged to develop the 5M?

What is interesting with the 5M is that we were already investigating what a really large turbine would look like back in 1999. That was still in the days of the Rendsburg pro & pro Energiesysteme GmbH, that later became REpower Systems AG. Just to put things into perspective, at that time the largest turbine in serial production was our prototype of the 1.5-megawatt turbine (MD70) that was erected in Kaiser-Wilhelm-Koog. The first plans for turbines off the German coast were being made at the time and it was becoming obvious that there would be numerous projects out there in deep waters. That was the starting point on which we based our considerations about what such an offshore product would be like – and needs to be like. One thing was obvious to us: it has to be big, as only then can the very high costs for foundations and sea cables be reduced in relative terms; after all, we want turbines that are more than 35 kilometres from the coast and in water deeper than 30 metres to be working profitably! It was our initiative that led to the North German Offshore Consortium, consisting of pro & pro, Jacobs and Nordex AG. Within this group of three we created a team that worked on a feasibility study for a 5-megawatt

turbine. Astonishingly, that ini-tial technical concept is not so different to the basic parameters for the current 5M.

How did you arrive at those parameters?
At the time, we went to the suppliers and asked them what sizes they would trust themselves to build. What makes economical and technical sense? That's how we arrived at those dimensions – and at the same time this gave us a framework for our further technical considerations. At the end of the day it was all about how much torque the gearbox would transmit and what rotor-blade length we imagined would be feasible.

Did you ever consider a direct-drive version?
At the beginning everything was possible. Of course, we looked into all possible types of drive train in the detailed studies: full converter, synchronous generator, double-fed system, multiple generators and direct-drive. At the end of the day we decided, based on the techni-cal assessment – and not least due to cost structures – on the double-

位于不来梅港的瑞能系统公司的制造车间。
View of the REpower Systems AG production facility in Bremerhaven.

主要的推动力 Key impetus 159

您是否考虑过直接驱动系统？

在开始的阶段任何事情都是可能的。我们当然也详细研究了所有可能的传动系统类型：全额转换器、同步发电机、双馈系统、多电流发电机和直接驱动系统。最后，我们基于技术评估结果以及成本结构而决定选择双馈系统，也就是今天的5兆瓦风机所使用的系统。从技术角度而言，5兆瓦风机并不是1.5兆瓦风机线性发展的结果。

随着瑞能公司的成立，海上风机的研发工作是否得以继续开展？

瑞能公司直接接受了海上风机的概念。2001年公司首次召开董事会议，弗里茨·瓦伦霍尔特教授是与会者之一，当时"海洋工程"这一主题就已出现在董事会议程之上。是追求海洋技术的发展，还是集中精力朝3兆瓦级风机方向努力以扩大产品线，面对这两个选项，我们选择了5兆瓦风机——这在当时绝对是一个大胆的决定！我们希望使用这一产品打响新成立公司在市场上的名声。所以在2002年年末，5兆瓦风机的概念已经基本确定下来了。

研发海上风机的战略定位对公司来说是否是一项风险？

所有开创性工作都具有风险性。当时的瑞能系统公司还是一家小公司，公司要考虑的主要问题是：海上风电项目是否存在实质性风险。我们必须学习MD 70的研发经验，即利用原型样品来资助研发工作。运行原型的收益覆盖了产品系列的研发费用。与此同时，我们继续经营1.5兆瓦及之后的2兆瓦风机，这两个产品已经获得了一定的市场认可。2002年，公司成立了海洋业务部，直到2008年年中，该部门一直由马丁·斯基巴博士精心管理。海洋业务部需要保证公司的长远发展计划不被日常的业务所混淆而渐渐淡出人们的视线，这对于一个需要投资很多成本，却不见任何收益的部门来说并不简单。所幸的是，5兆瓦风机一直不是公司的风险。如今，我们已经是这项技术的领先者，无论是过去，还是现在，5兆瓦风机的研发工作都对公司陆上业务的发展带来了积极影响。

5兆瓦风机的研发总成本是多少？

我们没有精确计算过成本，而且不知道哪

fed system, like the one found in the 5M today. Technically spea-king, however, the 5-megawatt turbine is not a linear further development of the 1.5-mega-watt turbine.

Did the work on the offshore turbine continue seamlessly with the founding of REpower?

The offshore turbine concept was taken over directly by REpower. The subject of 'offshore' was already on the agenda at the very first board meeting in 2001, at the time still with Prof. Dr. Fritz Vahrenholt. We had to make the decision on whether to pursue the develop-ment of offshore technologies or concentrate on extending our product portfolio in the direction of 3-mega-watt turbines. We chose the 5-megawatt turbine – and that was a daring decision at the time! We intended to use this product as a differentiating feature on the market for the new company. Thus, at the end of 2002, the concept for the 5M had already been more or less decided on.

Was the strategic orientation to develop offshore machines a business risk?

All pioneering work is a risk. For what was at the time a still-small REpower Systems AG it was pivotal whether the offshore project would turn out

to be a substantial risk or not. We had learned from the experience with the MD70 that we could finance the development with prototypes. At the end of the day, the development of this series had been paid off with running the prototype. At the same time we continued our everyday business with the 1.5 and later the 2-megawatt turbines, which had already established themselves on the market at the time. In 2002 we formed the 'Offshore' business unit, which Dr. Martin Skiba managed intensively until the middle of 2008. This unit was intended to ensure that our forward-looking development did not get lost amongst all the day-to-day business. It wasn't always easy for this company area, as it initially cost a lot of money but did not generate any income. Nevertheless, the 5M was never a corporate risk. On the contrary, nowadays we are the forerunners in this technology and the development of the 5M had, and still has, a positive impact on our onshore business.

What did the development of the 5M cost in total?

We haven't worked it out to the penny. And the question is always which overhead costs count as development and which not. And, moreover, we received subsidies from the state of Schleswig-Holstein from the Development Program 2000 as well as from the European Commission. The funds from both programmes all together added up to around three million euros.

Let's get back to the technology: we've talked about dimensions, but what special features does the offshore turbine have in particular?

If you have good engineers involved then you will quickly agree on the question of dimen-sions. What is interesting in this respect really are the details. We had listened around on the market beforehand and asked what turbine was really required by the clients. Never before, for any other product, had we conducted such an intensive market analysis. However, other than saying that they would like the turbine to be "as large as possible", we received widely varying and frequently vague responses. So we had to draw our own conclusions. There was one important consideration that we had to think a long time about, though: when repairs are required do we want to replace the complete nacelle or do we do the repairs on site? With the 5M we ended up deciding

左：5兆瓦风机机舱内部
Left: Inside the 5M nacelle.
右：轮毂已经关闭，工程即将收尾。
Right: The rotor hub is closed and the construction almost finished.

些间接成本需要计算到研发成本中，而哪些不需要。此外，我们的研发项目还获得了石荷州和欧洲委员会颁发的补贴。两个项目所获得的基金总数约为300万欧元。

回到技术话题：我们讨论过参数问题，那么海上风机独有的特点是什么呢？

如果你有一个优秀的工程师团队，那么他们在参数这个问题上将很快达成一致。而这里真正有趣的却是细节。我们必须事先了解市场，打听客户实际需要的风机类型。在这个项目之前，我们从未进行过如此详细的市场分析。然而，除了"我们希望风机越大越好"这一一般观点之外，其它回答要么差别很大，要么含糊不清。所以我们必须自己下结论。我们就这个问题讨论了很久，即风机需要维修时，是替换整个机舱，还是进行现场维修？针对5兆瓦风机我们决定采用模块化结构，从而可以在现场维修可能出现的故障。鉴于这一点，机舱内部设置了一台相对较大的移动式起重机。此外，我们选择了传统的叶轮轴承。轴系也相应配备了两个主轴承，这意味着可以在不移动叶轮的情况下取出齿轮箱。这一设计在海上具有明显优点，因为你不能随时随地放下任何东西。我们将机舱的内部空间设计得相对较大，从而为机械装配工腾出了工作空间。我们还在传动系统的上方边缘到机舱顶之间预留了很大的空间，原因很相似：为了能够轻松地操纵起重机。按照我们的设想，机舱必须完全预装好并完成线路连接工作，这样一来，所有设备在风机安装完毕后便能开始运转。

从您的叙述看来，5兆瓦风机的重量应该非常大吧……

首先，这么庞大的装置一定很重。但在我们看来，重要的不是海上风机的重量。而是必须有一个牢固的机器结构来保护机舱尾部的所有电子设备免受风浪引起的强烈振动。

5兆瓦风机运作时，机舱内是否处于正压，从而使含盐分的空气无法进入？

没有，我们没有这么做。人们总是高估海水的腐蚀性。拿我们公司位于澳大利亚沿岸的一个风电项目来说，那边由于波浪拍打海岸，空气中的含盐量要比北海上高得多。

瑞能公司是不是很早就开始考虑桩基的相关问题？

对，在这个领域积累一定的专业知识对我们来说非常重要。我们在研发阶段进行的销售宣传中就明确了这一点：若桩基的设计不合理，那么其成本将非常高。

这对瑞能公司来说是一个全新的领域，对吗？

是的。所以我们从项目一开始便从大学里招募了一名专家，他的任务就是不断地开发这个领域。如今，我们已经具备了足够的海上桩基技术知识。我们之所以想在这个新领域内研发出一些属于自己的技术，主要是为了能够成功地向客户提供一些成熟的建议，并不是因为我们想自己制造和提供该产品。我们公司苏格兰沿海的第一个项目正好能证明拥有自己专业能力的重要性。由于采纳了我们的建议，所以桩基最终成本仅为初始报价的一半。挪威OWEC Tower工程公司接受委托并设计了导管架。

开启海上风电项目之前，瑞能公司是否打算测试更多的陆上风机？

对，我们一开始是有这个想法的，即2004年11月在德国布伦斯比特尔完成原型测试后，先在陆上架几台5兆瓦风机以获取尽可能多的经验。但我们出乎意料地接到一个任务——在苏格兰Beatrice海上油田上建造两台风力发电机，我们当然不会放弃这一个机会，不久之后，第二台和第三台5兆瓦风机就已屹立在海上。到现在为止，这些小型项目以及合理的风险管理已经构成了我们的学习曲线：从一开始Beatrice的两台风机，然后是Thornton Bank的六台装置，以及阿尔法•文图斯的六台风机。接下来的爱尔兰海Ormonde项目将建造30台风机。之后我们将有信心接更大的项目。

Beatrice是海上风电业务的良好开端，对吗？

我们很幸运能接到Beatrice两台风机的项目！这个项目清晰地展示了风机在水中的工作性能。从2006年起我们就可以利用这宝贵的经验。早些时候我们就想表明这一点，即如果没有测试及示范风电场，那么2002年德国联邦政府批准的计划——2010年达到3000兆瓦——无论如何都无法完成。如果一开始就要建立80台风机，那么没人会参与这项巨大的投资。我们瑞能公司也绝对不会将Horns Rev这么大型的风电项目作为起家项目。虽然我们心中存在北德情结，但我们还是决定去苏格兰开始第一个项目。

……然后直接进入石油工业的中心？

……我并不认为这是件坏事。5兆瓦风机原型建立在德国布伦斯比特尔核电站附近，而公司的第二、第三台风机则建立在海上石油平台的周围。我觉得这一点非常具有吸引力。塔里斯曼能源公司和苏格兰及南方能源公司（SSE）都是我们在Beatrice项目中的合作伙伴，他们在其中所起的作用至关重要。塔里斯曼非常熟悉海洋工程业务，而其它一些传统的能源供应商（出于不同的企业文化）运用的是不同的风险管理方法。一般来说，一个数千欧元的项目必须经过五个管理层才能得到最终的审批答复。这种做法不适用于海洋工程业务。项目经理必须在现场作出快速决定，有时候这些决定涉及的成本非常高；你没有

on a modular construction, so that we could repair any damage on site wherever possible. Therefore, there was a relatively large, mobile crane integrated into the nacelle. Moreover, we chose a classic rotor bearing. Accordingly, the shaft was fitted with two main bearings, meaning that we could lift out the gearbox without removing the rotor. This is a great advantage at sea, as you can't put anything down anywhere out there. We took a generally spacious approach to the nacelle's design, as the mechanical fitters don't have much space to work at sea. We left a lot of space between the upper edge of the drive train and the roof for that very same reason: it needs to be possible to easily manoeuvre the crane. Our approach also took account of the need to have the nacelle completely ready and wired for installation so that it can go into operation immediately after being erected at sea.

All this means that the 5M has become quite a heavyweight ...

On the one hand, it's obviously going to weigh a bit due to the sheer size of this turbine. However, we consider the weight not to be that important at sea. Furthermore, we require a solid machine construction to protect the electronics, which are assembled completely in the back of the nacelle, from powerful vibrations caused by the wind and waves.

Is there a pressure in the nacelle when the 5M is running so that no salty air can get in?

No, we didn't do that. Corrosion at sea is overestimated anyway. We even get higher amounts of salt in places around the coast than we do on the North Sea, due to spray from the breaking surf – for example, with our projects on the coast of Australia.

Did REpower look into the offshore foundations early on?

Very much so. It was absolutely necessary for us to build up the necessary expertise in this area. Even during the development work, during our initial sales pitches it became obvious that the foundation structure would be very expensive if wrongly designed.

So this was a completely new area even for REpower, wasn't it?

Absolutely. That's why we brought in an expert from the university right from the start, who has been continually developing this area. Nowadays, we have the required know-how for offshore foundations. The motivation to develop something of our own in this new area was first and foremost our efforts to advise our clients successfully, less the desire to manu-facture and supply by ourselves. The first pro-ject off the coast of Scotland demonstrated just how important possessing your own expertise is. Thanks to our advice the foundations only cost,

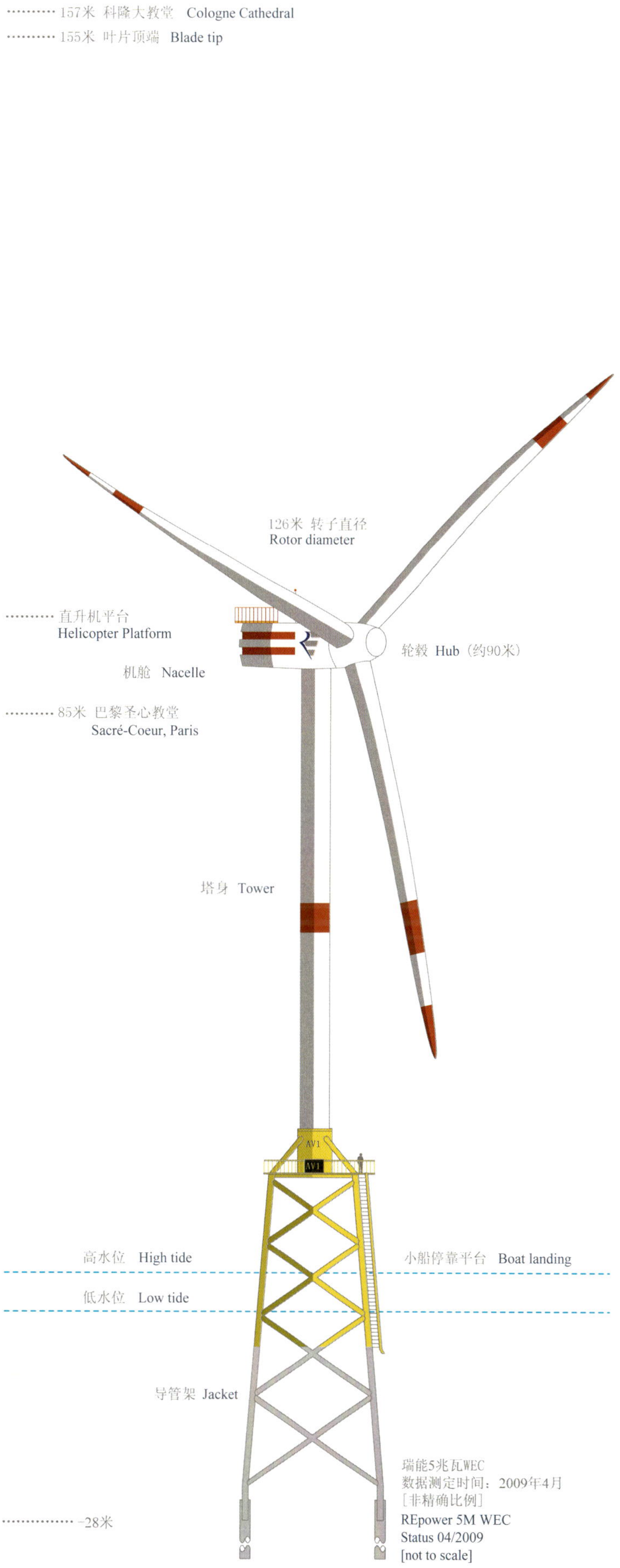

·········· 157米 科隆大教堂 Cologne Cathedral
·········· 155米 叶片顶端 Blade tip

126米 转子直径
Rotor diameter

·········· 直升机平台
Helicopter Platform

轮毂 Hub（约90米）

机舱 Nacelle

·········· 85米 巴黎圣心教堂
Sacré-Coeur, Paris

塔身 Tower

瑞能5兆瓦风机技术参数：
TECHNICAL DATA REPOWER 5M

从海底起的总高度： Overall height above seabed	185 m
额定功率： Rated capacity	5 MW
转速： Speed	5.9-14.8 rpm 5.9 to 14.8 rpm
接入风速： Cut-in wind speed	3.5 m/s（3级风力） 3,5 m/s (wind force 3)
额定风速： Rated wind speed	13.0 m/s（6级风力） 13,0 m/s (wind force 6)
切出风速： Cut-out wind speed	30 m/s（10级风力） 30 m/s (wind force 10)
叶尖速度： Blade tip speed	80 m/s（288 km/h）
机舱重量（带叶轮和轮毂）： Nacelle mass with rotor and hub	410 t
钢铁重量（基础结构、塔架、机舱）： Steel mass (foundation, tower, nacelle)	1.120 t
仅基础结构所用钢铁重量： Steel mass of foundation alone	500 t

高水位 High tide
小船停靠平台 Boat landing
低水位 Low tide

导管架 Jacket

············ -28米

瑞能5兆瓦WEC
数据测定时间：2009年4月
［非精确比例］
REpower 5M WEC
Status 04/2009
[not to scale]

主要的推动力 Key impetus

时间可以浪费。我们从塔里斯曼的项目管理过程中学到很多。

如果阿尔法·文图斯项目早进行两年，是否对瑞能公司更有利？

对，没错——这不单是对我们而言。

阿尔法·文图斯项目的进行过程是不是进两步退一步？

没有，绝对没有。学习曲线总是曲折的，你需要尝试和不同的合作伙伴合作、尝试在不同的国家工作。阿尔法·文图斯是一个重要的示范性项目，因为它反映出了德国近岸区的典型框架性条件。即使如此，仍有几个问题尚未得到解决，例如：哪些港口最适合进行项目？物流链中的瓶颈环节在哪里？如果我们真想做大项目，必须解决这些问题。在德国，我们必须再次严肃认真地考虑这些挑战。瓶颈的确存在，这就是为什么阿尔法·文图斯项目从荷兰埃姆斯港开始。

阿尔法·文图斯项目对瑞能有哪些影响？

对于我们公司来说，阿尔法·文图斯是我们进入德国海洋工程业务的发令枪，因此也是我们立足这个国内市场的重要依据。

瑞能公司从阿尔法·文图斯项目中获得了哪些经验？

从我们公司的角度看，我们通过项目学习了深水区域的物流问题。时间的有效利用是一个极为重要的因素。我们在阿尔法·文图斯试验场竖立风机的效率比在Thornton Bank项目中高很多。物流速度稍许提高一点，就能带来极为可观的节省。接下来，我们将从运营和维护过程中学习。优化成本结构的出发点在是什么？如果涉及到运营和维护，那么摆在我们面前的必然是一条很陡的学习曲线。

从您的观点看来，海洋工程业务中存在的最大挑战是什么？

风机的巨大尺寸。所需组件的尺寸都要比一般工业标准大或者大很多。当你作为制造商找到供应商，你无法得到批量生产的大尺寸组件——这就是最大的挑战。我们必须事先让供应商以工业标准制造这些组件。举两个例子：轴承和机架，乍一看这是两个简单、传统的组件。若这两个组件用于2兆瓦风机，那么欧洲很多公司都可以制造；但若是用于5兆瓦风机，情况就不一样了。整个欧洲能生产这些组件的公司屈指可数。这里有一点非常重要，即我们必须向这几家供应商解释市场前景，从而可以使他们将此类制造业务纳入长远计划之内。例如我们与RWE Innogy公司签订框架合同时非常重要的是向供应商证明其生产业务的可靠前景。

at the end of it all, half of what was quoted at the start. Our input lead to the Norwegian engineering company OWEC Tower AS being commissioned, who developed the jackets in a very elegant way.

Didn't REpower initially intend to test more offshore turbines on land before the premiere on the open sea?

That's correct. We initially had the idea, after running the prototype in Brunsbüttel in November 2004, to first set up several 5Ms on land, in order to gather as much experience as possible. Then all of a sudden we had the chance to set up two turbines in the Scottish offshore oil field Beatrice. Of course we didn't want to miss that opportunity and soon the second and third 5M was up and standing in water. We have, up to now, been able to climb our learning curve with small projects and sensible risk management: first Beatrice with the two turbines, then the next step was Thornton Bank with six and alpha ventus again with six. The next to follow is Ormonde in the Irish Sea with 30 turbines. Then we will also dare to take on the larger projects.

Beatrice was a good start into the offshore business, then?

Beatrice was, with the two turbines, a tremen-dous stroke of luck for us! We were able to demonstrate the performance of the machines on the water within manageable parameters. Since 2006 we have been able to make use of this very valuable experience. Early on we tried to make it clear that the very ambitious plans of the German Federal Government approved in 2002 – of 3,000 megawatts by 2010 – would not be possible anyway if we had no test and demonstration fields. No one is going to make this huge investment if they need to set up 80 turbines right from the outset. As REpower we would never have worked with offshore farms such as Horns Rev as start-up projects. Nevertheless, as North Germans we did slightly regret that we first had to go to Scotland.

… and then straight into the heart of the oil industry …

… I didn't think that was a bad thing at all. We set up our prototypes next to the Brunsbüttel nuclear power station and the second and third turbine at sea directly neighbouring an oil platform. I regard that as very appealing. Moreover, with the Beatrice project it was hugely important to have the right partners in Talisman Energy Inc. and Scottish and Southern Energy. Talisman had excellent knowledge of the offshore business. As opposed to this, some classic energy providers, simply due to their corporate culture, exercise a different risk management. There are frequently five levels of hierarchy that you have to go through to get decisions made on just a few thousand euros. You can't do that in the offshore business. The project

海上风电是不是风电产业的"思维转换"？

海上风电的确是一个全新的业务范围，客户、合作伙伴和供应商都是新的。如果你不能理解并接受这一点，那么你注定会失败。有些人可以应对这样的"思维转换"，而有些人不行。我们必须使其形成批量生产。举基础结构为例，如果我们依然停留在制造层面，基础结构的成本仍将非常高。所以我们在不来梅港进行实验，希望找到方法降低导管架结构的制造成本。导管架大致就是一个格子形塔架，从根本上来说，塔架所有连接点的几何结构也相同。如果必须手工焊接这些连接点，那么工作量会很大，且成本也会很高。所以我们在研究使用标准管，这样就能应用自动环缝焊接技术将其连接到铸造节点元件。

第一台6兆瓦风机将在何时进入海上？

它将紧接着5兆瓦风机进入海上。我们将2012到2014年计划为逐步转换期。我们位于丹麦边境附近Ellhöft的三台岸上原型机器其第一批试验结果非常令人满意，符合公司研发部门所预期的情况。对此，我们感到非常高兴。

有些专家已经开始讨论10兆瓦风机。你是否和他们一样也在计划更大型的风机？

事实上，我们也在讨论10兆瓦风机的问题——虽然市场对下一步的反应可能是7兆瓦。现在对我来说更重要的是如何改善5兆瓦和6兆瓦风机的工业制造可行性。我确信可以进一步大幅降低成本，不仅仅是风机本身，还包括基础结构、物流和在海上建立的过程。作为制造商，我们必须更加努力来优化这些问题，从而可以不依赖他人。我们希望涉及到所有方面。

以多高的强制光伏上网电价，海上风能才能显出其经济性？

这个问题不能单方面地解答。每个国家的产业发展架构条件不同。就德国近岸区而言，如果没有德国加速基础设施规划法规，那么风机的运营肯定不会经济。

您对海上电网发展持什么观点？

在许多问题的策划方面，德国人都是领先世界的佼佼者……但却没有一个针对电网的杰出策划。我们在这个问题上也没有太多进展，对此我个人也感到十分惊讶。如何将上述提及的、计划建造在北海和波罗的海上的20GW（gigawatt）设备发出的电能输送到岸上，这个问题也没有得到解决。有一个情况很令人惊讶：似乎每个人都知道完成这么大规模项目所需的时间。我们需要今天进行大量的额外投资来将明天的风电能源接入电网，这也将减弱融资的难度。银行是否真的愿意进入海上风电业务，取决于我们是否能够证明海上风能也能与陆上风能一样盈利。

manager has to make quick, sometimes very expensive decisions on the spot; you have no time to waste. We learned a lot from how Talisman managed the project.

Would it have been better for REpower if alpha ventus had come two years earlier?
Yes, that's right – but not only for us.

Was alpha ventus one step back after two steps forward?
No, not at all. You have to climb your learning curve a number of times, with various different partners, in various different countries. For that reason alpha ventus is a very, very important demonstration, as it illustrates the typical framework conditions that we find in German offshore waters. But there are still several unanswered questions in Germany: for example, which are the best ports to start from? Where are the bottlenecks in the logistics chain? These questions need resolving if we really do want to do great things. We have to take a serious look at these key challenges in Germany once again. There are bottlenecks. There was a reason why alpha ventus was set up from the Dutch port of Eemshaven.

What significance does alpha ventus now have for REpower?
For us it means the starting gun for our entry into the German offshore business and thus a very important reference on this market, which is also our domestic market.

What has REpower learned from alpha ventus?
From our perspective we have been able to learn the most from the logistics required in extreme water depths. Efficient usage of time is an extremely important factor. We were already able to erect our turbines in the alpha ventus test field more efficiently than in the Thornton Bank project. Even slightly quicker logistics can add up to incredibly large savings. The next learning process involves operation and maintenance. What starting points are there to improve cost structures? We certainly have a steep learning curve ahead of us when it comes to the areas of maintenance and operation.

What would you say is the greatest technical challenge in offshore matters?
The sheer size of the turbines. Components are required that have dimensions well over and above common industrial standards. As a manufacturer, if you go to the established suppliers you won't get equipment in these dimensions serially produced yet – that's the great challenge. We have to get the supp-liers to make these components in industrial dimensions beforehand. Let's look at two examples: bearings and mainframe, which at first glance are simple, classic machine components. In the 2-megawatt turbine area there are several companies in Europe that can manufacture them; this is no longer the case for the 5-megawatt turbine. There are only a handful of companies in the whole of Europe who can do it. It is extremely important to explain to these suppliers what the market perspectives are so they can enter into this type of production in the long term. That's why large framework contracts, like the ones signed by us with RWE Innogy, are very significant – to demonstrate reliable perspectives to the suppliers for their production.

Does offshore represent a paradigm shift for the wind energy industry?
Offshore really is a completely new business sector, with new clients, new partners and new suppliers. If you do not understand and accept this you will fail. Some can cope with this paradigm shift, others not. We have to get into serial production. Let's take the example of foundation structures, which will remain very expensive if we stay on the manufacturing level. That's why we are conducting experi-ments in Bremerhaven to find out how we can make our jacket structure cheaper to produce. The jacket is more or less a lattice tower and in principle there is the same geometry at all the connection points. If you have to weld these nodes by hand then that's a lot of work to do and it's expensive. We're therefore loo-king into using standard pipes that can then be connected to the cast node elements in an automated way, using circular weld joints.

When will the first 6M go offshore?
That will be the direct successor to the 5M. We're planning a stepwise transition from 2012 to 2014. The first results from our three prototypes onshore in Ellhöft near the Danish border are very good and they reflect what our Development Department predicted. We are therefore very happy!

Some experts are already talking about turbines of the 10-megawatt class. Are you also planning larger offshore turbines?
We are, in fact, also talking about 10-megawatt turbines – even though the market will presumably move on initially with 7 megawatts. What is more important to me at the moment is how I improve the industrial feasibility of the 5Ms and 6Ms. I am convinced that we will be able to further reduce the costs considerably. The issue is not only the turbine itself, but the foundation, logistics and erection at sea. As a manufacturer we have to do more to improve these things, so as not to be dependent on others. We want to get thoroughly involved in all these aspects.

At what feed-in tariffs does offshore wind power become economical?
That can't be answered in a one-dimensional way. There are framework conditions that differ from country to country. In German offshore waters,

到2020年,海上将有多少台瑞能公司的风机?

(考虑了一会儿)到那个时候,我们公司应该已经安装了1000台风机吧。

operation would certainly not be economically viable at the moment without the German Act on Accelerated Infrastruc-ture Planning.

What's your opinion on the development of the grid network at sea?

In many ways we Germans are world cham-pions at planning things ... but as yet there is no master plan for grid connections. We have not got very far with this topic – and I am very surprised. It is still not absolutely clear how we will bring the electricity from the aforementioned 20-gigawatt installations planned for the North and Baltic Sea ashore. This is astounding, seeing as everyone knows how long it takes to realize a project of these dimensions. We need large additional invest-ments today to feed tomorrow's offshore wind energy into the grid. This would also make the financing easier. Whether the banks really do get into the offshore wind energy business will certainly depend also on whether we can prove that wind energy at sea can be just as profitable as it is on land.

How many offshore turbines from REpower will there be standing in the sea by 2020?

(After a while of thinking) We should have installed our 1,000th offshore turbine by then.

未来已经来临
The future has already begun

2009年12月,世界各国都密切关注着哥本哈根世界气候大会。人们期待联合国气候委员会能制定出具有转折性意义的全球气候和能源政策。然而,结果却令人失望:近200个与会国家的元首或政府首脑对各国在气候变化中的作用存在较大分歧。虽然如此,此次会议仍就减少温室气体排放这一最小目标基本达成了协议,以期在2050年时全球气温最多上升2℃。

世界上许多地方已出现了气候变化的前期征兆,气候变化已经引起了很多灾难。但现在不是逃避的时候,也不能寄希望于这种现象会自动消失,即使目前还没有成功达成协议来替代《京都议定书》。相反,哥本哈根气候峰会上达成的基础协议再次清楚地显示出:如果后代子孙想要有一个适宜的生活环境或生存环境,现在急需根本转变。要达到这种效果,必须重构现代社会,包括汽车行业、运输行业、私营行业、工业,当然特别是能源行业。脱碳是关键词汇之一,意思是指从依赖于石油、汽油和煤的经济中转变。即使最具怀疑态度的人也不再继续争论,只有使用可再生能源才能实现这点,若要使世界摆脱二氧化碳的困扰,化石燃料和核能也将被逐步取代。此外,煤炭、石油、天然气和铀储量的减少正驱使能源价格上涨。只有那些早先投资于可再生能源的国家能够避免能源价格的急剧上涨,不依赖能源,确保他们的长期能源安全。

在这种情况下,风能是迄今为止的主要驱动力。仅二十年时间,风能已从一个细分市场发展为一个主要行业,世界范围内有几十万的人为它工作。目前,仅德国、丹麦、西班牙、中国和美国等为数不多的几个国家将风能视为发电的能源。风电装机容量每年都会打破新纪录。但仅这几个国家所作出的这些努力对于提高风能在总的发电市场中的份额还远远不够。所有专家一致认为扩大风电市场无法在陆上上实现,特别是人口密集的欧洲,那里没有足够的可利用空间。

更新发电设备是指用更大更先进的风机取代老旧风机,将来肯定会增加,同时,优先使用风能的地区也将扩大,但不是无限度的。因此,在发展陆上风能的同时,还必须着力发展海上风电装机容量。海洋为未来清洁能源提供了广阔的空间。继续推动扩大海上风电装机容量能够成功为传统发电厂创造可持续发电的未来资源。

向海上推进——无限扩张?

德国花了整整十年时间第一次向海洋时代迈出重大一步,实现了阿尔法·文图斯试验场的建造。冗长的政治讨论让一些先驱开发商在

In December 2009 the world watched events in Copenhagen, spellbound. The UN Climate Summit was supposed to be the turning point for global climate and energy policy. However, the results were disappointing: the leaders of almost 200 countries in attendance were too far apart in their positions. Yet at least there was basic agreement on a minimal goal – to reduce greenhouse gas emissions in an attempt to stop the planet warming by more than two degrees Celsius by 2050.

The first signs of a changing climate are already evident in many parts of the world, and climate change is already causing much damage. However, this is not the time to stick one's head in the sand and hope it goes away, even if there is not (yet) a successor agreement to the Kyoto Protocol. Quite the contrary: the exhaustive negotiations in Copenhagen once again showed clearly that a fundamental turnaround in outlook is needed more urgently than ever, if future generations are to have a chance of an acceptable quality of life, or even survival. To be effective, a restructuring of modern society is needed across all areas – mobility, transportation, private households, industry, and of course the energy industry in particular. Decarbonisation is one of the key words, meaning a shift away from an economy based on oil, gas and coal. Even the most sceptical no longer dispute that this will be possible only with the use of renewable energies. Fossil fuel and nuclear power will have to be replaced step by step if the world is to escape from the CO_2 trap. Furthermore, dwindling reserves of coal, petroleum, natural gas and uranium are driving up energy prices. Only countries that invest early on in renewable energies will be able to escape this price spiral, become energy-independent and ensure their own long-term energy security.

Wind-energy has thus far been the driving force in this scenario. In just two decades it has grown from a niche market to a major industry that employs several hundred thousand people worldwide. Wind energy is an established and accepted factor in electricity generation in Germany, Denmark, Spain, China and the US, to name just a few countries. The expansion of wind-energy capacity breaks new records year after year. But these efforts by themselves will not be enough to substantially boost wind's share in overall electrical generation. All the experts agree that such an expansion will not be possible on land alone. Especially in densely populated Europe, there is simply not enough space available.

Repowering, that means the replacement of older turbines with larger and more modern ones, will certainly increase in the future, and priority areas for wind energy use will be expanded, but this expansion cannot go beyond a certain limit. Therefore, along with growth in onshore wind energy, the development of offshore capacity must be pursued. The sea offers plenty of space for the clean energy of the future. A con-

还没启动项目前就耗完了资金。而且欧洲邻国后来居上，超过德国成为风能大国。但是进一步的观察表明，德国计划的搁置是有积极原因的。自然环境保护的倡议者、旅游业、渔业、海军和航运业的相关利益方表达了他们的担忧，能源业也表达了他们的保守意见。争论导致德国海工项目计划一再搁置，而不完善的经济框架，以及未并网问题阻碍了所有进程。但是这个漫长的过程仍为德国带来了利益。今日海上风机的额定功率远远高于几年前，而且德国联邦议院2006年通过了《加速基础设施建造规划法案》，让风电场并网更简单。此外，2009年《德国专属经济区域规划条例》为可持续海上经济活动提供了首份官方措施目录。这意味着德国海岸乱开发现象可以避免。这项基础条例对于早期防止海洋环境和海上风能需求之间的冲突有重大意义。和陆上一样，海上也建立了自然保护区，这就是为什么德国海工项目选址要远离海岸，与浅滩海国家公园保持安全距离。浅滩海国家公园是北海的"育儿地"，2009年被联合国教科文组织列为世界自然遗产。保护海洋环境是德国开发海上风电的主要挑战，在阿尔法·文图斯海上风电试验场进行生态研究具有高度重要性。

德国并不是唯一一个计划在北海和波罗的海进行海上风能开发的国家，几乎所有沿海的欧洲国家都计划在接下来的几年内转战海上。欧洲风能协会预测，到2030年，欧洲装机容量将达1500亿兆瓦。以今

tinued push to expand offshore wind energy capacity can succeed in creating a future source of sustainable electricity generation, on the scale of conventional power plants.

The offshore push – an unlimited expansion?

It took an entire decade for Germany to take its first major step into the offshore age with the realisation of the alpha ventus test field. Lengthy political discussions caused some of the pioneering developers to run out of funds before they could even get started. Meanwhile, European neighbours forged ahead, leaving Germany the leading wind-energy country, behind. But a closer look reveals that there were some good reasons behind the delays. Advocates of nature protection, tourism, fisheries, the Navy and shipping interests were able to make their concerns heard, and the energy industry also expressed its own reservations. The debate caused repeated delays of German offshore projects, while inadequate economic framework conditions, as well as unresolved issues with grid connections hindered all progress. But this long process has brought some benefits, too. Today's offshore wind turbines have much higher rated capacities than a few years ago, and the Infrastructure Planning Acceleration Law passed by the German Bundestag in 2006 has made grid connection easier. In addition, as of 2009 a planning ordinance for the German Exclusive Economic Zone (EEZ) provided the first official catalogue of measures for sustainable

星型叶轮安装高度令人叹为观止。这项工作需要经验丰富的施工队伍一丝不苟地高度集中注意力才能完成。
The rotor star is docked to the nacelle at breathtaking heights. Precision and maximum concentration are required from the experienced construction team.

economic activity at sea. This means that chaotic developments off the coasts of Germany will be avoided. This basic tool is of enormous importance for preventing conflicts between the needs of the maritime environment and offshore wind energy at an early stage. Just as on land, nature protection zones have been set up at sea, which is why the German offshore projects are located so far from shore, at a safe distance from the Wadden Sea National Park, the 'nursery' of the North Sea which became a UNESCO World Natural Heritage area in 2009. Protection of the maritime environment is one of the major challenges in the development of offshore wind energy in Germany, and ecological research is a high priority at the alpha ventus test field.

But Germany is not alone in its plans for offshore wind energy in the North and Baltic Seas. Almost all European countries with a coastline plan to go offshore in the next few years. The European Wind Energy Association (EWEA) predicts that up to 150 gigawatts could be installed in European waters by 2030. At today's output levels, that would translate into 30,000 wind turbines. A look at recent history and at what is currently feasible gives an idea of the prospects: "I predict that the growth rates in offshore wind energy will be comparable to the development on land during the last 20 years," says Andreas Wagner, Managing Director of the German Offshore Wind Energy Foundation. In 1995 there were only 2,500 megawatts of wind energy capacity installed across the entire EU. In early 2010, more than 75,000 megawatts have

天的发电水平计算，相当于3万台风力发电机。回顾这几年的历程以及目前的可行性，德国海上风能基金会执行总裁安德烈·瓦格纳对风能行业的发展前景提出了自己的观点："我可以预测海上风电的增长率将与近20年陆上风电的发展速度媲美"。1995年，全欧洲的风电装机容量仅为2500兆瓦。2010年初，超过75000兆瓦，其中2000兆瓦为海上装机容量。海上风电扩张的原因不难发现：目前，风能行业处在大规模经济地生产可再生能源的阶段。

欧洲前景

德国政府支持海上风电的发展已有时日。官方计划呼吁2030年前德国专属经济区域EEZ的风电装机容量达到25000兆瓦，为德国提供远远超过其它可再生能源的电能。根据德国环境部2008年发起的"2050年先期研究"，可再生能源最早在2030年就能满足德国50%的电力需求。其中1/3将由海上风电提供。

当然，北海和波罗的海的其它沿海国家也并不是悄然无息。英国政府特别制定了一系列宏伟计划，并确信北海将成为欧洲未来的发电主力。目前海上的装机容量数据显示，英国已居欧洲海上装机容量的首位。截止2009年，英国总装机容量已接近600兆瓦。英国首轮投标项目几乎已经实现，第二轮投标项目正在实施中，第三轮关于海上250亿兆瓦总体装机容量的项目投标结果在2010年初宣布。

海上电网

无论未来的主导趋势如何，未来几十年内北海和波罗的海将建造的风电场必须形成大型联网输电系统，因为电力供需不是恒常不变的。所以必须通过跨区域的电力交换来平衡区域供电波动，以实现经济供电，同时满足市场需求。未来海上风电场将不仅与其最近的陆地馈入点连接，风场之间也将实现连接，形成全欧洲的"超级电网"。克里格斯·弗拉克项目在波罗的海起到了先锋作用，来自丹麦、瑞典和德国的三个电网系统营运商计划建立互相连接的海上电网。通过德国、斯堪的那维亚、英国、法国、比利时、荷兰之间的海底电缆进行电力转换，长期以后可能在全北海实现。2009年末，北海临国发起倡议。最后达成的协议是，德国沿海风电场暂停供电时，由英国风电场为德国提供电力，反之亦然。此外，海上电力生产必须与陆上电力生产平衡。如果北海暴风使所有风电场的风机以额定功率运转10个或20个小时，传统电厂则必须限制电力生产。或者必须另外增加储电设施避免电过剩，例如挪威水电库。要充分做到这点，必须至少提前12或24小时了解天气情况。这意味着精确的风力预测系统将起到重要作用。风能研究机构与输电系统营运商协作开发配置此类系统已有多年。截至目前，该预测系统仅对德国陆上风电场的电力馈入起作用。迄今为止从中获得的积极经验促使人们计划将该预测系统推广运用到海上风电场。除先进的天气预测系统和电网扩大之外，电子汽车和电子移动系统也将根据市场需要为智能电网集成提供新的可能性，目前，这在技术上已具有可行性。未来，大量电子汽车能在其电池中储存海上电能。

been installed across the EU, of which about 2,000 megawatts offshore. The reasons for the new dynamism in offshore wind expansion are not hard to find: today, the wind industry is in a position to generate renewable energy economically and on a large scale.

European outlook

The German government has been supporting the expansion of offshore wind energy for some time now. Official plans call for up to 25,000 megawatts to be installed in the German EEZ by 2030, delivering more power than any other renewable energy source in the country. According to the 'Lead Study 2050' commissioned by the German Environmental Ministry in 2008, renewable energy could cover 50 percent of Germany's electricity requirements as early as 2030. Just under a third of this is to be generated by offshore wind farms alone.

Of course, other countries around the North and Baltic Sea have not been sleeping. The British government in particular has set itself ambitious goals and is betting on the North Sea as the future powerhouse of Europe. Measured in capacity currently installed at sea, Great Britain has become the European leader. By the end of 2009 there were already just under 600 megawatts of generation capacity off the British Isles. The first Round of British tenders has been almost fully realised, a second one is being implemented, and the results of Round 3 with a total offshore potential of 25 gigawatts were announced in early 2010.

Offshore grids

Whatever the future holds, the wind farms that are to be set up in the North and Baltic Seas in the next few decades will need to grow into one large, networked power transmission system - because neither supply nor demand for electricity are constant. It will therefore be necessary to balance regional power feed-in fluctuations via a cross-regional power exchange, to offer a power supply that is economical and meets demand. Offshore wind farms of the future will not just be connected to their nearest feed-in point ashore, but will also be interconnected with each other to create a pan-European 'supergrid'. The Kriegers Flak project could play a pioneering role in the Baltic Sea, where three system operators from Denmark, Sweden and Germany intend to establish an interconnected joint offshore grid. Power-supply exchange via submarine cables between Germany, Scandinavia, Great Britain, France, Belgium and the Netherlands will be possible just about everywhere in the North Sea in the long run. An initiative by these North Sea-neighbouring countries was launched in late 2009. Finally, wind farms off the UK will supply their electric power to Germany when there is a lull in the wind off the German coast, and vice-versa. Furthermore, the power produced at sea must be balanced with that generated on land. If a storm over the North Sea makes all wind farms run at rated capacity for ten or twenty hours, conventional power plants will need to be throttled back. Alternatively, new additional storage capacities such as Norwegian hydropower reservoirs will have to be integrated in order to avoid excess power generation. To do this well, it is necessary to know meteorological conditions at least twelve or even 24 hours in advance. This means that accurate wind-forecasting systems will become even more important. Wind-energy researchers have already deployed these systems for a couple of years in collaboration with transmission system operators. To date, forecasting has only concerned the feed-in of power produced by the German onshore wind

如果德国北海要在2030年前实现25000兆瓦的风电装机容量，还需要做出巨大努力。这要求新的物流概念实现风机安装、营运和维护。目前沿海区域正在另外建造生产基础设施和风机所需的设施。生产自动化在不断进步，几年后标准风机的功率可能达到10兆瓦。风能仍将是德国乃至全欧洲就业率增长的主要驱动力。EWEA认为，到2030年，全欧洲将有375000人在风能行业工作，其中将有215000人在海洋风电领域工作。

阿尔法·文图斯海上风电试验场不仅是德国，也是全欧洲海上工业的里程碑项目，因为这个先驱风电场证明了深海项目不再是遥远的梦想。

未来已经来临。风能业和能源业正迎来一个崭新的时代。荷兰早期的风能研究领军人物和奥尔登堡大学的荣誉博士约斯·博伊尔斯肯斯说："建造风力发电系统在70年代是一件困难却令人激动的事，未来30年会更加成熟。"就像业内其他人一样，他对未来充满信心。深海项目的机遇广阔，然而面临的挑战也将更大。

farms. However, the experience gained thus far has been so positive that it is planned to extend the forecasting systems to offshore wind farms. In addition to sophisticated weather forecasting techniques and physical grid expansion, electric cars and e-mobility systems offer promising new possibilities on the demand side for smart grid integration, already technically feasible today. In future, large fleets of electric cars may be able to store a part of the electricity generated at sea in their batteries.

If 25,000 megawatts are indeed to be installed in the German North Sea alone by 2030, tremendous efforts will need to be made. New logistics concepts are already required for setting up, operating and maintaining these turbines. Additional manufacturing capacity is currently being built for the construction of foundations and wind turbines along the coast. Production automation will make progress, and a standard turbine could have a capacity of ten megawatts or more in a few years' time. Wind energy will remain an important driver of job growth in Germany and throughout Europe. The EWEA assumes that by 2030 some 375,000 people will be working in the wind-energy industry Europe-wide, of which 215,000 alone will be employed in the offshore sector.

The alpha ventus test field is a major milestone – not just for the German offshore industry but for the whole of Europe, because this pioneering wind farm proves that projects in deep waters far out at sea are no longer just a distant vision.

The future has already begun. A new era is dawning for wind power as well as for the energy industry. "Building wind-power systems from scratch back in the 'seventies was already exciting, but this will be even more true over the next three decades," says Jos Beurskens, Dutch wind pioneer of the early days and honorary Doctor at Oldenburg University. Just like the rest of the industry, he is very positive about future prospects. Yet while the opportunities out at sea are big, the challenges ahead may be even bigger.

附录 Appendix

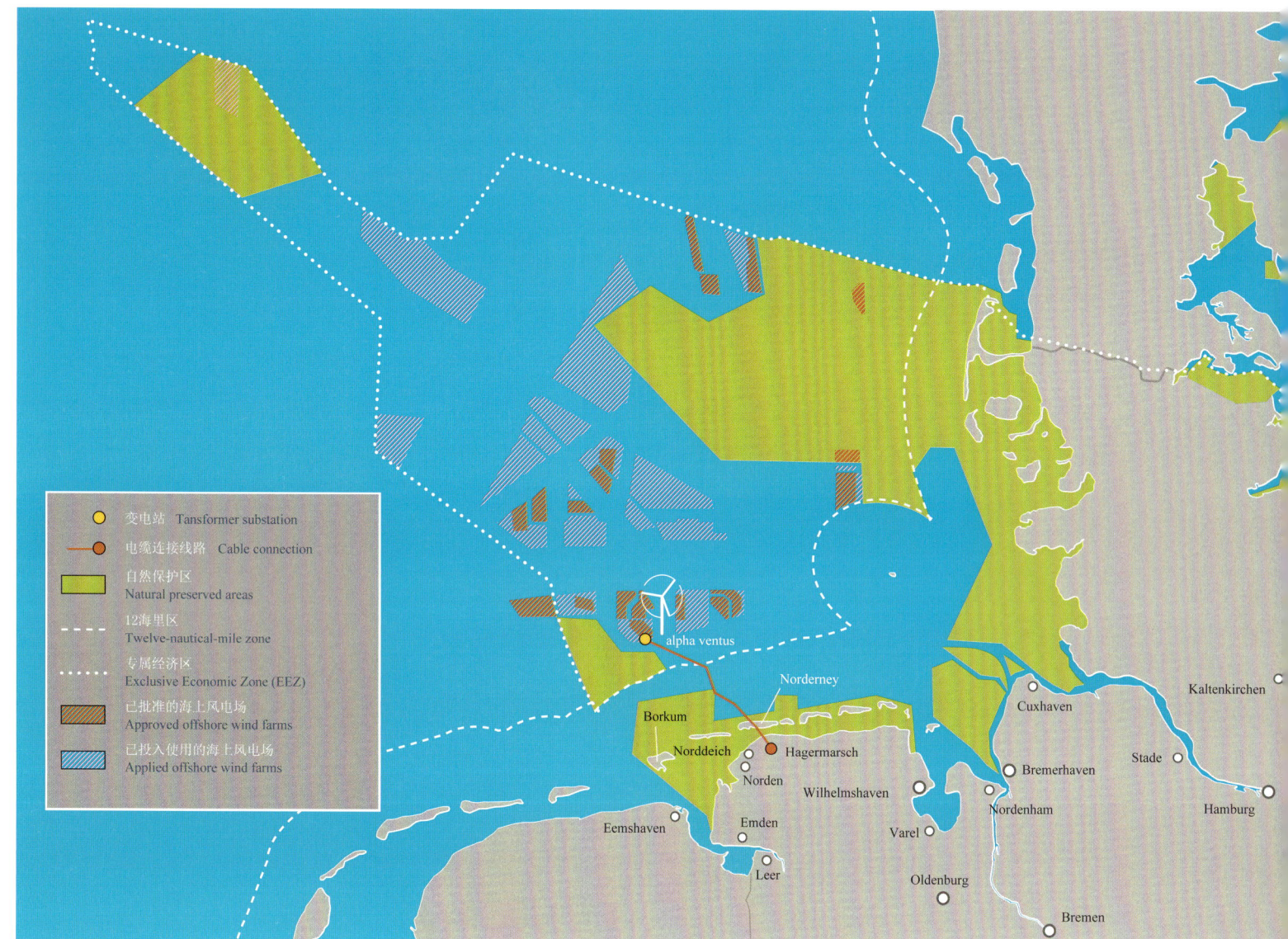

阿尔法·文图斯的运营商、发起者及审批机关
Operators & Initiators & Approval Authority for alpha ventus

柏林 BERLIN
德国联邦环境、自然保护及核能安全部（BMU）
Federal Ministry for Environment,
Nature Conservation and Reactor Safety (BMU))

汉堡 HAMBURG
德国联邦海事与水文局（BSH）
Federal Maritime and Hydrographic Agency (BSH)
Vattenfall AG, 欧洲大瀑布电力有限公司

慕尼黑 MÜNCHEN
德国意昂气候与可再生能源公司
E.ON Climate & Renewables GmbH

诺尔登 NORDEN
阿尔法·文图斯控制中心
alpha ventus control centre

诺德代希 NORDDEICH
阿尔法·文图斯服务港 Service port

奥尔登堡 OLDENBURG
EWE公司

瓦雷尔 VAREL
德国海上风能基金会
German Offshore Wind Energy Foundation

阿尔法·文图斯建造过程中涉及到的制造商、安装公司及物流公司
Companies involved in manufacturing, installation and logistics

拜罗伊特 BAYREUTH
transpower有限责任公司

挪威 卑尔根 BERGEN Norway
NorWind瑞能5兆瓦导管架式桩基设计、建造与安装的总承包商
General contractor for REpower 5M jacket design, construction and installation
电缆铺设自升式平台 Barge cable installer

不来梅 BREMEN
AMBAU有限责任公司 5兆瓦和M5000塔架制造
5M and M5000 tower manufacturing

不来梅港 BREMERHAVEN
阿海珐Multibrid股份有限公司 M5000机舱制造
M5000 nacelle manufacturing
瑞能系统有限责任公司 5兆瓦机舱和轮毂制造
5M nacelle and hub manufacturing
WeserWind有限责任公司 联营变电站
Transformer station consortium

苏格兰 巴提斯兰德 BURNTISLAND Scotland
巴提斯兰德制造有限公司 导管架式桩基制造
Jacket manufacturing

库克斯港 CUXHAVEN
DEWI认证及海上风能研究中心 海上样机试验场
Test field for offshore-prototypes

德累斯顿 DRESDEN
阿海珐能源技术有限公司 变电站（30/110Kv）
Transformer station (30/110 kV)

迪拜 DUBAI (VAR)
NICO Middle East Ltdo 电缆铺设船
Cable-laying ship

哈格马施 HAGERMARSCH
陆上变电站
Substation onshore

汉堡 HAMBURG
豪赫蒂夫建筑公司 Odin自升式平台
Odin jack-up barge
联营变电站
Transformer station consortium

卡尔滕基兴 KALTENKIRCHEN
孟克有限公司 三脚式桩基打夯工作
Ramming works for tripod

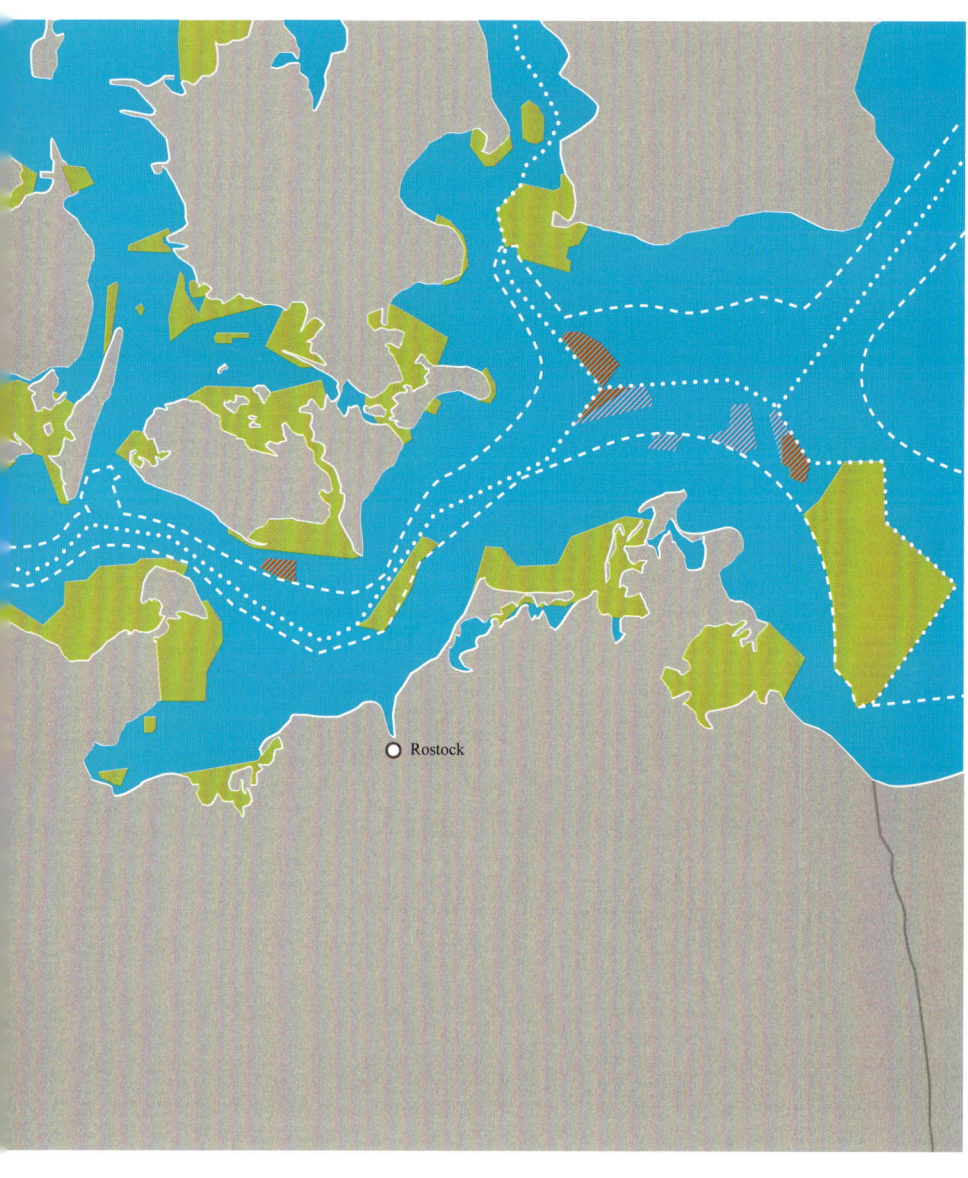

莱尔 LEER
海上风能技术有限公司（OWT）
M5000桩基和塔架包覆工程
Engineering of M5000 foundation structure
and tower cladding
Briese船舶公司 Mega Motti顶推自升式平台
Mega Motti pusher barge

荷兰 莱顿 LEIDEN Netherlands
Heerema海事承包商
"Thialf"号重吊船
Thialf heavy-lift ocean vessel

丹麦 伦纳斯考 LUNDERSKOV Denmark
艾尔姆玻璃纤维制品有限公司 5M叶轮
5M rotor blades

曼海姆 MANNHEIM
比尔芬格柏格集团 联营变电站
Transformer station consortium

苏格兰 梅西尔 METHIL Scotland
巴提斯兰德制造有限公司 瑞能5M导管架式桩基制造
Jacket manufacturing for REpower 5M

苏格兰 蒙特罗斯 MONTROSE Scotland
ICH制钢有限公司 导管架式桩基样板制造
Template manufacturing for jackets

诺尔登哈姆 NORDENHAM
北德电缆有限公司
用于内场布线的Stemat 82电缆铺设船
Stemat 82 cable laying barge for infield cabling

荷兰 鲁尔蒙德 ROERMOND Netherlands
Sif集团公司 三脚式桩基钢管
Tubular elements for tripods

罗斯托克 ROSTOCK
EEW机械制造有限公司 导管架式桩基
Piles for jackets

荷兰 鹿特丹 ROTTERDAM Netherlands
斯米特起重机 "Taklift 4"号浮吊
Taklift 4 floating crane

荷兰 斯利德雷赫特 SLIEDRECHT Netherlands
自升式平台公司
JB114和JB115自升式平台
JB 114 and JB 115 jack-up platform

施塔德 STADE
PN叶轮有限公司 阿海珐Multibrid叶轮叶片制造
Rotor blade manufacturing AREVA Multibrid

挪威 韦尔达尔 VERDAL Norway
M5000三脚式桩基建造
Tripod construction for M5000

威廉港 WILHELMSHAVEN
变电站导管架式桩基安装
Transformer station jacket assembly

比利时 兹韦恩德雷赫特 ZWIJNDRECHT Belgium
Buzzard自升式平台导管架式桩基打夯作业
Ramming works for jackets, Buzzard jack-up platform

大事记
CHRONOLOGY

1998

Aerodyn能源系统股份有限公司第一次在汉诺威展览会上呈现额定功率为5兆瓦的Multibrid风机的基本技术概念。

Aerodyn Energiesysteme GmbH presents for the first time at the Hanover Fair the basic technical concept for the Multibrid turbine with a rated output of five megawatts.

1999

瑞能系统公司的前身为Rendsburger pro & pro 能源系统公司，其工程师首次考虑多兆瓦级海上风力发电机。

Engineers at the Rendsburg pro & pro Energiesysteme, later to become REpower Systems AG, consider an offshore multi-megawatt turbine for the first time.

9月

Prokon北方能源系统公司向德国联邦海事与水文局申请博尔库姆西海上风电场建造许可。

September Prokon Nord Energiesysteme GmbH applies to the German Federal Maritime and Hydrographic Agency (Bundesamt für Seeschifffahrt und Hydrographie, (BSH) for a construction permit for the Borkum West offshore wind farm.

2000

年末时，Pfleiderer 公司建立了Multibrid开发公司，并与aerodyn公司签署了一份专利许可协议。

Towards the end of the year Pfleiderer AG founds the Multibrid Entwicklungsgesellschaft mbH and signs a patent license agreement with aerodyn.

12月

德国联邦经济和技术委员委托项目管理和执行组织Projekttrager Julich（PTJ）调查海上试验场地的建设。生产商、制造业、认证机构和VDMA（德国机械设备制造业联合会）都要求发表谈话。

December The German Federal Ministry of Economics and Technology (Bundesminis-terium für Wirtschaft, BMWi) commissions the project management and executing organi-zation Projektträger Jülich (PTJ) to investigate the construction of an offshore test field. Manufacturers, industry, certifiers and VDMA (German Engineering Federation) are all called upon to make a statement.

2001

2月

德国联邦经济技术部、德国联邦环境、自然保护及核能安全部（BMU），以及德国机械设备制造业联合会同意将UMTS无线频率销售所得资金中的部分用于建设海上试验场和研究平台。

February The BMWi, the German Federal Ministry for the Environment, Nature Conservation and Nuclear Safety (Bundesministerium für Umwelt, Naturschutz und Reaktorsicherheit, BMU) and the German Engineering Federation (VDMA) agree that funds from the sale of UMTS wireless frequencies should be used for the erection of an offshore test field and research platforms.

4月

瑞能公司董事会决定进一步开发和建造额定功率为5兆瓦的海上风力发电机。

April The Board of REpower Systems AG decides to further develop and construct an offshore turbine with a rated output of five megawatts.

春季

用于建造海上试验场和海洋研究平台的资金显然不足。BMU承担海上风力发电相关的生态学研究。联邦政府部门最初考虑资助连接试验场地的海底电缆；然而这项提议不久就被驳回。BMWi现在决定专注于海洋研究平台的建造。

Spring It becomes clear that the funds for promoting an offshore test field and the construc-tion of research platforms are insufficient.
The BMU takes on the accompanying ecological research for offshore wind power. Initial considerations are made at ministerial level about subsidizing the submarine cable for connecting up a test field; however this idea is later rejec-ted. The BMWi now decides to concentrate on the construction of research platforms.

7月

位于汉堡的德国劳氏船级社风能有限公司接受委托评估海洋研究平台的建造工作。接着确定了海洋研究平台在北部和波罗的海的位置。FINO 1将建造在博尔库姆西。

July Hamburg-based Germanischer Lloyd WindEnergie GmbH is commissioned with the job of pushing forward the construction of research platforms. Locations are subsequently defined for the research platforms in the North and Baltic Seas (Forschungsplattformen in Nord- und Ostsee, FINO). FINO 1 is to be erected in Borkum West.

11月

Prokon北方公司获得主管部门（BSH）对博尔库姆西项目的建造许可。成为第一个获批的海工项目。

November Prokon Nord is granted construction approval for Borkum West by the responsible authority (BSH). This is the first consented off-shore project.

2002

2月

德国联邦政府宣布"利用海上风能的战略文件"。计划于2006年达到500MW装机容量，2010年达到2000MW至3000MW。长期目标（2030年前）达到25000MW。

February The German Federal Government announces its 'Strategy paper for utilizing wind power at sea'. 500 megawatts are planned by 2006 and 2,000 to 3,000 megawatts by 2010. The long-term goal (by 2030) is to achieve 25,000 megawatts of installed capacity.

6月

在欧洲招标后，FINO 1的建造合同正式签署。该项目由汉堡F+Z建筑公司和不来梅Bugsier航运与打捞公司公司共同承担。德国劳氏风能有限公司负责协调项目的建造、安装和调试。

June After a European-wide invitation to tender, the construction contract for FINO 1 is signed. The task goes to the consortium of F + Z Baugesellschaft mbH, Hamburg, and Bugsier Reederei- und Bergungsgesellschaft mbH & Co, Bremerhaven. Germanischer Lloyd WindEnergie GmbH (GL Wind) coordinates construction, erection and commissioning.

12月

BMU负责研究可再生能源以及海洋研究平台。

December The BMU takes over responsibility for researching renewable energies and therefore also for the research platforms.

2003

安装FINO 1。在海洋研究平台上开始进行测量。

FINO 1 is erected. Measurements start on this research platform.

12月

Prokon北方能源系统公司从Pfleiderer公司接管Multibrid开发公司。

December Prokon Nord Energiesysteme GmbH takes over Multibrid Entwicklungsgesellschaft mbH from Pfleiderer AG.

2004

10月

完成位于布伦斯比特尔的瑞能5兆瓦样机的安装。并于11月16号并网。

Enercon股份有限公司完成了屹立于埃姆斯河畔E-112的安装。它是德国第一个近岸风力发电机。

October The erection of the prototype of the REpower 5M in Brunsbüttel is completed; on 16th November it is connected up to the power grid.

Enercon GmbH completes the erection of an E-112, standing in direct proximity to the embankments of the River Ems. It is Germany's first near-shore wind turbine.

12月

不来梅港的Multibrid 5兆瓦样机投入运营。

December The prototype of the Multibrid M5000 goes into operation in Bremerhaven.

2005

1月

第四届德国国家海事会在不来梅举行。国家政要、组织机构、协会和风机生产商第一次组建海上风电专题研讨会。与会者向政要表达了建造多兆瓦级风机试验场地的愿望。

January The 4th National Maritime Conference of the German Federal Chancellor takes place in Bremen. For the first time, state politicians, organizations, institutions and manufacturers of wind turbines set up a workshop for off-shore wind power. Participants in the workshop express their desire to the politicians to set up a test field for multi-megawatt turbines.

6月/7月

成立了"利用和开发海上风能的德国工业基金会",简称"海上风能基金会",并向BMU提出申请要求支持购买德国海上试验场地的许可权。

June/July The German Industry Foundation for the Use and Exploration of Wind Energy at Sea (Stiftung der deutschen Wirtschaft für die Nutzung und Erforschung der Windenergie auf See), shortened to the 'Offshore Wind Energy Foundation', is formed. It makes an application to the BMU for support in purchasing the license rights to a German offshore test field.

8月

海上风能基金会获批五百万欧元拨款。

August A grant of 5 million euros to the Offshore Wind Energy Foundation is approved.

9月

海上风能基金会用五百万欧元向Prokon北方能源系统公司购买了博尔库姆西海工项目的使用权。

September The Offshore Wind Energy Foundation buys the utilization rights to the Borkum West offshore project from Prokon Nord Energiesysteme GmbH for five million euros.

2006

4月

德国总理府召开德国能源峰会。能源供应商意昂公司、EWE公司和大瀑布电力公司同意默克尔总理的提议,建立和运营德国海上试验场地。

April Energy summit in the German Chancel-lery. The energy suppliers E.ON, EWE and Vattenfall agree to Chancellor Merkel's pro-posal to set up and run a German offshore test field.

5月

BMU战略内容为Bad Zwischenahn的风能研究。生产商和业界机构就试验场地的研究项目和目标进行了讨论。

BMU宣布将5000万欧元投入海上试验场地的计划研究。

八家领先风能机构为研究项目提案,协调工作由德国Kassel太阳能技术研究机构承担,该研究所于2009年1月与新成立的弗劳恩霍夫风能及能源系统技术研究所合并。

May BMU strategy talks on wind-energy research in Bad Zwischenahn. Discussions are held with manufacturers and institutes regarding research projects and goals for the test field.

The BMU announces that 50 million euros are being made available for the planned research in the offshore test field.

Eight leading wind energy research institutes make proposals for research projects – coor-dinated by the Kassel Institute for Solar Energy Supply Technology (Institut für Solare Energie-versorgungstechnik, ISET), which merged in January 2009 with the newly-founded Fraun-hofer Institute for Wind Energy and Energy System Technology (Fraunhofer-Institut für Windenergie und Energiesystemtechnik, IWES).

7月

EWE、意昂和大瀑布电力公司建立德国海上试验场地和基础设施。

July EWE, E.ON and Vattenfall establish the German Offshore Test Field and Infrastructure (Deutsche Offshore- Testfeld und Infrastruktur) GmbH, abbreviated to DOTI.

8月

瑞能系统公司第一次在海上建立5兆瓦风力发电机。该风机位于苏格兰东海岸的Beatrice油田附近,安装在44米水深的导管架式桩基上。

August For the first time a 5M from REpower Systems AG is erected at sea. It is located near the offshore oil field Beatrice off the east coast of Scotland, standing on a jacket foundation in a depth of water of 44 meters.

9月

BMU发布了支持风能部门的措施,重点在于试验场地研究方面。在这之前对各种研究项目的内容和重要性进行了集中讨论。

September The BMU publishes support measu-res for the wind-energy sector, with emphasis on research in the test field. Preceding this had been an intensive discussion about the content and importance of various research projects.

秋季 海上风能基金会组织了集中讨论，就电缆连接问题达成一致意见，成立了并网公司GbR，该公司拥有八个潜在风电场项目组织机构的代表，他们同意共用穿过德国诺得尼岛的电缆线。该电缆不受浅滩海国家公园规定的制约。

Autumn Lead-managed by the Offshore Wind Energy Foundation, intensive discussions lead to agreement on the issue of power-cable connections. The Netzanschlussgesellschaft (grid connection company) GbR is founded, in which the eight potential wind-farm project organizers are represented and who then agree on a common cable route through the island of Norderney. This cable route is exempted from the regulations covering the Wadden Sea National Park.

12月

海上风能基金会和DOTI签署了租赁协议。DOTI必须积极支持试验场的研究。

DOTI发出需要提供12台风力发电机的请求。

《德国加速基础设施建造规划法案》开始生效。它强制电网营运商意昂公司资助并建立电缆连接设施。

December A lease agreement is signed between the Offshore Wind Energy Foundation and DOTI. DOTI is obliged to support the research in the test field actively.

DOTI issues a Request for Tenders for twelve test-field turbines.

The German Act on Accelerated Infrastructure Planning (Infrastruktur-Planungsbeschleunigungsgesetz) comes into force. It obliges the grid operator E.ON Netz GmbH to finance and to build the cable connections.

2007

1月

BMU挑选计划研究项目。DOTI与ISET、DEWI、BSH和PTJ等相关研究机构协调内容。

德国风能研究机构与DOTI共同定义了独立项目的主要测量技术要求。

所谓的"空导管"建设工程在诺德奈启动，电缆将穿过"空导管"，连接风电场和陆地接入点。

January The BMU selects planned research projects. DOTI coordinates the contents with the research institutes involved: ISET, DEWI, BSH and PTJ.

The German Wind Energy Institute (Deutsche Windenergie-Institut, DEWI) defines the technical requirements for the individual projects for a central measurement concept, coordinated with the DOTI.

Construction work commences on Norderney for the so-called 'empty conduit', through which the cable is later to be run that will connect the wind-farm with the onshore feed-in point.

2月

诺德克斯公司完成了N90风机的建造和安装，该风机的标准输出功率为2.5MW，位于罗斯托克油港岸壁前方500米处。这个项目被载入史册成为德国第一台海上风力发电机。

DOTI发出基础设施建设招标书。

February Nordex AG completes the construction and installation of the N90 wind-energy generator, with a nominal output of 2.5 megawatts, 500 metres in front of the quay wall of the Rostock oil port in Breitling, a shallow, brackish body of water that opens into the Baltic Sea. This goes down in the books as the first German offshore wind turbine.

DOTI issues a Request for Tenders for foundations.

9月

阿海珐公司从Prokon北方能源系统公司收购了Multibrid 51%的股权。

September Die AREVA erwirbt von der Prokon Nord Energiesysteme GmbH 51 Prozent der Multibrid GmbH.

2008

4月14日

建筑工作在哈格马斯陆上变电站启动。这里将是未来海上电力接入110kV电网的场所。

14th April Construction work starts on the onshore transformer station in Hagermarsch. This is where the power produced at sea will be fed into the 110 kV grid in future.

5月8日

BMU批准了试验场的大部分研究项目。BMU在下萨克森州代表团柏林办事处举行了开幕典礼后，以RAVE（阿尔法•文图斯研究工作）的名义开始了研究项目。

8th May BMU approves most of the research projects in the test field. The BMU research initiative starts work under the name RAVE (research at alpha ventus) at an opening ceremony in the offices of the Lower Saxony state delegation in Berlin.

6月

德国联邦议院通过了《可再生能源法案》（EEG）修订案，增加海上风能的补偿。

June The German Bundestag (lower house of the Federal Parliament) passes the EEG (renewable energies law) amendment, allotting improved remuneration for offshore wind energy

春季，第一根连接风电场的电缆穿过诺得尼岛的"空导管"。

The first cable is inserted through the empty conduit completed in spring on Norderney to connect up the wind farm.

5月到8月

从Hilgenriedersiel到哈格马施变电站铺设了4.5公里长的陆地电缆。

May to August The 4.5 kilometre-long land cable is laid from Hilgenriedersiel to the transformer station in Hagermarsch.

9月5日

第一部分电缆穿过下萨克森州的浅滩海国家公园。需要约两周的时间铺设穿过泥滩、近五公里长的电缆。

5th September The first metres of cable section are laid through the Lower Saxony Wadden Sea National Park. Around two weeks are required to lay almost five kilometres of cable through the mudflats.

9月19日

海上建筑工作启动。变电站第一次打桩。

19th September Construction work begins at sea. The first blow to drive the foundation piles of the transformer station is struck.

9月27日

55公里左右的海底电缆从公海开始一直铺设到距离变电站的1000米处。

27th September Around 55 kilometres of submarine cable are laid from the open sea right up to the last 1,000 metres from the transformer station.

大事记 Chronology 183

9月28日

海上变电站峻工。未来阿尔法·文图斯风电场的第一步构造完工。剩余的建造工作因恶劣气候而中断。哈格马斯的变电站如今也已完工。

28th September The offshore transformer station is completed. This is the first structure completed for the future alpha ventus wind farm. The remaining construction work is subsequently interrupted due to bad weather. The transformer station at Hagermarsch is also now completed.

10月28日

德国联邦环境部部长西格马·加布里尔正式宣布BARD 5.0为德国第一台北海海上风机。这台由BARD工程公司提供的5兆瓦试验样机屹立在霍克西尔港Jade河河口引人注目的三脚式桩基上。

28th November Germany's Federal Minister of the Environment, Sigmar Gabriel, officially commissions BARD 5.0 as the first German offshore turbine in the North Sea. The five-mega-watt test and demonstration turbine from the company BARD Engineering GmbH stands in the estuary of the River Jade off Hooksiel, on a striking tri-pile foundation.

2009

1月1日

EEG修订案生效。

1st January The EEG amendment comes into force.

4月23日

经过冬天的停顿之后重新开始进行建筑工作。

23rd April Construction work is recommenced after the winter break.

5月5日

据报道，风电场并入110kv电网并接通。海底电缆和海上变电站准备运行。

5th May It is reported that the 110 kV grid connection for the wind farm has been switched on. The submarine cable and offshore transformer station are ready for operation.

6月1日

六根三脚式桩基被固定在海底。

1st June The six tripod foundations are firmly anchored onto the seabed.

7月15日

EEZ的第一台德国海上风力发电机阿海珐Multibrid 5兆瓦安装完毕。

15th July The first German offshore wind turbine in the EEZ – an AREVA Multibrid M5000 – is erected.

8月12日

阿尔法·文图斯风电试验场第一次将电力输送到大陆。

12th August The first power flows to the mainland from the test field alpha ventus.

9月9日

世界最强大的浮吊——海上作业船"Thialf"开始安装瑞能风机的六根导管架式桩基。这项工作几天之内就完成了。

9th September The high-seas work-ship 'Thialf', the most powerful floating crane in the world, starts erecting the six jacket foundations for the REpower turbines. The work is completed within just a few days.

秋季 六台瑞能风机组装完毕，安装在阿尔法·文图斯风电场的公海上。

Autumn The six REpower turbines are assembled and installed on the open sea at the alpha ventus site.

11月16日

第六台阿尔法·文图斯5兆瓦风机安装结束。拥有12台风机的阿尔法·文图斯风电场现已建成。

16th November The sixth 5M from REpower is erected. The alpha ventus wind farm, with its twelve turbines, has now been completed.

术语
GLOSSAR

A

Accompanying ecological research Analyses and measures aiming to improve knowledge of the con-structional and operational impact of offshore wind farms on the marine environment. They also aim to develop climate and ecosystem-friendly offshore wind power.

附属生态研究
为了进一步认知海上风电场在建造和运营时对海事环境产生的影响所使用的分析方法。也用于开发气候和生态友好的海上风电。

B

Beaufort Scale A 12-stage scale to estimate the wind force and classify wind speeds. It is named after the British admiral Francis Beaufort. Offshore *wind-energy converters can produce electricity from Wind Force 3 (gentle breeze, 4.0 to 5.5 metres/second). They reach their rated power at wind force 6 (strong breeze, 11.5 to 14.0 metres/second). Depending on turbine type, they cut off automatically at 25 metres/second (Wind Force 10, storm) or 30 metres/second (Wind Force 11, violent storm).

蒲福风级
用12级风力来估计风力大小和风速等级。以英国人海军军官Francis Beaufort名字命名。海上风能转换系统在3级风力时可进行发电（微风，4.0-5.5米/秒）。在6级风力（强风，11.5-14米/秒）时可达到额定功率。因风机型号不同，转换系统在25米/秒（10级风力，风暴）或30米/秒（11级风力，强风暴）时自动断开。

Benthos The entire group of small, seabed-dwelling immobile and mobile flora and fauna (including snails, mussels, worms and crabs).

底栖生物
生活在海底的固着或爬行的小动植物群（包括蜗牛、蚌、蠕虫和螃蟹）。

BMU The German Federal Ministry for the Environ-ment, Nature Conservation and Nuclear Safety, based in Berlin: www.bmu.de

BMU
德国联邦环境、自然保护及核能安全部，位于柏林：www.bmu.de

BSH The German Federal Maritime and Hydrographic Agency (FMHA) located in Hamburg. The BSH decides on the approval of offshore wind farms in the *EEZ. www.bsh.de

BSH
德国联邦海事与水文局（FMHA），位于汉堡。BSH负责审批在专属经济区域上建立海上风电场。

C

Cable-laying ship *Work-ship used for laying submarine cables.

电缆铺设船
用于铺设海底电缆的工作船。

Connection point Connection point is an onshore substation where the wind power produced at sea is fed into the power grid.

连接点
连接点是陆上变电站，将海上风电馈入电网。

D

DEWI The German Wind Energy Institute in Wilhelmshaven. Some of this research facility's responsibilities are to measure wind velocities at the FINO 1 research platform and to coordinate upcoming research projects as part of *RAVE. www.dewi.de

DEWI
位于威廉港的德国风能研究所。该研究所的一部分职责是测量FINO 1研究站的风速，协调即将开始的RAVE部分研究项目。www.dewi.de

DOTI German Offshore Test Field and Infrastructure GmbH & Co.KG. In July 2006, the three energy utilities E.ON, EWE and Vattenfall established DOTI as a joint venture in order to pool their activities effectively.

DOTI
德国海上试验风场与基础设施公司。2006年7月，意昂公司、EWE和大瀑布电力公司三家能源公司共同出资组建DOTI，以有效地共同开展海上活动。

E

EEG Renewable Energy Act – REA. It has governed the feeding-in of electricity produced from renewable energy into the public grid since 2000. The following applies to the feed-in of power generated in offshore wind farms: 13 eurocents/kWh are paid within the first twelve years of operation. The tariff rises to 15 cents per kilowatt hour if the project will be operational by December 31, 2015. It is reduced to 3.5 cents per kilowatt hour after 12 years of operation. However, the high initial tariff is paid for longer than twelve years if the wind farm is located more than twelve nautical miles off the coast and is set up in water depths of over 20 metres.

EEG
可再生能源法案——REA。2000年以来，该法案对可再生能源馈入到公共电网进行了相关规定。以下是关于海上风电电力馈入的具体规定：运营的前12年是13欧分每千瓦时。若该项目到2015年12月31日仍在运营中，则期间电价涨到15欧分。运营12年后电价减少到3.5欧分每千瓦时。然而，若风电场距离海岸12海里以上，并且建址水深超过20米，高初始电价将持续12年以上。

EEZ Exclusive Economic Zone. Coastal waters that lie beyond the 12-nautical-mile zone and are limited by the territorial waters of the neighbouring countries. In Germany the Federal Maritime and Hydrographic Agency (BSH) is responsible for issuing construction permits within the EEZ.

EEZ
专属经济区域。超过12英里的沿海水域，以邻国的水域为界。德国联邦海事与水文局（BSH）负责颁发EEZ的建造许可证。

EIA Environmental impact assessment. A procedure for examining projects whose impacts are likely to be detrimental to the environment. The EIA's report must be considered in project licence decisions.

EIA
环境影响评估。审核可能对环境造成危害的项目的程序。在决定发放项目许可证时必须考虑EIA报告。

F

FFH area Flora-Fauna-Habitat protection area. An area designated according to the EU's FFH directive for the protection of natural flora, fauna and habitats. Bird sanctuaries of equal status are also included. The objective is to link these areas together across Europe (Natura 2000 project). The areas are proposed by the German federal states and registered after analysis by the EU Commission. In late 2008, 22,945 regions throughout the EU with a combined land sur-face area of 661,503 km^2 (13.3 % of EU land area) along with maritime territory of 92,893 km^2 were designated as areas of Europe-wide interest. Some 4,675 areas with a land surface of 54,343 km^2 (9.9 % of land surface) and maritime territory of 19,134 km were in Germany. This includes almost the entire Wadden Sea off the German North Sea coast.

FFH区域
动植物栖息地保护区域。根据欧盟的FFH指令设立的保护区域，旨在保护大自然动植物及其栖息地。也包括对鸟类栖息地的保护。目的是将全欧洲的动物保护区汇总（2000年自然保护规划）。该区域是由德国联邦州提议，经欧盟委员会的分析后通过申请注册。2008年末，全欧洲22945个区域进行了汇总，陆地表面积达到661503平方公里（占欧洲陆地面积的13.3%），海事面积92893平方公里，作为欧洲共同利益区域。德国拥有4675个区域，陆地面积达54343平方公里（9.9%为陆地面积），海洋面积达19134平方公里。这些区域几乎包括了德国北海沿线的整个浅滩地。

FINO Abbreviation of Forschungsplattform in Nord- and Ostsee (Research Platform on North and Baltic Seas). To date three platforms have been set up: FINO 1 at the rim of the alpha ventus test field, FINO 2 in the Baltic Sea, about 30 kilometres north of the island of Rügen and FINO 3 in the North Sea, about 80 kilometres west of the island of Sylt. The chief task of these research platforms is measuring the wind velocity and wind direction at various heights. Furthermore, they collect all the meteorological information, such as oceano-graphic and ecologic data. www.fino-offshore.de

FINO
北海和波罗的海研究站。截止目前，已建立三个研究站：FINO 1位于阿尔法·文图斯海上风电试验场边缘；FINO 2位于波罗的海，大约在Rugen岛北30公里处；FINO 3位于北海，约在Sylt岛西80公里处。这些研究站的主要任务是测量风速和不同高度的风向。此外，他们也收集所有的气象信息，如有关海洋和生态的数据。www.fino-offshore.de

Floating crane A mobile crane floating on waters which belongs to the *work-ship class. It is normally used for lifting and moving especially heavy or large objects.

浮吊
漂浮在水上的一种移动式起重机，属于工作船的一种。常用于起吊和移动大件重物。

Foundation structure Foundation of an offshore *wind-energy converter. It may consist of steel or concrete. In the alpha ventus test field, two different steel foundation structures are used. A three-legged structure (tripod) and a lattice structure (jacket). The simplest foundation structure consists of a steel tube which is driven into the seabed (monopile). This, however, is only suitable for low water depths and therefore was not an option for the alpha ventus test field.

基础结构
海上风能转换系统的桩基。由钢或混凝土构成。在阿尔法·文图斯试验场中使用了两种钢制桩基，三脚式桩基和导管架式桩基。最简单的桩基由打入海底的钢管构成（单桩）。然而，这只适合于浅水域中，因而阿尔法·文图斯试验场的建造并未采用该桩基。

Fraunhofer IWES The Fraunhofer Institute for Wind Energy and Energy System Technology. In January 2009 the Institute was formed after the amalgamation of the Institute for Solar Energy Supply Technology (ISET) in Kassel and the Fraunhofer Center for Wind Energy and Maritime Technology (Fraunhofer CWMT) in Bremerhaven. The Fraunhofer IWES is located both in Bremerhaven and Kassel. www.iwes.fraunhofer.de

Fraunhofer IWES
弗劳恩霍夫风能及能源系统技术研究所。成立于2009年1月，由位于卡塞尔的太阳能供应技术研究所（ISET）和位于不来梅港的弗劳恩霍夫风能和海事技术中心（Fraunhofer CWMT）合并而成。在不来梅港和卡塞尔均有办事处。

H

HSE Health, Safety and Environment (also called Environment, Health & Safety, EH&S). The collective name given to a variety of environmental and work safety management systems applied by many major companies.

HSE
健康、安全和环境（也称环境、健康和安全，EH&S）。该集合名称用于评价众多大企业采用的不同环境和工作安全管理系统。

Hub Component of a *wind-energy converter (wind turbine). The hub is mounted on the end of the main drive shaft, to which the three rotor blades are attached.

轮毂
风能转换系统（风力发电机）的组成部件。该部件安装在主驱动轴的尾部，上面装有三个叶轮。

Hub height Distance of the wind turbine hub's centre point to the ground, or mean sea level.

轮毂高度
风力轮毂中心与地面或平均海平面的距离。

HVDC High-voltage, direct-current transmission. Electrical energy transmission with direct current voltages in the range from 100,000 to 1,000,000 volts. The three-phase AC current supplied by electricity generators (such as wind turbines) is first rectified to DC and then re-inverted to three-phase AC current at the end of the transmission line. HVDC is suitable for power transmission over longer distances and to transfer higher power capacities. A three-phase AC line is sufficient for the alpha ventus test field. However, offshore wind farms that are further than 100 kilometres off the coast will be connected by HVDC lines with connection points onshore in the years to come.

HVDC
高压直流输电。直流电压在10万伏到100万伏范围内电力的传输。发电机（如风力发电机）产生的三相交流电首先经过整流变成直流，然后在传输末端再次转换成三相交流电。HVDC适用于远距离电力传输和转换大容量电力。一条三相位交流电传输线对于阿尔法•文图斯海上风电试验场而言已经足够。然而在未来几年内，距离海岸100公里以上的风电场将由HVDC线路连接陆地的连接点。

I

Infield cabling Electrical interconnection of *wind-energy converters within a wind farm. The power cables from six wind turbines each will be formed into a ring and then routed as a submarine cable to the offshore transformer station in the alpha ventus test field.

内场布线
风电场内风能转换系统的电路连接。将六台风力发电机每台的电缆绕成一个环，然后作为海底电缆对阿尔法•文图斯风电试验场的变成站进行布线。

Infrastructure Planning Acceleration Act German law to accelerate planning procedures for large-scale infra-structure projects. It came into force on December 17, 2006 and obliges transmission grid operators to equip offshore wind farms with connections to the grid in their balancing zone.

《加快基础设施规划法案》
德国为加快规划大规模基础设施建设而通过的法律文件。于2006年12月17日生效，强制要求电网运营商在其平衡区域为海上风电场装备并网连接设备。

ISET Institute for Solar Energy Supply Technology in Kassel. By joining forces with the Fraunhofer Center for Wind Energy and Maritime Technology (Fraunhofer CWMT), Bremerhaven, in January 2009 it formed the *Fraunhofer IWES. Its brief is to coordinate the *RAVE programme.

ISET
位于卡塞尔的太阳能供应技术研究所。2009年1月与位于不来梅港的弗劳恩霍夫风能和海事技术中心（Fraunhofer CEMT）合并成为弗劳恩霍夫风能及能源系统研究所。机构的精简是为了合作研究阿尔法•文图斯项目。

IWES See *Fraunhofer IWES.

IWES
参见Fraunhofer IWES

J

Jacket *Foundation structure of an offshore *wind-energy converter.

导管架式桩基
海上风能转换系统桩基。

Jack-up platform Seagoing craft in the form of a pontoon, with legs that can be lowered at each of the four corners to support it securely on the sea floor. The platform is jacked up to permit working at sea even when the sea is rough. Jack-up platforms which are equipped with one or several cranes belong to the *work-ship class. Jack-up platforms with no drive
of their own are towed by tugs.

自升式平台
一种海上平底自升式平台，四个角都有支腿，支腿可下降固定在海底，牢牢支撑着平台。即使海况恶劣，也可升起平台继续作业。装备一个或多个吊机的自升式平台属于工作船，它没有发动机，要靠拖船牵引。

L

LIDAR Light Detecting And Ranging. Measuring the wind speed using a laser beam. Backscattering of the bundled laser light is measured by the ever-present dust particles and aerosols. The method has a range of several hundred metres.

LIDAR
光达技术。用激光测量风速。通过粉尘和悬浮微粒来测量激光束的反向散射。该方法测得的范围为几百米之内。

M

Marine Facilities Ordinance An ordinance regulating the installation and operation of facilities in the area of the *EEZ. Installation and operation must be approved by the *BSH. Attention has to be paid to the *regional planning objectives.

海洋设施条例
该条例用于规范指导专属经济区域的设施安装和运营。安装和运营必须取得BSH的许可。必须注意《区域规划》的目标。

Monopile One of several possible *foundation structures of offshore *wind-energy converters.

单桩
海上风能转换系统几种可能的桩基中的一种。

N

Nacelle Component of the *wind-energy converter where mechanical is converted into electrical energy. It accommodates drive train and generator. In some offshore wind turbines, converters and transformers are also integrated into the nacelle.

机舱
风能转换系统的组成部件，机械能可转换为电能。机舱中装备了传动系统和发电机。在一些风机中，变频器和变压器也设置在机舱内。

National Maritime Conference A regular event hosted by the German Federal Ministry for Economy and Technology on maritime economic issues (shipping, shipbuilding, offshore technology, etc.). Six of these conferences took place between 2000 to 2009. In 2005, a workshop was devoted solely to offshore wind power for the first time.

国际海事会议
由德国联邦经济技术部主持的常规会议，会议内容是关于海事经济问题（航运，造船，海洋工程技术等）。2000年至2009年已举行过六次会议。2005年首次为海上风电专门组织了研讨会。

Near-shore wind farm A wind farm set up at sea but less than one kilometre offshore.

近海风电场
建立在海上的风电场，但是离岸不到1公里。

O

Offshore wind farm Wind farm set up on the open sea.

海上风电场
建立在开放海域上的风电场。

Onshore wind farm Wind farm on land.

陆上风电场
建立在陆地上的风电场。

OWEC Offshore *wind-energy converter

OWEC
海上风能转换系统。

P

Pile Pile tube, about one metre in diameter, that is driven into the seabed to securely anchor *foundation structures. The piles are pushed through pile sleeves which are welded to the foundation structure's base points.

桩
直径约一米的管桩，可打入海底牢牢固定基础结构。由焊接在基础结构基点上的桩套筒推进。

Porpoise Marine mammal that belongs to the toothed whale family. It is found on central and southern European coasts, but also in the lower reaches of some rivers. It can grow to about two metres long.

海豚
海中哺乳动物，属鲸类。出没于欧洲沿海的中部或南部，一些河流下游也可发现。长成后可达2米。

R

RAVE Research at Alpha Ventus. A programme integrating the accompanying research at the alpha ventus test field. RAVE is financed by the German Federal Environment Ministry (BMU) with a total of 50 million euros. All the research activities are divided up into 15 individual projects.

RAVE
阿尔法•文图斯研究项目。该项目包括阿尔法•文图斯风电试验场的附带生态研究。由德国联邦环境部（BMU）资助5千万。整个研究项目分为15个独立项目。

Regional planning Multidisciplinary, top-level planning that extends beyond the area of land of the smallest territorial division (municipality) in Germany. Its responsibility and mission is to provide sustainable spatial development and to align social and economic requirements with ecological aspects, in order to apply them long term to large surface areas.

区域规划
超越德国最小领土区域（自治区）的跨学科顶级规划。其责任和使命是提供可持续的空间开发，使空间开发的社会和经济要求与生态系统平衡，从而可长期在大面积领域内实施。

Rotor star Component of the *wind-energy converter consisting of the three rotor blades and the *hub. Or in short: rotor.

星型叶轮
风能转换系统的组成部件，由三个叶轮和轮毂组成，简称叶轮。

S

Service ship Vessel for transporting service personnel, tools and smaller spare parts.

工作船
运输工作人员，工具和小零部件的船舶。

T

Template A template which is laid on the seabed and determines the exact position of the *piles, before these are driven into the seabed.

板
置于海底，在桩腿打入海底之前为其提供精确的着落位置。

Traffic Separation Scheme – TSS Area with separate shipping lanes for different directions. They primarily serve to channel shipping traffic on busy shipping lanes to reduce the risk of collisions. Traffic separation schemes are arranged similarly to motorways. They consist of one zone for each traffic direction as well as a separation zone in the middle where sailing is forbidden. The alpha ventus test field is located between two Traffic Separation Schemes.

分道航行系统——TSS
为不同航向设置了独立的航道的区域。主要服务繁忙航道，以减少因船舶航道拥挤造成碰撞的风险。分道航行的规划跟高速公路相似。每个航向一个区，中间设有禁止通行的航道。阿尔法·文图斯试验场位于两个分道航行系统的中间。

Transformer substation Facility for changing the supply voltage using transformers. The transformer substation consists of a switchgear unit, transformers and a control centre with the measurement and safety equipment.

变电站
使用变压器改变供应电压的设施。变电站由开关设备、变压器、控制中心以及测量和安全设备组成。

Tripod One of several possible *foundation structures of offshore *wind-energy converters.

三脚式桩基
海上风能转换系统几种可能的桩基中的一种。

Twelve-nautical-mile zone Coastal waters that are the sovereign territory of a coastal state and extend twelve nautical miles (22.2 kilometres) into the sea. In Germany the state authorities concerned are responsible for issuing project licences within the twelve-nautical-mile zone.

12海里区域
沿海国家领水区域，即离岸12海里（22.2公里）的沿海水域。在德国，国家政府负责对12海里区域内的项目颁发许可。

W

Wadden Sea National Park An extensive nature conservation area off the German North Sea Coast, characterized by mudflats that surface at low tide. The Wadden Sea is subject to strict nature conservation regulations and tight restrictions as far as its usage is concerned. Legally this area consists of three national parks: the Schleswig-Holstein Wadden Sea National Park, the Lower Saxony Wadden Sea National Park and the Hamburg Wadden Sea National Park. Since 2009, UNESCO has recognized these as World Natural Heritage sites.www.wattenmeer-nationalpark.de

浅滩海国家公园
德国北海沿岸的一个面积辽阔的自然保护区，以浅滩著称。浅滩海受严格的自然保护条例制约，相关利用也受到严格限制。从法律上讲，该区域由三个国家公园组成：石荷州浅滩海国家公园，下萨克森州浅滩海国家公园和汉堡浅滩海国家公园。自2009年来，联合国教科文组织将该国家公园认定为世界自然遗产。www.wattenmeer-nationalpark.de

WEC See *wind-energy converters.

WEC
参见风能转换系统。

Wind energy converter (WEC), also wind turbine generator (WTG) A power generator which converts the kinetic energy from wind into electric energy. A wind-energy converter essentially consists of a tower, *machine housing and *rotor star. Wind turbines installed at sea require a specific *foundation structure.

风能转换系统（WEC），即风力发电机（WTG）
一种能将动能转换成电能的发电装置。一台风能转换系统一般由一个塔架、电机外壳和叶轮组成。风机安装在海上需要专门的基础结构。

Wind Force See *Beaufort Scale

风力
参见蒲福风级。

Workship A type of ship that is designed for work on, or from water; work-ships include *jack-up barges, *cable-laying ships and *floating cranes, amongst other types.

工作船
水上工作船。包括自升式平台，电缆铺设船和浮吊等等。

功率单位

容量
1兆瓦=1,000千瓦
1十亿瓦=1,000兆瓦=1,000,000千瓦
1太瓦=1,000十亿瓦=1,000,000兆瓦=1,000,000,000千瓦

经比较，ICE-3型的高速传动系统的额定输出功率为8兆瓦，而一个大型核电站（如德国北部的格龙德）的额定功率可达1300兆瓦。

功率
1十亿瓦时=1,000兆瓦时=1,000,000千瓦时
1太瓦时=1,000十亿瓦时=1,000,000,000千瓦时

经比较，十亿瓦时电力约为250户四口家庭平均每年的消费量。德国每年的净电力消费总量约为540太瓦时。

图片来源
PHOTO CREDITS

Matthias Ibeler
© DOTI/Ibeler: 封面
© DOTI/Ibeler: P.15, 17, 39, 53, 75, 78, 79, 83, 90 t., 106, 124/125, 126/127, 134, 137, 138, 139, 140, 141, 142, 144, 145, 147, 148, 149 b., 150/151, 152/153 156/157, 167, 168, 170, 171, 174/175
© WeserWind/Ibeler: P.70, 72, 73, 86, 87, 88, 89, 113 r.b.

Jan Oelker
© Areva Multibrid/Jan Oelker: P.12, 14, 16, 19, 21, 22, 23, 25, 26/27, 28/29 30/31, 32/33, 36, 48/49, 50, 51, 52, 61, 62/63, 65, 67, 69, 95 b., 110, 114 b., 115
© Offshore-Stiftung/Repower/Jan Oelker: P.40, 109 t., 109 b.l., 146, 149 t., 154/155, 161
© Offshore-Stiftung/Multibrid/Jan Oelker: P.76, 90 b., 92, 95 t., 114 t., 128/129, 130/131, 132/133
© Offshore-Stiftung/Jan Oelker: P.77, 176
© Repower/Jan Oelker: P.44/45, 103 t., 159
© ProkonNord/Jan Oelker: P.57
© Jan Oelker/Agentur Focus: P.91, 99, 100/101, 103 b.

Detlef Gehring
© Offshore-Stiftung/Multibrid/Gehring: P.35
© Offshore-Stiftung/REpower/Gehring: P.109 r.
© Offshore-Stiftung/Gehring: P.112 und b.r., 160
© Offshore-Stiftung/transpower/Gehring: P.116, 118, 119, 120, 121

Weitere

AREVA Multibrid/Heike Winkler: P.34

Karin Desmarowitz (Porträt Christian Dahlke): P.54

Ralf Grömminger, P.158

Industrie- und Handelskammer zu Schwerin (Porträt Jörgen Thiele): P.52

Privat: P.11, 64

Sebastian Fuhrmann: P.97

编后记

敬爱的读者：

您对今天的一些"热词"，如低碳、减排、可持续发展、可再生能源、风能、海上风电一定耳熟能详。尤其是海上风电，近年来异军突起，发展势头强劲。

但是，您可知道，海上风力发电的发展历程是怎样的？前景如何？人们在规划、设计、建造和营运一个海上风力发电厂时的关键之处是什么？会遇到怎样的挑战？

上述问题的答案，您都能从这本书中找到。在此感谢中船重工704所及《船舶工程》杂志邀请德国劳氏参与本书的审校工作。通过这一国际团队的通力合作，我们为您呈现了一本关于海上风电的翔实、生动、精美的中文版百科全书。

本书作者Dierk Jensen和Detlef Koenemann博士详尽介绍了参与阿尔法•文图斯海上风电项目的德国风能公司阿海珐（AREVA）Multibrid、瑞能（Repower）、DOTI如何在德国联邦环境部的支持下，创造性地规划、设计、建造了这一里程碑式的海上风电场。两位作者以德国人特有的认真、严谨、系统、实用的态度，对这一了不起的工程进行了记录和总结，明白易懂地回答了当人们在规划、设计和建设海上风电场时必须考虑的问题，例如：

- 项目资金运作及保险
- 法规、主管机构及审批程序
- 环境调查及风场选址
- 项目运作方式、合同、管理
- 风机设备及基础选型
- 海上安装作业及安装设施
- 并网运营

对海上风电业的工程师、经理人，抑或是有意了解该领域的普通读者来说，本书不仅读来有趣且有启迪意义。

作为全球风电，尤其是海上风电的领军人，德国劳氏集团（Germanischer Lloyd Group）的风能分部（GL Wind）曾承担了阿海珐 Multibrid和瑞能5兆瓦的风机认证和整个阿尔法•文图斯项目的海上风电场认证。今天，我们又非常荣幸地应邀参与本书的编译工作，并作此编译后记。

中国的海上风电产业是一个极具发展空间的未来产业，但它的发展还面临着包括技术挑战在内的重重挑战。德国劳氏及旗下的GL Noble Denton和GL Garrad Hassan将凭借我们的专业技术、专家队伍、信息资源、服务网络为中国海上风电的发展提供涵盖整个风电产业链的一站式技术支持和服务。

衷心希望本书能对中国海上风电行业应对并战胜这些挑战有所裨益，这将会成为我们最大的满足。

德国劳氏船级社（中国）有限公司

2013年11月，于上海

# 中船重工(重庆)海装风电设备有限公司
CSIC (Chongqing) Haizhuang Windpower Equipment Co., Ltd.

5MW海上风机特点

- 三叶片、上风向、水平轴、大轴承结构
- 三级增速、可选高速永磁/双馈
- 适应海上特点的主控
- 满足GL海上标准的CMS系统
- 极限载荷控制技术
- 迷宫式密封技术、内循环空空冷却系统
- 自然对流空油冷却系统
- 标配消防系统
- 电网适应性好

设计理念

- 标准化、系列化、模块化设计：除叶片、增速箱外，5.0MW各种规格零部件完全互换。
- 适度冗余的可靠性设计。
- 要求正面维护，可维护性好；强调零部件可靠性，可维修；操作、运行、体验安全。
- 整体抗恶劣环境处理。
- 主流技术路线，新技术比例适当控制，传统与创新相结合。
- 适当预留技术演进空间。
- 可满足现有工程施工条件。
- 单位kW发电量高。

地址：重庆市北部新区经开园金渝大道30号　　传真：023-63023178
电话：023-63023100　　网址：www.hzwindpower.com

电气与自动化工程学院
Electrical Engineering & Automation

天津大学电气与自动化工程学院前身是1933年成立的北洋大学电机系，素以严谨治学、务实求真而闻名。先后培养出以原清华大学校长高景德院士，北京邮电大学名誉校长叶培大院士，发电工程与设备专家梁维燕院士，电力系统继电保护专家、俄罗斯工程院院士贺家李教授，电力系统分析、规划与仿真专家余贻鑫院士，国际电机领域知名专家陈之藩教授，电力系统著名华人企业家荣智健先生等为代表的一大批各类杰出人才。

学院现有电气工程、控制科学与工程学科均为博士、硕士学位授权一级学科，并分别设有博士后流动站。在学院所属的8个二级学科（电力系统及其自动化、电机与电器、高电压与绝缘技术、电力电子与电力传动、电工理论与新技术、控制理论与控制工程、检测技术与自动化装置和模式识别与智能系统）中，电力系统及其自动化、检测技术与自动化装置为国家重点学科。学院设有电气工程及其自动化、自动化2个宽口径的本科生专业。每年本科生招生规模在330人左右，研究生在300人左右（硕士研究生约240人，博士研究生约60人）。

学院有一支高效、精干、勇于开拓的师资队伍，现有中国工程院院士1人，俄罗斯工程院院士1人，国家"千人计划"引进人才1人，长江学者创新团队1个，长江学者特聘教授2人，长江学者讲座教授1人，"973"首席科学家2人，国家杰出青年基金获得者2人，国家百千万人才2人，教育部新(跨)世纪优秀人才14人，天津市"千人计划"引进人才2人。

学院现拥有各类科研和教学实验室20余个，其中包括：智能电网教育部重点实验室、天津市电力系统仿真控制重点实验室、天津市过程检测与控制重点实验室、教育部新型飞行器联合研究中心（先进制导与控制分中心）、天津市配电系统规划及自动化技术推广中心，以及与国内外知名企业共建的楼宇自动化中心（与美国霍尼韦尔公司共建）、电力研究与培训中心（与华北电力公司、天津电力公司、河南电力公司、天津大港电厂等单位共建）、天津大学——三菱电机自动化实验室（与三菱电机(中国)公司共建）、天津市电力新能源与智能配用电技术工程中心（与天大求实公司共建）、天津市锻压装备技术工程中心（与天锻压力机公司共建）等多个科研和实训平台。现拥有各类实验仪器设备3000余台套，设备总值近亿元，实验室总面积近万平米。多数实验室和研究平台可对在校学生和企业开放，用于培养学生的创新能力和解决企业的实际问题。

学院拥有雄厚的科研实力，近5年来，共完成科研项目400余项（包括两项国家973项目），获2012年国家技术发明二等奖、2011和2010年两项国家科技进步二等奖，2009年中国高校十大科技进展以及其他各省（部）级科学技术进步奖20余项，发表科技论文1500多篇，取得了丰硕的科研成果。2012年全院承担的科研项目经费超过5000万元，且已形成多个在国内、外具有一定影响的特色研究方向，如：电力系统规划、评估与优化，电力系统安全性与运行控制，分布式发电与微网，电力系统保护与控制，新型电机及其控制技术，电器系统优化与节能，高电压与绝缘材料，新型传感器与流动参数检测，自动化装备与过程控制，智能系统检测、建模与控制，智能信息处理与应用，航空制导技术，机器人控制技术，新能源动力汽车控制技术，等等。

地址：天津市南开区卫津路92号　邮编：300072
电话：(022)27406272　E-mail: autju@163.com

中船重工（重庆）海装风电设备有限公司
CSIC (Chongqing) Haizhuang Windpower Equipment Co.,Ltd.

5MW海上风机特点

- 三叶片、上风向、水平轴、大轴承结构
- 三级增速、可选高速永磁/双馈
- 适应海上特点的主控
- 满足GL海上标准的CMS系统
- 极限载荷控制技术
- 迷宫式密封技术、内循环空空冷却系统
- 自然对流空油冷却系统
- 标配消防系统
- 电网适应性好

设计理念

- 标准化、系列化、模块化设计：除叶片、增速箱外，5.0MW各种规格零部件完全互换。
- 适度冗余的可靠性设计。
- 要求正面维护，可维护性好；强调零部件可靠性，可维修；操作、运行、体验安全。
- 整体抗恶劣环境处理。
- 主流技术路线，新技术比例适当控制，传统与创新相结合。
- 适当预留技术演进空间。
- 可满足现有工程施工条件。
- 单位kW发电量高。

地址：重庆市北部新区经开园金渝大道30号　传真：023-63023178
电话：023-63023100　　　　　　　　　　　网址：www.hzwindpower.com

电气与自动化工程学院
Electrical Engineering & Automation

天津大学电气与自动化工程学院前身是1933年成立的北洋大学电机系，素以严谨治学、务实求真而闻名。先后培养出以原清华大学校长高景德院士、北京邮电大学名誉校长叶培大院士、发电工程与设备专家梁维燕院士、电力系统继电保护专家、俄罗斯工程院士贺家李教授、电力系统分析、规划与仿真专家余贻鑫院士、国际电机领域知名专家陈之藩教授、电力系统著名华人企业家荣智健先生等为代表的一大批各类杰出人才。

学院现有电气工程、控制科学与工程学科均为博士、硕士学位授权一级学科，并分别设有博士后流动站。在学院所属的8个二级学科（电力系统及其自动化、电机与电器、高电压与绝缘技术、电力电子与电力传动、电工理论与新技术、控制理论与控制工程、检测技术与自动化装置和模式识别与智能系统）中，电力系统及其自动化、检测技术与自动化装置为国家重点学科。学院设有电气工程及其自动化、自动化2个宽口径的本科生专业。每年本科生招生规模在330人左右，研究生在300人左右(硕士研究生约240人，博士研究生约60人)。

学院有一支高效、精干、勇于开拓的师资队伍，现有中国工程院院士1人，俄罗斯工程院院士1人，国家"千人计划"引进人才1人，长江学者创新团队1个，长江学者特聘教授2人，长江学者讲座教授1人，"973"首席科学家2人，国家杰出青年基金获得者2人，国家百千万人才2人，教育部新(跨)世纪优秀人才14人，天津市"千人计划"引进人才2人。

学院现拥有各类科研和教学实验室20余个，其中包括：智能电网教育部重点实验室、天津市电力系统仿真控制重点实验室、天津市过程检测与控制重点实验室、教育部新型飞行器联合研究中心（先进制导与控制分中心）、天津市配电系统规划及自动化技术推广中心，以及与国内外知名企业共建的楼宇自动化中心(与美国霍尼韦尔公司共建)、电力研究与培训中心(与华北电力公司、天津电力公司、河南电力公司、天津大港电厂等单位共建)、天津大学——三菱电机自动化实验室(与三菱电机(中国)公司共建)、天津市电力新能源与智能配用电技术工程中心(与天大求实公司共建)、天津市锻压装备技术工程中心(与天锻压力机公司共建)等多个科研和实训平台。现拥有各类实验仪器设备3000余台套，设备总值近亿元，实验室总面积近万平米。多数实验室和研究平台可对在校学生和企业开放，用于培养学生的创新能力和解决企业的实际问题。

学院拥有雄厚的科研实力，近5年来，共完成科研项目400余项（包括两项国家973项目），获2012年国家技术发明二等奖、2011和2010年两项国家科技进步二等奖，2009年中国高校十大科技进展以及其他各类省（部）级科学技术进步奖20余项，发表科技论文1500多篇，取得了丰硕的科研成果。2012年全院承担的科研项目经费超过5000万元，且已形成多个在国内、外具有一定影响的特色研究方向，如：电力系统规划、评估与优化，电力系统安全性与运行控制，分布式发电与微网，电力系统保护与控制，新型电机及其控制技术，电器系统优化与节能，高电压与绝缘材料，新型传感器与流动参数检测，自动化装备与过程控制，智能系统检测、建模与控制，智能信息处理与应用，航空制导技术，机器人控制技术，新能源动力汽车控制技术，等等。

地址：天津市南开区卫津路92号　邮编：300072
电话：(022)27406272　E-mail: autju@163.com

武昌船舶重工有限责任公司
WUCHANG SHIPBUILDING INDUSTRY CO., LTD.

科技创新　　引领发展

武昌船舶重工有限责任公司,简称"武船",是中国以造船为主的大型现代化综合性企业和重要的军工生产基地。

武船始终注重以科技和创新引领发展,是国家船舶工业"创新能力十强"企业,拥有国家级的企业技术中心,拥有舰船设计所、三维设计研究所、海洋工程船舶设计公司、新产品研发中心、特种材料应用技术研究所、信息集成公司等多个研究机构,具有独立设计、联合设计、重大工艺技术攻关、核心工艺技术创新与应用的业绩和能力。

目前,我公司正在进行海上风机安装船设计研发工作,右下图为已形成的海上风机安装船概念模型:

地址:湖北武汉市武昌区紫阳路2号　邮编:430060
电话:027-68887174/7175/7176/7177/7178
传真:027-88077801
E-mail:wsqls@163.com

风机塔筒生产线

风机安装船概念图

 中国电力工程顾问集团
华东电力设计院
EAST CHINA ELECTRIC POWER DESIGN INSTITUTE
OF CHINA POWER ENGINEERING CONSULTING GROUP

    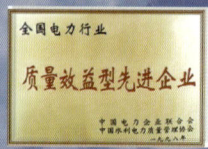 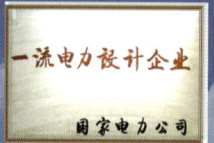

中国能建中电工程华东电力设计院（简称"华东院"）1953年创建于上海，是中国勘察设计单位综合实力百强和获得国家质量管理体系、环境管理体系、职业健康安全管理体系认证证书单位，是具有工程设计综合、工程勘察综合、工程监理、工程咨询、工程造价咨询、环境影响评价、测绘、水土保持方案编制、节能评审/评估等甲级证书和对外经营权的独立法人。华东院主要承担电力系统规划、火电、核电、新能源和输变电项目的勘察、设计、咨询、监理、总承包等业务。

华东院技术力量雄厚、专业配套齐全。截至2012年底共有在职职工1149人，其中工程技术人员有978人。华东院拥有全国工程勘察设计大师2人、历年享受政府特殊津贴的专家22人，现有教授级高级工程师113人，高级工程师402人，工程师239人，国家注册建筑师15人，注册建造师30人，注册结构工程师56人，注册土木工程师22人，注册电气工程师53人，注册公用设备工程师35人，注册造价工程师27人，注册监理师38人，注册咨询工程师44人，环境影响评价工程师11人，注册地震安全性评价工程师6人等。此外，华东院还拥有一批资深的、经验丰富的老专家，在工程勘测设计工作中发挥着技术支撑作用。

华东院始终坚持"精心设计、优质服务、艰苦奋斗、改革创新"的企业精神和"生存、发展、诚信、和谐"的企业核心价值观，努力为顾客提供优质的勘测设计产品和服务，切实履行好社会责任。多年来，华东院被国家、行业和地方有关管理机构授予"全国重合同守信用单位"、"中国勘察设计百强单位"、"中国工程设计企业60强"、"全国电力行业质量特别奖"、"全国电力行业优秀企业"、"全国一流电力设计企业"、"上海市文明单位"、"上海市高新技术企业"、"上海市科技小巨人企业"等荣誉称号并被分别评为中国建设系统、电力行业、电力规划设计行业、外经贸行业 "企业信用AAA级单位"和上海市合同信用等级AAA级企业。

海上风机维护　　　　　　　　　　　　风机海上运输、安装

风电市场从陆地到海洋　　　　　　　　海上及滩涂风电场建设

精心设计　　优质服务　　艰苦奋斗　　改革创新

地址：上海武宁路409号　　邮编：200063　　　　邮箱：ecepdi@ecepdi.com
电话：86-21-22015888　　传真：86-21-62574087 62577326　　网址：www.ecepdi.com